CAPITAL UNGOVERNED

# CAPITAL UNGOVERNED

## Liberalizing Finance in Interventionist States

MICHAEL LORIAUX
MEREDITH WOO-CUMINGS
KENT E. CALDER
SYLVIA MAXFIELD
SOFÍA A. PÉREZ

CORNELL UNIVERSITY PRESS

ITHACA AND LONDON

First published 1997 by Cornell University Press.


Printed in the United States of America

⊗ The paper in this book meets the minimum requirements of the American National Standard for Information Sciences—Permanence of Paper for Printed Library Materials, ANSI Z39.48–1984.


Library of Congress Cataloging-in-Publication Data

Capital ungoverned : liberalizing finance in interventionist states / Michael Loriaux . . . [et al.].
    p.  cm.
    Includes bibliographical references and index.
    ISBN 0-8014-3176-X (cloth : alk. paper). — ISBN 0-8014-8281-X (pbk. : alk. paper)
    1. Monetary policy.  2. Capital movements.  3. Credit control.  I. Loriaux, Michael Maurice.
HG230.3.C367   1996
332.4'6—dc20
                                        96-23238

*To Robert Gilpin*


*for his teaching, scholarship, and Menschlichkeit*

# Contents

# CAPITAL UNGOVERNED

# The End of Credit Activism
# in Interventionist States

## MICHAEL LORIAUX

The oil crisis of 1973–74 sparked interest among academics in the adjustment strategies adopted by interventionist states. Japan confounded the world by turning its vulnerability to external supply shocks into a huge trade surplus. There was also much dissection of policies that, for a brief period in the late 1970s, placed France in third place among the world's exporting nations. Both France and Japan relied heavily on the state's capacity to influence or control the allocation of credit to pursue a strategic course of adjustment to global economic change. Activist credit policy had been an important tool of state interventionism in both countries for decades. In the 1980s, however, both France and Japan renounced credit activism and surrendered much of the state's power over the flow of capital to the market.

South Korea, Mexico, and Spain once exercised similar control over the allocation of credit and used that control to facilitate economic adjustment as well as longer-term industrial development. These countries, like Japan and France, also liberalized their financial systems in the 1980s, stripping the state of much of its power to control how credit was allocated.

Aside from their experience with activist credit policy, these countries do not have much in common. They span a wide range of levels of economic development, display great diversity in political and social structures, and occupy strikingly different geopolitical situations. Some of them experienced great success using control over the allocation of credit to promote economic adjustment and development, others less. Yet, because credit activism was abandoned almost simultaneously in five such dissimilar countries, one can reasonably infer that the force driving that process was common to all of them and must have had roots in the evolution of the broader global political economy.

Each of the five countries has been the focus of a book-length investigation by one of the authors of this volume.[1] Although each of the country studies presented here stands on its own, the juxtaposition of the five cases creates the opportunity to identify common factors and address the question of how the global political economy is evolving and how state institutions are adapting to that evolution.

## State Control over Credit Allocation

State control over financial policy in general and credit policy in particular was a hallmark of the political economy of a number of countries throughout much of the twentieth century. But, before the economic crisis of the 1970s, activist credit policy did not attract much attention among students of politics. It was Peter Katzenstein's pathbreaking volume, *Between Power and Plenty*, which appeared in 1978, that, along with his studies of policy making in the small states of northern Europe, inspired a generation of scholars to pay closer attention to the politics of economic adjustment.[2] Not only did *Between Power and Plenty* attract scholarly attention to the relationship between domestic institutional structure and policy response to economic crisis, it alerted scholars to the importance of financial policy and policy-making institutions in

[1]  Kent Calder, *Strategic Capitalism: Private Business and Public Purpose in Japanese Industrial Finance* (Princeton: Princeton University Press, 1993); Michael Loriaux, *France after Hegemony: International Change and Financial Reform* (Ithaca: Cornell University Press, 1991); Sylvia Maxfield, *Governing Capital: International Finance and Mexican Politics* (Ithaca: Cornell University Press, 1990); Jung-en Woo (Meredith Woo-Cumings), *Race to the Swift: State and Finance in Korean Industrialization* (New York: Columbia University Press, 1991); Sofia Pérez, *Banking on Privilege: The Politics of Spanish Financial Reform* (Ithaca: Cornell University Press, 1997).

[2]  Peter Katzenstein, ed., *Between Power and Plenty: Foreign Economic Policies of Advanced Industrial States* (Madison: University of Wisconsin Press, 1978). Peter Katzenstein, *Corporatism and Change: Austria, Switzerland, and the Politics of Industry* (Ithaca: Cornell University Press, 1984), and *Small States in World Markets: Industrial Policy in Europe* (Ithaca: Cornell University Press, 1984).

conditioning that response. Two contributors to that volume, T. J. Pempel and John Zysman, focused particularly on the apparent capacity of Japan and France to promote adjustment by controlling and directing the allocation of credit.

John Zysman, in his seminal work, *Governments, Markets, and Growth*, argued subsequently that "by knowing the financial system one [can] predict the nature of the process of adjustment." Governments of countries with strong and active capital markets tend not to intervene at the level of the sector or firm to try to dictate or influence adjustment strategies, while governments of countries with credit-based systems and administered prices intervene much more frequently at that level. In France, he observed, the weakness of the capital market obliges firms to turn to lending institutions. Business dependence on institutionally supplied capital in turn allows the government bureaucracy "to orient the adjustment of the economy by explicitly influencing the position of particular sectors, even of individual companies."[3] France's credit-based system assured the success of economic planning; it allowed the government to subject certain sectors to a market-induced process of decline while assuring investment funds to sectors whose expansion was essential for development; and it gave the state the power to serve "as crutch and prod in the transformation of French industry away from an insular world in which small-scale production and intercompany connections slowed change toward an international marketplace in which a more modern industry composed of hierarchically managed giant corporations could compete with its counterparts."[4]

The countries examined in this volume have resembled Zysman's France at one time or another. In Japan, the state stepped in between banks and industrial borrowers, particularly during the 1940s and 1950s, to control and guide the allocation of credit. Bank of Japan discount rates[5] were set lower than short-term rates (three months to a year or so) offered by banks, making it possible for banks to borrow from the central bank and to lend elsewhere at a profit.[6] The state also intervened

---

[3]  John Zysman, *Governments, Markets, and Growth: Financial Systems and the Politics of Industrial Change* (Ithaca: Cornell University Press, 1983), p. 91.

[4]  Ibid., pp. 168–69.

[5]  The discount rate is the interest rate that the central bank charges other banks when it lends them money.

[6]  Calder, *Strategic Capitalism*, p. 88.

through such institutions as the Loan Mediation Bureau to facilitate the transformation of liquid deposits into long-term loans (five years and longer) to industrial firms.[7] Growing bank dependence on discounting by the Bank of Japan increased the central bank's power to regulate bank activity. Regulatory controls gave certain kinds of borrowers the guarantee of rediscounting by the central bank at privileged rates and so induced banks to direct their activities to sectors of the economy that benefited from that guarantee.

Financial activity in the Republic of Korea was also marked by active state involvement and control. As in Japan, credit policy was designed to mobilize capital and funnel it toward industrial investment. The state insulated the financial market from the world and regulated the flow of foreign capital into the Korean economy. The government nationalized the banks and used them to extend loans to industrial investors at interest rates that were often negative in real terms. Like the Japanese, the Koreans established several specialized financial programs, such as the Machine Industry Promotion Fund, the National Investment Fund, and the export loan program, which provided targeted sectors with investment capital on attractive terms.

Before World War II, Mexico created institutions to finance roads, irrigation, and energy production to improve agricultural output and spur industrial development. During the war and again in the early 1950s, the government instituted a system of reserve requirements,[8] which, though initially implemented to slow inflation by controlling the growth of credit, was soon being used to support a more interventionist program of discretionary credit allocation. When the government became more concerned about the pace of productive investment in the 1970s, it developed credit institutions, the *fideicomisos,* that provided preferential credit to selected sectors of the economy. Between 1970 and 1973, the amount of money distributed by the *fideicomisos* grew by 25 percent annually. The trend toward increasing government intervention

[7]    An asset is said to be "liquid" if it can be spent on real, that is, nonfinancial goods, or if it can easily be converted into an asset that can be spent on real goods. Cash is completely liquid. Stocks and bonds are less liquid, since they have to be sold for cash before the value locked up in them can be used to buy goods. Savings accounts that impose penalties on early withdrawals are less liquid still. Capital assets, such as machines and real estate, are very unliquid, because they are hard to convert into cash.

[8]    Reserve requirements generally stipulate that banks must not lend more than some specified ratio of their deposits or assets.

in financial markets culminated in 1982, when the government nationalized the banking sector.

In France, as in Japan, the state mobilized various lending institutions to help overcome the postwar shortage of capital and put in place a system of direct state investment subsidies, which initially distributed Marshall Plan funds. But the state gradually withdrew from the business of subsidizing the economy directly and acted instead through intermediaries: public and semi-public lending institutions in the 1950s and deposit banks (the three largest of which were state-owned) in the 1960s and 1970s. When fully developed, the French system relied on the capacity of the state to place limits on credit expansion by banks, while exempting certain kinds of borrowers (exporters, for example) from those limitations and compensating other sectors through functionally specific and narrowly targeted credit programs. Because the banks were dependent on central bank support, they respected the limits placed on their activity; but they lent generously to sectors that were exempted from limits. This system gave the state considerable control over both credit allocation and aggregate monetary growth. The state used that control to aid investment in new industries, to promote social stability by alleviating economic stress in traditional sectors, and to contain inflation.

In Spain, the fiscal and economic consequences of World War I led the state to get involved in developing and regulating the banking sector. But generous backing by the central bank and granting of regulatory privileges gave rise to an oligopolistic banking sector. Generalissimo Franco tried to exploit this system to finance economic autarky but succeeded only in producing rents for the banks.[9] In the wake of financial collapse and intervention by the International Monetary Fund (IMF) in 1959, Spain rejected autarky and gained admission into international financial and commercial institutions. Financial reforms accompanied this new orientation and produced Spain's first effective activist credit policy, which was used to support a system of indicative planning on the French model.[10] As in the other

---

[9]  The term "rent" designates the remuneration that is offered to some factor of production in excess of the equilibrium price as determined by the unimpeded encounter of supply and demand on the market.

[10]  Indicative planning was pioneered in France. It is similar to central planning as implemented by Soviet bloc countries in that it revolves around the determination of medium-term

countries, the financial sector was compartmentalized. Specific credit institutions were created to assure the financial support of specific sectors and activities.[11] Compartmentalization gave rise to privileged financing circuits within which authorities intervened to control the allocation of credit. And, as in France, rediscounting by the central bank was used to provide privileged treatment to certain kinds of loan. Credit activism allowed Spain to finance an industrial investment strategy that facilitated its integration into the global liberal commercial order.

## Global Forces Contributing to Financial Deregulation

All five states intervened forcefully to direct the allocation of credit. They did so to finance projects and deploy programs that they deemed important for the general welfare of their nations. In some countries these tasks were defined in strictly economic terms; in others they addressed broader security issues, as in Korea, or issues of social and economic stability, as in France. Moreover, it would appear on first examination that at least some of these countries used their capacity to direct credit effectively. This, of course, is a contentious issue. Japan and Korea both succeeded in developing into highly industrialized, export-oriented economies. The French economy also grew rapidly during the 1950s and 1960s, but growth slowed in the recessionary 1970s (though it slowed less in France than in other European countries). But it is more difficult to gauge the benefits of credit activism in Spain and Mexico. Nevertheless, activist credit policy, whether it sped growth and

---

(generally five years) growth targets for the economy and for specific sectors within the economy. It differs from central planning in that the state has much less control over actual investment. The state must rely to a large extent on private investors, which it coaxes and prods with the aid of public purchases, fiscal and credit policy, and information about government intentions and forecasts regarding the evolution of the national and global economic environment. Its impact on actual investment by private firms has been disputed, but the French continue to find the plan useful, even in these times of economic liberalization.

[11]  A compartmentalized financial market is one that is divided up among various productive sectors. Instead of there being one unified, market-determined price for capital that applies to the economy as a whole, there are a variety of sector-specific, administratively fixed prices. The flow of capital from one "compartment" to another is hampered by regulations and interventionist institutions.

industrial development or not, did appear to supply these countries with something they all wanted: a degree of autonomy to pursue national ambitions, however idiosyncratic those ambitions might be. Why, then, did these countries dismantle the institutions that gave them the power to control the allocation of credit, thereby surrendering much of that power to the market?

Though the literature on credit activism in interventionist states is not extensive in English, the literature on financial liberalization in general terms is voluminous. Explanations of financial liberalization tend to converge on two arguments, one privileging the role of market forces and the other underscoring the importance of policy decisions in financially powerful states. Theories that focus on market forces tend to interpret liberalization as a relentless transformative process driven primarily by the development of new technologies and more sophisticated financial instruments. Regulatory frameworks do not supply the state with as much control over financial transactions as they once did. Theories that focus on the policy decisions of financially powerful states, on the other hand, tend to concentrate primarily on the United States and the changes it has wrought in the international regimes that govern international monetary and capital movements.

According to the market-centered interpretation, the origins of global financial liberalization go back to the development of the Eurocurrency market in the late 1950s and early 1960s. At that time, the growing volume of international trade was increasing the demand for commercial credit in foreign currencies, especially the dollar. But because bank regulations and exchange controls made foreign currencies scarce, such credit was expensive and hard to get. A number of enterprising banks profited from this situation by moving some of their operations "offshore," where they could cater to this demand out of reach of regulatory legislation. This was the beginning of the Eurocurrency market, that is, the market for credit in currencies other than the national currency of the borrower.

The oil shock of 1973 reinforced this trend. Oil-producing states deposited windfall oil revenues in the banks of the industrialized "North." But because the crisis depressed domestic demand for credit in the North, banks turned to the Euromarket to prospect for foreign borrowers, which they found in great numbers among the developing countries of the "South." In the same year, floating exchange rates[12] goaded holders of financial assets to increase their holdings in foreign currencies in order to hedge the risk of holding assets in a single currency denomination. This development had two effects. First, it reinforced the demand for speculative credit in non-national currencies. Second, it gave rise to a sizable demand for interest-bearing bonds denominated in non-national currencies. Investors wanted to compose risk-minimizing portfolios by mixing assets denominated in a variety of currencies. The subsequent "securitization" of the Eurocurrency market, that is, the move from non-interest bearing currencies to interest-bearing and revenue-generating financial assets, spurred domestic banking interests to press for deregulation so as not to be left in the cold either by the development of offshore banking or by the growth of the Eurobond market.

The trend toward international financial deregulation, described by some as "the end of geography," raises forcefully the question of what role the state can and should play.[13] Indeed, we have only begun to wit-

---

[12]    Beginning in 1973, the value of a currency in terms of other currencies (e.g., the price of the dollar in French francs) was no longer determined by international agreement between governments but rather by market transactions. Consequently, the value of the currency now floats, that is, rises and falls in response to variations in the supply and demand of that currency on the currency market.

[13]    Richard O'Brien, *Global Financial Integration: The End of Geography* (New York: Council on Foreign Relations Press, 1992), pp. 1–2. The "end of geography" refers to the situation in which the geographical location of lenders and borrowers no longer matters, since financial market regulators no longer hold full sway over their regulatory territory. By focusing on two paradigmatic explanations of international financial liberalization, I recognize that I am passing over many excellent and important studies that have appeared on the topic. These include: Benjamin J. Cohen, *Crossing Frontiers: Explorations in International Political Economy* (Boulder, Colo.: Westview Press, 1990); Jeffry A. Frieden, *Debt, Development, and Democracy: Modern Political Economy and Latin America, 1965–1985* (Princeton: Princeton University Press, 1991); Jeffry A. Frieden, *Banking on the World: The Politics of American International Finance* (New York: Basil Blackwell, 1989); Stephen Gill and David Law, *The Global Political Economy: Perspectives, Problems, and Policies* (Baltimore: Johns Hopkins University Press, 1988); John Goodman, *Monetary Sovereignty: The Politics of Central Banking in Western Europe* (Ithaca: Cornell University Press, 1992); Robert Guttmann, *How Credit-Money Shapes the Economy: The United States in a Global System* (Armonk, N.Y.: M. E. Sharpe, 1994); Stephan Haggard and Chung H. Lee, eds., *Financial Systems and Economic Policy in Developing Countries* (Ithaca: Cornell University Press, 1995); Stephan Haggard, Chung H. Lee, and Sylvia Maxfield, eds., *The Politics of Finance in Developing Countries* (Ithaca: Cornell University Press, 1993); Ethan Kapstein, *Governing the Global Economy: International Finance and the State* (Cambridge: Harvard University Press, 1994); Paulette Kurzer, *Business and Banking: Political Change and Economic Integration in Western Europe* (Ithaca: Cornell University Press, 1993); David M. Meerschwam, *Breaking Financial*

ness the pressures that the end of geography is placing on the capacity of national governments to regulate financial markets. As late as 1980, financial internationalization was still relatively shallow, since one could still detect a close correlation between levels of domestic savings and investment. But much has changed since then. More recent studies reveal that the correlation between domestic savings and investment has weakened appreciably, indicating a rising degree of capital mobility.[14] In other words, the internationalization of the financial market is a recent phenomenon corresponding to the period that interests us: the 1980s and early 1990s.

The second theoretical explanation does not dispute the impact of market pressures but ascribes the emergence of those pressures to policies adopted by financially powerful states. Susan Strange has argued that the United States, by forsaking many of the market-regulating responsibilities that it assumed in the 1950s and 1960s, has permitted the growth of a "casino capitalism" that defies government control and threatens international financial collapse. In contrast, Henry Nau, who served on the National Security Council during the Reagan administration, claims that it is not through negligence but by design that the United States used its hegemonic influence to promote the development of free markets and to force countries like France to pursue pro-market policies.[15]

Eric Helleiner, in his excellent examination of the history of exchange controls in the post–World War II era, shows how the United States and Great Britain colluded to bring down the Bretton Woods regulatory framework. For Helleiner, it was American and British initiatives that gave rise to the Euromarket in the 1960s. In the 1980s, Great Britain, by deregulating its financial centers, and the United States, by amassing a

---

*Boundaries: Global Capital, National Deregulation, and Financial Services Firms* (Boston: Harvard Business School Press, 1991); Louis Pauly, *Opening Financial Markets: Banking Politics on the Pacific Rim* (Ithaca: Cornell University Press, 1988); Rob Steven, *Japan and the New World Order: Global Investments, Trade, and Finance* (New York: St. Martin's Press, 1996); Ingo Walter, *Global Competition in Financial Services: Market Structure, Protection, and Trade Liberalization* (Cambridge, Mass.: Ballinger, 1988).

[14] O'Brien, *Global Financial Integration*, pp. 88–89. O'Brien cites M. Feldstein and C. Horioka, "Domestic Saving and International Capital Flows," *Economic Journal* 90 (1980). Shelley Cooper, "Cross-border Savings Flows and Capital Mobility in the G7 Economies," *Bank of England Discussion Papers*, no. 54 (March 1991).

[15] Susan Strange, *Casino Capitalism* (Oxford: Basil Blackwell, 1986); Henry Nau, *The Myth of America's Decline* (New York: Oxford University Press, 1990).

huge budget deficit which the Federal Reserve Board refused to monetize,[16] unleashed a process of "competitive deregulation" that compelled other countries to introduce liberalizing reforms into their own financial markets. They did so to prevent capital from leaving the country to cash in on opportunities created by U.S. and British policy. The United States did not pursue such policies under the compulsion of irresistible market forces. It acted purposefully to "utilize its dominant position in the open, liberal international financial system to encourage foreigners both to finance and to bear the burden of adjustment to its growing current account and fiscal deficits."[17] Great Britain and Japan seconded American initiatives, the first in an effort to defend the internationally predominant financial position of the City of London, the second to assume a position of leadership that its growing weight in global financial affairs had begun to confer on it. This second interpretation is broadly compatible with hegemony theory in its more historicist formulation, as developed by Robert Gilpin, and provides support for the notion of "predatory hegemony."[18]

## Global Liberalization and the Dismantling of Activist Credit Policies

Difficulties emerge when we turn from global forces to credit policy reform at the national level. The evidence from our five countries does not allow us to explain the dismantling of activist credit policies as simply the result of either irresistible market forces or direct and indirect

---

[16]   The central bank monetizes government debt when it inscribes the money needed to cover the debt directly onto the government's account. The act of inscribing money onto the government's account creates money *ex nihilo*, just as the act of inscribing money on to the account of any borrower by any bank creates money *ex nihilo*. This is why the lending activity of banks must be regulated and controlled. In the absence of credit extended by the central bank, the government must finance its debt by selling bonds. This does not create money *ex nihilo*, since the money that is lent to the government is already being held as assets by the lender.

[17]   Eric Helleiner, *States and the Reemergence of Global Finance: From Bretton Woods to the 1990s* (Ithaca: Cornell University Press, 1994), p. 202.

[18]   Robert Gilpin, *U.S. Power and the Multinational Corporation* (New York: Basic Books, 1975). On "predatory hegemony," see Robert Gilpin, *The Political Economy of International Relations* (Princeton: Princeton University Press, 1987), pp. 90, 345. Gilpin borrows the term from John Conybeare, *Trade Wars: The Theory and Practice of International Commercial Rivalry* (New York: Columbia University Press, 1987). Helleiner also makes reference to the concept in *States and the Reemergence of Global Finance*, p. 13.

pressures generated by dominant financial powers. Market pressures are evident in all cases, but they manifest themselves differently from country to country. Similarly, although the United States exerted indirect policy pressure and sometimes direct diplomatic pressure to force several countries to alter policy, this pressure affected some countries more than others.

In Japan, a virtuous circle of growth, success in foreign trade, and reinforcement of the capital base of Japanese industrial firms created the conditions for a gradual reform in financial institutions and practices. The process of reform began in the mid-1970s and continued through the 1980s. Market opportunities appear to have played the dominant role. The financial situation of Japanese firms changed as their success in export markets grew. As Kent Calder tells us in Chapter 2, by the late 1970s the financial situation of Japanese industrial firms was such that they could borrow money on the basis of market criteria without reference to state priorities. Revenues from foreign trade, combined with a fall in the demand for credit occasioned by the post–oil shock recession, created the opportunity for Japanese firms to diminish their level of indebtedness vis-à-vis institutional lenders. Indeed, Japanese industrial firms were soon supplying capital to the rest of the economy. In the late 1970s banks began to borrow from industrial firms as well as lend to them. In 1979 the banking industry introduced certificates of deposit to facilitate industrial investment in the banking sector. Government control over the allocation of credit grew weak as a swelling supply of capital cut the cost of borrowing and decreased dependence on such government financial institutions as the Japan Development Bank. The Japanese do not appear to have been pushed to abandon activist credit policy by market forces or by the reverberating effects of policy in powerful countries. Rather, they were drawn out of that practice by the opportunities generated by success in international trade.

Financial liberalization in Korea was more dependent on state initiative. As in Japan, the state had sought in the decades following World War II to hasten and give direction to the process of industrial development by extending state-backed and sometimes state-funded credit to industrial firms. But as Meredith Woo-Cumings argues in Chapter 3, security concerns weighed heavily in Korean policy. Korea, a front-line state in the cold war, adopted industrial development policies that contributed to its military independence and strength. As such, it was the object of much financial solicitude by the United States and, at U.S.

insistence, by Japan. The United States tolerated Korea's state-led development policies "as long as it remained in the interstices of global capitalism and on the forefront of the cold war."[19] State efforts to hasten industrialization produced inflation, which often exceeded 20 percent in the 1970s. But inflation did not necessarily foster economic instability, even in the aftermath of the oil crisis. Tariff rates were high enough to dampen the impact of rising domestic prices on the country's trade balance, and the military dictatorship was able to ward off inflationary wage-price spirals through labor repression.

But in the 1980s domestic and international pressures led to a reform in financial practices. Domestically, it became imperative to restrain the use of credit to socialize risk "as the amount of non-performing loans skyrocketed in the 1980s."[20] Internationally, the United States was applying heavy pressure on Korea to reduce tariffs and to open up its economy to U.S. financial services. High inflation, meanwhile, was leading Koreans to see virtue in both tariff reduction and financial reform. The Korean government liberalized its trade legislation and accompanied this liberalization with an all-out assault on inflation. It cut back drastically on state-supplied credit and adopted a rigorous plan of monetary stabilization. Domestic credit expansion fell from a very high rate of 41 percent in 1980 to 30 percent in 1982 and 13 percent in 1984. The state acted to fill the financial void it created by attracting private lenders with pro-market reforms. Banks were privatized, ceilings on interest rates were lifted, barriers to foreign banks and financial institutions were abolished, and specialized credit programs that would have competed with private lenders were eliminated.

Financial reform in Mexico occurred at about the same time as in Korea. The turnabout in credit policy was perhaps more dramatic, if only because Mexico's creation of *fideicomisos* and its nationalization of banks were such recent events (1970 and 1982 respectively). In 1986, however, the government began to cut back on the volume of preferential credit allocated through public development banks. In 1989, credit controls were lifted, the size and role of the public development banks were reduced, the banks were denationalized, reserve requirements were reduced from 90 to 30 percent, and interest rates were liberalized.

---

[19]    Woo-Cumings, *Race to the Swift*, p. 202.
[20]    Ibid., p. 192.

Commercial bank activity was deregulated and foreign investment was encouraged. In 1990, the government sold its two-thirds holding in the nationalized commercial banks after amending the constitution to acquire the legal authority to do so. Finally, in a move that bears much resemblance to parallel developments in France, the government encouraged the adoption of "multiple" or "universal" banking practices on the German model, encouraging the banks to increase their involvement in industrial financing and to take on some of the responsibilities previously assumed by the state.

Sylvia Maxfield's analysis of reform in Mexico (Chapter 4) assigns a privileged place to international factors. Above all, preserving the value of the peso, needed to prevent a massive shift of assets from the peso to the dollar, was a "fact of life" for Mexican officials that affected policy throughout the period examined here. Mexican governments originally instituted state control over the allocation of credit not to promote industrial development but to fight inflation and defend the value of the peso. Structural pressure on Mexican policy was amplified in the early 1980s by the debt crisis—the consequence of heavy borrowing during the oil boom of the 1970s and of the rise in interest rates and the value of the dollar in the 1980s under the influence of Reaganomics. It was in response to the debt crisis that the government of López Portillo nationalized the banks and tried to impose greater control over capital movements. The new government that assumed power in 1983 rejected nationalist solutions, however, and worked to attract foreign capital back to Mexico in order to offset the outflow of money that serviced the debt. To achieve this, the government deregulated the capital market and enacted pro-market reforms.

In France, as in Mexico, interventionism was crowned in 1982 by bank nationalization. But, as in Mexico, liberalizing reforms were enacted within a few years of nationalization. Ironically, these reforms were implemented by a Socialist government that had assumed power with the intention of pursuing a more interventionist economic policy but was now forced to retreat because of speculation against the franc. The speculation was of such intensity and duration that the franc had to be devalued (within the framework of the European Monetary System) three times in 1982 and 1983.

But, as I show in Chapter 5, the source of France's monetary woes goes back farther—to the monetary crisis of the early 1970s which caused the collapse of the Bretton Woods system. The new regime of floating rates exposed the French economy to destabilizing spirals of inflation and currency depreciation, to which the French responded in 1976 by pegging the franc to the Deutsche mark. To support that policy, the French borrowed heavily on foreign markets while tightening their control over credit allocation. These policy responses, however, seemed only to hamstring French industry, debilitate the French political economy, and increase its vulnerability to external shocks. The French then took a serious look at more radical liberalizing reforms that subjected the growth of credit, and thus the growth of the money supply and inflation, to greater market discipline. The elections of 1981 interrupted that effort. Speculation against the franc compelled the Socialist government to reinstate a strong franc policy in 1983, however, and to support that policy with pro-market financial reforms. It had become clear that the strong franc policy was incompatible with institutions and habits that had for the past several decades encouraged French firms to borrow from lenders that were owned, controlled, or regulated by the state. The Socialists embraced the cause of financial market reform to wean French industry away from its dependence on state-allocated or -controlled credit and to impose greater discipline on monetary creation.

Liberalization in Spain, as analyzed by Sofía Pérez in Chapter 6, bears some resemblance to both the Korean and French cases, on the one hand, and the Japanese case on the other. Spain in the 1980s abolished regulations requiring banks to grant low interest loans to certain categories of borrowers and liberalized regulations controlling access to the Spanish market by foreign financial institutions. But those reforms were the culmination of efforts undertaken in the 1970s to bring credit creation under tighter control by shifting regulatory powers from the planning bureaucracy to the central bank. These efforts had been undertaken in response to the failure of the 1967 devaluation to stabilize the peseta. As monetary instability persisted in the 1970s, central bank officials acquired greater influence over economic policy. In the 1980s, policy turned monetarist as Spanish officials assigned a high priority to the fight against inflation and currency depreciation. Fighting inflation, however, did not mean subjecting credit to greater interventionist control, as in France in the 1970s, but rather subjecting the state to greater market discipline. Like the French in the 1980s, the Spaniards sought to use liberalizing reform as the foundation on which to deploy policies that would slow the flow of credit to the economy and bring greater stability to prices and the currency. But the Spaniards, unlike the French, did not adopt this course after giving interventionism a second and even a third chance; they began experimenting with liberal reforms relatively early on. Consequently, liberalization in Spain, as in Japan, was a more protracted process.

## Similarities and Dissimilarities across the Five Experiences of Reform

As we survey these five experiences of liberalizing reform, it becomes apparent that liberalization was not a simple process, despite similarities in the institutions and practices being reformed or abolished and despite the contemporaneity of the reforms in the five countries. Market forces do not seem to have had the same impact on the five countries, nor do policy shifts by financial powers, notably the United States, appear to have had the same repercussions.

France and Korea seem to provide the greatest evidence for the claim that policy shifts in the United States produced liberalizing reforms elsewhere. But the evidence points to a different kind of impact in each country. U.S. policy intervened indirectly in the French case by forcing change in the rules of international monetary relations on which French credit policy depended, thus forcing the French to change practices and reform institutions. The United States intervened in a more direct and instrumental manner in the Korean case by placing pressure on the Koreans to liberalize both their trade policies and their banking regulations. In the Mexican case, U.S. policy has imposed and continues to impose major indirect structural constraints. But domestic factors assume greater importance in the cases of Japan and Spain. Neither Japan nor Spain liberalized because they were overwhelmed by innovations in global finance or by the repercussions of U.S. policy decisions. And yet the domestic factors that drove liberalization in each case were distinct. Market-related factors prevailed in the Japanese case, state policy–related factors in the Spanish case.

From afar, we see what appears to be a single phenomenon, the dismantling of activist credit policies (and of the institutions through which those policies were implemented) occurring in different places during the same decade, roughly 1975–85. And yet as we examine the phenomenon at closer range, similarities evaporate and differences accumulate. We are therefore compelled to exercise caution in fashioning an overarching interpretation. In Chapter 7, I advance two claims. First, the importance of international political factors cannot be discounted, even though market and technological forces themselves cannot be ruled out. This is an important observation if only because it empowers us to receive interpretations inspired by neoclassical economic theory with a measure of skepticism. Second, we can interpret both the international political factors that we detect and many of the differences that we perceive in the process of liberalization across the five countries as the manifestation of uneven growth in the international political economy. Uneven growth, Robert Gilpin reminds us, is a corrosive power in the international political economy. Evidence of uneven growth reinforces the admonition that we treat purely market-based interpretations of recent trends with circumspection.

# Assault on the Bankers' Kingdom: Politics, Markets, and the Liberalization of Japanese Industrial Finance

KENT E. CALDER

**P**olicy-making, it is increasingly clear, presents a great dialectic between established institutions for decision making and the broader social problems with which they seek to cope.[1] Institutions tend to be conservative and function quite consistently over time. In the case of Japanese industrial institutions forged in World War II or American social-policy structures forged in the Depression of the 1930s, they tend to mirror, often for decades, the preconceptions and priorities of the turbulent times in which they were founded or sweepingly transformed. The more powerful and the more complex an institution, the stronger this endemic conservatism tends to be.[2]

Japan's industrial-credit bureaucracy has clearly been powerful and complex in comparative international terms. But substantial internationalization and economic liberalization have shifted, especially since 1970, the parameters within which Japanese policy is made, while the nature of the policy process itself has shifted with them. The bureaucracy's ability to respond sensitively to changing international circumstances, however, is impeded by the natural conservatism of established state institutions.

This chapter details the changing economic and political context of Japanese industrial-credit policies from the classic Bankers' Kingdom period of nominally state-directed credit allocation, administered and

---

[1]  See Jeffrey Pfeffer and Gerald Salancik, *The External Control of Organizations: A Resource Dependence Perspective* (New York: Harper and Row, 1978).
[2]  Anthony Downs, *Inside Bureaucracy* (Boston: Little, Brown, 1966).

effectively controlled by the long-term credit and city banks during the 1950s and 1960s, to the less interventionist but more politicized patterns prevailing in the late 1980s, and finally to the situation arising in the mid-1990s, in which a cautious but significant movement toward reregulation and the reassertion of some degree of state control has taken place.[3] The Bankers' Kingdom credit structure evolved a maze of formal controls: artificially low interest rates, a quasi-governmental committee to regulate bond issues, window guidance by the Bank of Japan, and in reserve another range of sanctions ready to be invoked in extremity. Private entrepreneurship did make strategic manipulation of these controls difficult. But the presence of the controls themselves, and the leverage that capital shortages gave to the state in an era of high-speed, capital-intensive industrialization, gave birth to a complex, brokerage-oriented, often clientelistic politics of industrial credit in which the industrial-policy bureaucracy had major advantages. This chapter examines how those advantages were eroded over the course of the 1970s and 1980s and how a more liberal financial system, albeit one subject to some continuing bureaucratic intervention, ultimately emerged.

## Forces for Change in Financial Structure

Many of the advantages of the Japanese state in directing industrial credit began slowly to unravel during the early 1970s. The first pillar of the Bankers' Kingdom edifice to weaken was corporate demand for externally generated funds. With capital deepening and tax treatment for corporations growing increasingly favorable, depreciation ratios at major Japanese firms rose steadily from 17.9 percent of total corporate

---

[3]  On the "Bankers' Kingdom" concept, denoting a political-economic situation in which private banks dominate the terms of credit allocation due to below-equilibrium nominal interest rates, credit shortages, strong banking-sector political influence, and limited bureaucratic intervention, see Kent E. Calder, *Strategic Capitalism: Public Purpose and Private Enterprise in Japanese Industrial Finance* (Princeton: Princeton University Press, 1993), chap. 5. The term "city banks" refers to standard commercial or retail banks as found in most countries aside from the United States. They manage deposit accounts for the public and offer loans and other financial services. Most countries have about a half dozen. Banking laws in the United States prevent such dominance of the retail market for banking services by a small number of large banks. Long-term credit banks specialize in long-term loans to businesses and generally rely on their own capital or on capital raised on the financial market to do so.

funds during 1966–70 to 28.0 percent during 1976–80 and to 34.5 percent during 1981–82.[4] Rising international competitiveness, coupled with trade policy developments such as voluntary export restraints on steel, color televisions, and automobiles also intensified Japanese corporate profitability, and with it the availability of internal corporate funds for investment. At the same time, the slump in global economic growth after 1973, combined with rising foreign protectionism and a structural shift in the Japanese economy away from capital intensive sectors like steel and shipbuilding, reduced the overall corporate demand for funds. Total corporate liabilities in Japan fell astoundingly from ¥181.6 trillion in fiscal 1975 to ¥9.5 trillion in 1980 to only ¥8.3 trillion in fiscal 1985.[5]

Many industrial firms not only reduced their borrowing and other means of raising capital but even developed substantial surpluses, which they began lending to others, thus intensifying domestic excess liquidity. Across the manufacturing sector as a whole, financial assets in proportion to liabilities rose from 42.6 percent in 1975 to 66.3 percent in 1984.[6] Portfolio assets of Japanese firms rose from ¥7.8 trillion in 1975 to ¥23 trillion in 1985.[7] Toyota Motors and Matsushita Electric even by the late 1970s had accumulated such great surpluses that they became known as "banks."[8] By 1984 they enjoyed annual financial earnings—unrelated to their manufacturing operations—of ¥48.9 billion ($211.7 million) and ¥57.7 billion ($249.8 million) respectively.[9]

By 1987 Toyota's financial profits had tripled even from 1984 levels to ¥149.6 billion, with its total cash hoard swelling to ¥1.7 trillion ($13.4 billion), or enough to buy Honda.[10] By 1995 they had spiralled to over $25 billion. Matsushita's financial profits were less spectacular, but still impressive—in 1987 they totaled ¥109.2 billion or nearly double 1984 levels.

[4]   Sakakibara Eisuke and Nagao Yoriyuki, eds., *Study on the Tokyo Capital Markets* (Tokyo: JCIF Policy Study Series No. 2, March, 1985), p. 60.
[5]   Bank of Japan Research and Statistics Department (Nihon Ginkō Chōsa Tōkei Kyoku), *Keizai tōkei nenpō* (Economic statistics annual), flow of funds data from selected issues.
[6]   Bank of Japan (Nihon Ginkō), *Shuyō kigyō no keiei bunseki* (Management analysis of major firms), 1984.
[7]   Bank of Japan, *Keizai tōkei nenpō*, 1976 and 1986, flow of funds data.
[8]   See *Toyota Shōhō-Matsushita Shōhō* (Toyota's and Matsushita's way of doing business) (Tokyo: Nihon Jitsugyo Shuppan, 1977).
[9]   C. T. Ratcliffe, ed., *Zaitech* (Tokyo: Kinyū Zaisei Jijō Kenkyū Kai, 1986), pp. 7–9.
[10]   "Japan Inc.'s Most Profitable Factory," *The Economist*, June 25, 1988, p. 75.

*Table 2.1.* Financial profits at major Japanese manufacturing firms (fiscal 1987)

| Manufacturing firm | Financial profits (¥ billion) | Percentage of pre-tax nonoperating profits |
|---|---|---|
| Toyota Motor | 149.6 | 37.6 |
| Matsushita Electric | 109.2 | 58.8 |
| Nissan Motor | 89.4 | 65.3 |
| Sharp Electric | 28.0 | 73.2 |
| SONY | 27.2 | 62.8 |
| Honda Motor | 22.7 | 26.1 |
| Sanyo Electric | 21.5 | 134.2 |
| Isuzu Motors | 16.4 | 1962.4 |

*Source:* Wako Economic Research Institute.

By the mid-1980s financial manipulations known as "Zaitech" ("financial technology") had become the most important source of profitability for a broad range of Japan's major electronics, automotive, and precision machinery producers. As Table 2.1 indicates, for many of Japan's best-known manufacturers, highly entrepreneurial financial operations have become a major source of corporate profits and a cushion against losses in more conventional operations. Zaitech played a major role in enabling these firms to withstand the steep revaluation of the yen during 1985–87, which made manufacturing for export from Japan suddenly less and less profitable. Zaitech was also important, although less so, in cushioning the sharp yen appreciation of 1994–95.

A second supportive pillar of the Bankers' Kingdom was a strong corporate reliance on indirect financing through commercial banks. As corporate demand for funds began to fall after the 1973 oil shock, firms gained greater freedom to diversify their modes of financing, since they became less vulnerable to oligopolistic bank pressures. Regulatory changes also facilitated this tendency toward diversification. During the period from 1970 to 1974, bank lending accounted for an average of 84 percent of cross-industry corporate financing in Japan. By 1980–84 this share had fallen to an average of 60 percent, and in 1984 itself to 44 percent.[11]

When government policies discouraged equity and bond finance, as happened frequently during the early 1970s, changing patterns in the flow of funds emboldened firms to diversify into new modes of financ-

[11]    *Far Eastern Economic Review,* April 9, 1987, p. 54.

ing. The securities firms, in close alliance with key concentrations of political power, in turn used these changes in the corporate incentive structure to generate support for more market-oriented vehicles of corporate finance. The traditional system of issuing equities at par value, long enforced by bank pressure and Ministry of Finance (MOF) administrative guidance, began to erode in favor of the system of issuing equities at market prices. This development greatly reduced the cost of equity capital, as did the steady rise in Japanese share prices. MOF authorizations for convertible bond issues also increased. By 1985 straight equity issues alone accounted for 36.3 percent of the funds raised by Japanese corporations—double the share of the 1970s.[12]

The third pillar of the Bankers' Kingdom regulatory structure was the banking sector's heavy reliance on the Ministry of Finance and the Bank of Japan, particularly heavy in the case of the city banks at the core of major industrial groups. It had been a truism that "corporations are in debt to the banks, who are in debt to the Bank of Japan." But after 1970 the changes in the flow of funds dramatically altered the bargaining relationships between private banks and the bureaucracy. Excess liquidity, for example, decreased the attractiveness of the Bank of Japan's discount window to commercial banks; such borrowings fell from 5.8 percent of total liabilities and net worth of the city banks in 1970 to only 2.3 percent by 1986.[13]

Even more important in this erosion was the explosion of government debt after 1973. As indicated in Table 2.2, the total value of all Japanese national government bonds outstanding increased over twelve times in nominal terms and five times in real terms between 1973 and 1985. Between 1966 and 1975, the Bank of Japan (BOJ) repurchased the bulk of all government bonds absorbed by the major banks a year after they were issued. After 1975, however, the BOJ greatly reduced such repurchases as part of a major policy shift designed to encourage the gradual development of a secondary market in treasury bonds. With the slowdown in economic growth, the BOJ clearly realized that the new macroeconomic situation did not facilitate credit rationing. It saw that central bank operations on an Anglo-American style money market were much better adapted to the needs of a low-growth economy than

[12]  Ibid.
[13]  Bank of Japan, *Keizai tōkei nenpō*, 1986, pp. 43–44.

the more interventionist Japanese variant that had previously prevailed. The BOJ's holdings of government debt outstanding fell from 37.5 percent of total debt in 1975 to 17.0 percent in 1980 and to only 8.4 percent in 1985.[14]

The Ministry of Finance, in an effort to cushion the impact of the BOJ's policy shift on both the private banks and its own borrowing costs, negotiated terms with the private banks for their purchase of this vast body of obligations. This task became increasingly difficult during the early 1980s, as ten-year government bonds issued in large quantities around the time of the 1973 oil shock and the subsequent slowdown in economic growth began to mature. National bond refunding issues rose, as indicated in Table 2.2, from around ¥3.3 trillion in 1980 to ¥24.3 trillion by 1985.

The surge of refundings, combined with the pressure to liberalize the financial system that the United States exerted through the Yen-Dollar talks of the mid-1980s, gave the larger city banks leverage in securing other market-oriented changes to increase their liquidity. Among these changes were relaxation of regulations on secondary-market bond sales and the introduction of certificates of deposit (1979) and money-market certificates (1985) to increase the fund-raising capabilities of such institutions as the city banks.

A final pillar of the classical Bankers' Kingdom was the network of exchange controls that insulated the domestic Japanese financial system, with all its finely calibrated defiance of market logic, from an international financial environment where market forces held sway. Only somewhat amended, the Foreign Exchange and Foreign Trade Control Law (FEFTCL) of 1948 and the Foreign Investment Law of 1950 prohibited in principle all foreign exchange transactions unless specifically permitted by the government. These laws conferred on regulatory authorities great discretion in mediating between the domestic financial system and its global environment. They also provided the basic legislative framework that governed foreign exchange transactions for more than a generation. Justified as this control structure once might have been by the chronic foreign exchange shortages that plagued Japan until the late 1960s, rapidly rising Japanese trade and current account

---

[14]   Figures are for domestic Japanese holdings of short- and long-term government securities combined for the Japanese fiscal years in question. See ibid., pp. 201–2.

*Table 2.2.* Explosion of Japanese national government debt, 1965–1985 (¥ billion)

| Year | Total national government debt | National government bonds outstanding (domestic) | Refunding bonds | Foreign currency bonds | Liabilities to trust fund bureau |
|---|---|---|---|---|---|
| 1950 | 554 | 240 | — | 100 | 2 |
| 1955 | 1,057 | 425 | — | 88 | 19 |
| 1960 | 1,340 | 446 | — | 81 | 41 |
| 1965 | 1,766 | 688 | — | 57 | 198 |
| 1970 | 6,226 | 3,597 | — | 54 | 504 |
| 1973 | 13,154 | 8,267 | 606 | 39 | 948 |
| 1975 | 22,795 | 15,776 | 1,677 | 33 | 2,677 |
| 1980 | 95,011 | 71,905 | 3,299 | 15 | 10,894 |
| 1985 | 163,571 | 136,610 | 24,295 | 0.7 | 16,188 |

*Source:* Bank of Japan Research and Statistics Department (Nihon Ginkō Chōsa Tōkei Kyoku), *Keizai tōkei nenpō* (Economic statistics annual), 1986, pp. 233–34.
*Notes:* (1) All figures are as of the end of the Japanese fiscal year for the years indicated (i.e. March 31 of the following calendar year). (2) Aside from the three major subcategories of government debt indicated, the Japanese national government also borrows in smaller amounts through short-term "food bills" and "silk bills," and through transfers from the general and special accounts as well as from postal life insurance and postal annuity funds. (3) Treasury borrowings from postal savings are included under the figure above for liabilities to the Trust Fund Bureau. (4) Refunding bonds are government bonds issued not to cover a specific expenditure, but to redeem government bonds previously issued.

surpluses erased the foreign-exchange rationale for such barriers early in the next decade. Japan no longer needed these controls since it was rapidly accumulating a chronic foreign exchange surplus.

The fiscal crisis in Japan also undermined the MOF's ability to maintain a separation. In return for underwriting huge quantities of government bonds domestically, Japanese banks had to be given increasing opportunities to deal in securities, expand overseas operations, raise funds abroad by the most flexible means, and repatriate those funds freely.[15] In 1972, for example, the MOF gave Japanese banks permission to float certificates of deposit on the New York and London financial markets. The banks also gained a rapidly increasing range of business opportunities in corporate finance outside Japan, albeit subject to the 1975 Three Bureaus Agreement that Japanese banks neither serve as lead managers for offshore bond issues by

---

[15]   See James Horne, *Japan's Financial Markets: Conflict and Consensus in Policymaking* (Sydney: George Allen and Unwin, 1985), p. 77.

Japanese corporations nor "act against the spirit of Article 65 of the Securities Exchange Act" separating the business activities of Japanese banks and securities firms.[16]

The December 1980 Foreign Exchange and Trade Control Law (FETCL) did not initiate or result in the categorical relaxation of Japanese foreign exchange controls.[17] Other incremental steps had been taken previously. Furthermore, important provisions for exchange controls to be invoked in times of financial crisis remained even after the new FETCL came into effect. But the removal in principle of controls in normal times helped ratify and accelerate the historical movement of Japanese corporate finance away from the reliance on domestic bank loans, which had been central to the Bankers' Kingdom political economy of the 1950s and the 1960s. This erosion of exchange controls, begun during the 1970s and accelerated by the new FETCL, led Japanese corporations en masse to issue straight and convertible bonds overseas, particularly in the Euromarkets. There the absence of collateral requirements and mandatory prospectus issues—together with the broad range of financial instruments, swaps, and exchange-rate hedging mechanisms not available in Japan—made raising funds cheaper, quicker, and more convenient than in Japan itself.

Starting in 1961 with Sumitomo Metals and Kawasaki Steel, Japanese corporations had periodically issued bonds abroad during the high-growth period. But the total was small: during the early 1970s the Euromarkets only accounted for 1.7 percent of Japanese corporate financing, a share that had risen by the late 1970s to 19.6 percent, mainly to finance offshore operations. In the early 1980s reliance on offshore finance began to rise even more sharply, primarily through large-scale corporate bond issues in the Euromarkets.

The Japanese surge abroad was driven by both expectations of a strong yen (in the case of foreign-currency-denominated issues) and the more flexible issuing conditions outside Japan. In 1979 the total of straight and convertible bonds of Japanese corporations issued within Japan totaled over ¥1.6 trillion, more than double the total of offshore

[16] This agreement was reached by the Ministry of Finance's banking, securities, and international finance bureaus in August 1975. It came in response to the underwriting activities in the Euromarkets of the Industrial Bank of Japan's merchant-banking subsidiary, IBJ International.

[17] See Horne, *Japan's Financial Markets*, pp. 164–72.

issues;[18] but by 1985 total Japanese corporate bond issues offshore had risen by ¥3.3 trillion to a figure greater by 25 percent than the total for all Japanese corporate issues within Japan itself.[19] Total Euromarket financial issues, with terms dictated by markets rather than by bureaucratic fiat, supplied over half of all Japan's corporate bond financing and one third of its total corporate finance, despite the low cost of capital to domestic issuers within Japan.

The explosion of offshore financing by Japanese corporations during the early 1980s, particularly the rapid increase in unsecured corporate bond issues, further intensified the pressures building within Japan for financial liberalization. In addition to undermining any qualitative allocation powers remaining to the Bank of Japan and the Ministry of Finance, this flight offshore also rendered increasingly irrelevant the activities of the Bond Committee (Kisai Kai), a powerful grouping of private banks and securities firms that since the 1930s had set issuing conditions in the corporate bond market.[20] By the mid-1980s only four percent of all Japanese corporate funds were raised through the domestic bond market, which the Kisai Kai had dominated for half a century. In 1985 the Ministry of Finance announced plans to consider a bond rating system,[21] which effectively circumscribed the Kisai Kai's ability to determine bond-issuing conditions.

Offshore financing by Japanese corporations also increased the pressure to relax issuing restrictions, especially those on collateral requirements. Such requirements did not prevail in many of the Euromarkets where Japanese firms were ever more intensively seeking capital. The banks had long opposed any relaxation of collateral requirements within the domestic bond market, from whose stringency many reaped considerable income from fees. But they began to reassess this position during the early 1980s as the rush offshore cut back their share of corporate financial business.

Foreign governments and financial institutions also developed a rapidly growing interest in internationalization and liberalization of the

---

[18]   Ministry of Finance (Ōkurashō), *Ōkurashō kokusai kinyū kyoku nenpō* (International finance bureau yearbook), 1982, p. 116.

[19]   Ministry of Finance, *Kokusai kinyū kyoku nenpō*, 1986, p. 148.

[20]   On the details of Kisai Kai operations, see Calder, *Strategic Capitalism*, pp. 29–30 and pp. 164–66.

[21]   *Japan Economic Journal*, January 22, 1985.

Japanese financial system, particularly as Japan became a massive international creditor with huge international surpluses. During the 1970s Japan's current-account surpluses had averaged only $1.9 billion a year; Japan's external assets at the end of 1981 totaled only $10.9 billion, compared to $140.7 billion for the United States.

Within five years, however, Japan's weakness had been more than reversed, with the United States becoming a net debtor and Japan emerging with over $200 billion in external assets. As major actors in global markets, with broad expertise in both underwriting and funds management, Western financiers saw major competitive opportunities as Japanese domestic capital markets and pension funds began to grow along with Japanese investments elsewhere. Foreign manufacturers, eyeing a remarkably weak yen, also pressed for regulatory changes to internationalize and strengthen the currency. Foreign governments, particularly the Americans and the British, strongly backed their financiers and manufacturers in calling for regulatory change as Japanese trade and financial surpluses soared upwards during the first half of the 1980s.

## Skewed, Uneven Liberalization of Private-Sector Finance

Market forces building over the past twenty-five years finally undermined the Bankers' Kingdom institutions and patterns of credit allocation. Although industrial borrowers, corporate investors, securities houses, city banks, foreign governments, and even the Bank of Japan all had their reasons for seeking to liberalize the regulatory status quo of the last two generations, market forces, both global and domestic, helped them achieve their objectives. But the process of financial liberalization from the late 1970s into the 1990s was not simply a triumph of market forces. Market forces gained considerable salience in some areas, but in those parts of the financial system bearing on the allocation of credit they failed to make much headway. Here government structure and interest group pressure alike skewed the liberalization process. In some areas there was actually informal reregulation: after the financial bubble of the 1980s burst and the long-standing one-party conservative regime collapsed in 1993, the hand of the MOF and the BOJ grew strong once again.

Three factors strengthened the role of the bureaucracy in Japanese corporate finance in the 1990s: (1) the distress Japanese banks confronted when the financial bubble burst; (2) the intense rivalry of banks and securities companies to enter one another's turf as long-standing regulatory barriers eroded; and (3) the collapse of the ruling Liberal Democratic Party, which during the 1980s had been steadily intruding on ministerial prerogatives. The MOF's reviving influence led to a more prominent government role in some parts of the financial system, in contrast to the dominant long-term liberalization tendency. One concrete manifestation of bureaucratic influence was the Cooperative Credit Purchasing Company, set up at MOF initiative in January 1993 for the purpose of unloading bad debts (estimated to total over ¥15 trillion at the twelve Japanese city banks alone in late 1994).[22] Another was the Financial System Reform Law of 1993. Although this legislation formally allowed banks and securities firms to venture into one another's territory by acquiring subsidiaries in other sectors of finance, strong controls and heavy licensing and reporting requirements effectively enhanced MOF powers vis-à-vis the private sector.

Liberalization, despite its limitations, proceeded during the 1970s, 1980s, and 1990s on at least five axes, with crucial implications for the allocation of credit throughout the economy as a whole. Perhaps the most important move was Japan's adoption of fundamentally new mechanisms for allocating credit toward the financing of long-term Japanese public debt. Until the early 1980s virtually all of this debt was underwritten at rates well below the market, set either through syndicates of banks and securities firms or by the MOF-controlled Trust Fund Bureau. Secondary markets in government debt were virtually nonexistent, both because of the small scale of debt offerings and because of the huge capital losses that investors would incur upon reselling debts whose unreal prices had originally been absorbed by the underwriting syndicates. But around 1978 serious conflict began to develop between the MOF and the syndicates over the huge prospective risks that the syndicates confronted as government bond issues grew very large.[23] In at least seven monthly offerings between July 1981 and July 1984, the banking syndicate actually refused to buy bonds at the

[22]   Nikkei Weekly, *Japan Economic Almanac 1995* (Tokyo: Nihon Keizai Shimbun Sha, 1995), p. 70.
[23]   Horne, *Japan's Financial Markets,* pp. 65–70.

price levels determined by the MOF, forcing the MOF to suspend the offerings and to reissue them later at prices more closely reflecting market realities.[24]

In 1980, the Bank of Japan began marketing a portion of this debt through tender offers, which accounted for 25 percent of all new government debt issues by 1985.[25] And as the scale of refunding issues expanded steadily after 1981 (from ¥890 billion in 1981 to ¥8.95 trillion during the succeeding four years alone), the government was forced to countenance the issuing of treasury securities—even those underwritten by syndicates—at close to market prices. By 1985 the syndicates were reselling over 70 percent of their total purchase amount of government bonds and had to choose between outright refusal and huge capital losses if the MOF did not price its offerings in accordance with prevailing market rates.[26]

There were also important steps toward market orientation in the regulation of corporate bond issues, which made the control-minded policies of the Bond Committee more difficult. Collateral had in principle been required for all Japanese corporate bond issues between 1933 and the early 1980s, although the MOF had construed the definition of collateral broadly enough to permit a few issues of unsecured convertible bonds by such firms as Mitsubishi and Marubeni Corporations, Kawasaki Steel, and Komatsu Limited during the early 1970s. Keidanren had called for relaxation in this collateral requirement as early as 1971,[27] with the MOF's Securities Exchange Council and MITI's Industrial Structure Deliberation Council later echoing this recommendation. In March 1979 Sears Roebuck became Japan's first noncollateralized convertible bond issuer, followed the next month by Matsushita Corporation and twenty-one other firms during 1979–84.[28] In January 1985 the large magnetic tape manufacturer TDK undertook the first unsecured straight bond issue in the Japanese domestic market since 1932; by February 1987 more than 350 other firms had also been

---

[24]   Edward J. Lincoln, *Japan: Facing Economic Maturity* (Washington, D.C.: The Brookings Institution, 1988), pp. 144–45.

[25]   Bank of Japan, *Keizai tōkei nenpō*, 1986, p. 205.

[26]   In 1985 12.3 percent of the total amount of government bonds initially purchased by the underwriting syndicate was ultimately resold, up from 20.3 percent of a much smaller amount in 1981. See ibid.

[27]   Nagatomi Yūichirō. *Antei seicho jidai no kōshasai shijō*, (Government and corporate bond markets of the stable growth period) (Tokyo: Ōkura Zaimu Kyōkai, 1978), pp. 206–7.

[28]   *Japan Economic Journal*, November 13, 1984.

authorized to do so.[29] In 1985 the MOF's Securities Exchange Council proposed the eventual abolition of the collateral rule, a change facilitating the flow of capital toward consumer and service-oriented firms at the expense of capital-rich heavy industry. As was suggested earlier, the relaxation of foreign exchange restrictions and the rapid expansion of offshore bond issues by Japanese firms during the early 1980s seem to have done much to bring about the authorization of these noncollateralized issues at home.

A third area of financial liberalization has been the MOF's increasing acceptance of market- as opposed to par-value securities issues. Through issues at market prices, corporations have been able to lower the cost of equity capital. They have also gained further incentives to reduce reliance on debt, accelerating their move away from dependence on the commercial banks.

Foreign-exchange trading has undergone important deregulation since the introduction of the 1980 Foreign Exchange and Foreign Trade Control Law. In April 1984, the Ministry of Finance abolished the so-called real demand rule, which had long prevented firms from effectively hedging or speculating in foreign exchange markets, by requiring banks to verify that all foreign-exchange trades were based on real commercial transactions. In February 1985, the MOF also allowed banks to deal directly with one another in yen-dollar trades instead of through the eight Tokyo foreign exchange brokers.[30]

Liberalization of deposit rates has been relatively slow due to the threat that liberalization poses to small, less efficient financial institutions, which are so numerous in Japan and so closely connected to the political process. In April 1979 certificates of deposit in minimum amounts of ¥500 million were introduced, in the first major step toward deregulation. In March 1985 money market certificates were also introduced in denominations reduced to ¥3 million by June 1989.[31] Interest rates on time deposits with commercial banks have also gradually been liberalized, beginning with deposits of over ¥1 billion in October 1985 and continuing to total deregulation by June 1993. In October 1994, the MOF completed the interest-rate liberalization process with the deregulation of rates on liquid deposits.

[29]  Lincoln, *Japan*, p. 203.
[30]  *Far Eastern Economic Review*, April 9, 1987, pp. 73–74.
[31]  Ibid., p. 53.

Deregulation has meant higher costs for financial institutions short of funds. It has had a particularly sharp impact on the city banks, which prior to deregulation traditionally procured one-third of their funds in various interbank markets. Banks have generally passed these higher costs on, where they have had the power to do so, in the form of higher lending rates throughout the financial system. This dynamic was moderated in the early days after deregulation by the sluggish demand for funds during the recession of the mid-1990s and by the consequent reluctance of banks to raise deposit rates to compete for such funds.

Since 1979–80 Japan has become increasingly innovative in the introduction of new financial instruments, although it remains substantially behind the major liberalized Anglo-Saxon financial systems in this regard.[32] Aside from certificates of deposit and money-market certificates in large denominations, Japan has introduced other, more modern financial instruments such as yen bankers' acceptances, unsecured call deposits, and government bonds of less than six months maturity. In late 1986 the MOF also inaugurated an offshore market formally analogous to New York's International Banking Facility (IBF). But various regulatory complexities, such as stamp duties and corporate taxes levied against offshore market transactions, continued to impede the effective progress of liberalization at the end of the 1980s.

By Anglo-American standards, the liberalization of the Japanese financial system still has a long way to go. As of the mid-1990s, consumer lending through credit card overdrafts beyond thirty days was still proscribed. Bank branching authorizations were still a centrally allocated prerogative of the Ministry of Finance, used to maintain the MOF's strong "moral suasion." Life insurance companies, major financial actors in their own right, also faced complex mazes of restrictions, such as fiduciary requirements limiting their overseas investments to 30 percent of assets. The net effect of these remaining restrictions on capital flows is virtually impossible to calculate with precision. But they clearly seem to reinforce the remaining prerogatives of the traditionally favored institutions of the Bankers' Kingdom (principally the smaller banks and the Bank of Japan), together with the traditional flow of funds toward manufacturing rather than to services.

---

[32]    For details on early innovations and a comparative analysis of developments elsewhere in the industrialized world, see Nihon Keizai Shimbun, *Atarashi kinyū-shihon shijō* (The new financial and capital markets), 4 vols. (Tokyo: Nihon Keizai Shimbun Sha, 1987).

## Market Forces and the Future of Government Finance

Among the distinctive features of the postwar Japanese financial system has been the public sector's unparalleled access to a large captive pool of private funds. In absolute magnitude, the Japanese postal savings system represents by far the largest deposit base of any financial institution in the world. This system also looms large relative to other financial intermediaries in Japan. Postal savings in Japan make up more than 30 percent of total savings deposits—over double the percentages in France, West Germany, and the Netherlands, where the postal system also manages savings accounts. The United States and Canada have no postal savings systems at all.[33]

For many years, the existence of a huge pool of private capital, subject to state control, was of immense strategic benefit to Japan's government finance programs. The cost of funds to the government through postal savings was substantially lower than what it would have been had the government raised funds through capital markets in the Anglo-American fashion, although this saving was somewhat offset before 1987 by the fact that savings deposits were tax exempt. Low liquidity and related high levels of risk in the volatile Tokyo capital markets encouraged risk-averse Japanese investors to prefer postal savings and bank deposits to securities, even at relatively low rates of return. The cost of postal savings funds to government financial institutions was also highly competitive with the cost of funds incurred by Japanese private banks, due to government subsidies for the operation of the postal savings branch network. In nine of the twelve years from 1974 to 1985, the postal savings special account was in deficit due to an excess of expenses over revenues,[34] with the deficit being covered by the government's general account. Between 1981 and 1984 this deficit averaged ¥105.3 billion annually.[35]

---

[33]   For a fuller description of the Japanese postal savings system and its role in the industrial finance of contemporary Japan, see Kent E. Calder, "Linking Welfare and the Developmental State: Postal Savings in Japan," *Journal of Japanese Studies* 16 no. 1 (Winter 1990): 31–59.

[34]   Tanaka Shin, "Itaku kinri hikisage mondai to jiyu unyoron o kaibo suru" (Analyzing arguments about self-management and the problem of reducing interest rates on lending to the Trust Fund Bureau), *Kinyū zaisei jijō*, October 28, 1985, p. 19.

[35]   Ministry of Post and Telecommunications Savings Bureau (Yūseishō Chōkin Kyoku), *Tokubetsu kōwa shiryō* (Special lecture data), June 4, 1987 (unpublished), p. 121.

The existence in Japan of an unusual pool of captive private funds for public allocation allowed the Japanese goverment bureaucracy to avoid heavy reliance on private banks and other financial institutions to finance strategic government programs. This gave the bureaucracy a degree of autonomy that the American, British, West German, and even to some degree the French governments could not achieve. The huge assets of postal savings and postal life insurance also provided the MOF with a most useful pool of capital for covering fiscal deficits, independent of capital markets and underwriting syndicates. The MOF used this pool extensively during the late 1970s and the 1980s to ease the impact of rapidly expanding government bond issues on a financial system that still lacked well-developed capital markets. Between fiscal 1978 and fiscal 1985, Trust Fund Bureau purchases of government debt rose twenty-six times from ¥300 billion to ¥7.9 trillion, accounting in 1985 for 39.7 percent of all government bond issues.[36] As indicated earlier, by the end of fiscal 1985 the Trust Fund Bureau held 11.8 percent of all national government bonds outstanding.

Yet rigidities built into the Japanese postal savings and government finance systems as they evolved through the 1970s threaten their viability in a market-oriented financial environment. During the politically turbulent early 1950s, when Japan was both rebuilding industrially and also developing extensive subsidy programs for domestic agriculture and small business, there was severe competition between heavy industry and the conservative political world for budgetary resources. Since 1946–47 the Ministry of Finance had been devoting much of the general account budget to industrial subsidies, especially to priority sectors such as steel, shipping, coal mining, and railways. Under the fiscal stringency imposed after 1949 under the so-called Dodge Line, political opposition to this support for basic industry rose steadily. Finally, in 1953 the Trust Fund Bureau Law (Shikin Unyōbu Hō), introduced at Diet insistence a floor of 6.05 percent on the lending rate for Trust Fund Bureau loans (itaku kin) to the government financial institutions, except in specially authorized circumstances.

Although originally introduced by the agricultural lobby to prevent heavy diversion of general account funds toward interest-rate subsidies for industry, the floor on Trust Fund Bureau lending rates—the cost of

---

[36]    Bank of Japan, *Keizai tōkei nenpō*, 1986, p. 205; 1979, p. 197.

funds for government banks—had very different implications in the highly liquid, increasingly market-oriented Japanese financial system of the 1980s. This mandatory floor made it more difficult for the government financial institutions to preserve the cost advantages over private financial institutions, which had made government credit more attractive to private borrowers and consequently had allowed the Japanese state to use government credit to encourage private-sector support of government strategic goals.

As the surplus of savings over investment in Japan began to intensify during the early 1980s, long-term interest rates that had been gradually liberalized from the early 1970s on began to fall in response to market forces. Japan's long-term prime rate, for example, dipped from 9.5 percent in mid-1980 to 6.4 percent by early 1986. Government administrative policies were unable to determine the interest rate structure, especially given the growing integration of international and Japanese domestic capital markets. By 1985 the decline in long-term market interest rates had erased the two-percent differential between the long-term prime rate and the Fiscal Investment and Loan Program (FILP) cost of funds, below which the Japan Development Bank and other public institutions could not lend without subsidies.[37] Private-sector loans thus rivaled the cost of unsubsidized government credit for the first time in Japanese history.

The crisis of government credit in the Japanese financial system of the mid-1980s can be seen more clearly when one examines closely the interest-rate structure of this system in the process of liberalization. By late 1985 the cost of funds encountered by government financial institutions when borrowing from the Trust Fund Bureau was around 0.7 percent higher than the cost of funds encountered by long-term credit banks and other issuers of corporate debentures. Government funds were also more than one full percentage point costlier than those paid by city and local banks on their time deposits. Yet prospective competition from both private banks and direct financial issues, including cor-

---

[37] The Fiscal Investment and Loan Program was an off-budget system of government financing funded by postal savings rather than government bonds (which were frequently monetized by the central bank during the period of capital scarcity). It was assembled in 1953, and made possible noninflationary credit allocation in support of a strategy of industrial development. It is in many regards the Japanese equivalent of the French Treasury circuit, described in Chapter 6.

porate bonds and even equities, made it difficult for government financial institutions to raise their lending rates and remain attractive to private borrowers. In a buyers' market for credit, Japan's government banks labored under substantial disadvantages due to their forced reliance on high-cost funds drawn from politically protected postal savers.[38]

## Three Options for Transformation

These market developments confronted the Japanese government financial system by the mid-1980s with a highly unpalatable dilemma. The government had three options for action, each of which held significant prospective political and economic costs.

One option was to let market forces take their course, without changing the underlying structure of the system. This route would seriously threaten the ability of the government banks to lend, because of competition from private sector institutions in a market-oriented, highly liquid financial system. The government banks had unusually high costs in this system. One reason was high research-related overhead expenses, supporting elaborate national facilities like the Japan Development Bank's Capital Investment Research Institute (Setsubi Toshi Kenkyū Jo). Expensive benefits packages for senior executives, many of them high-level retirees from top government ministries, were another element. Rationalization, especially of expensive but long-standing retirement bonuses for top executives, was politically difficult.

The second possibility was to subsidize government credit institutions—a course that necessitated specific budgetary outlays. Given the elaborate traditional structure of those institutions, which were supported by a system of shrinking noneconomic rents, such a course promised to be expensive. Meanwhile both the business world and consumers were growing ever more intolerant of subsidies.

The third option was to begin dismantling the government financial system itself. Such a move would automatically cut the system's huge overhead costs, centering on retirement payments to senior government

[38] On the relative cost of funds incurred by banks and the postal savings program during the first half of the 1980s, see *Nihon kōgyō shimbun*, October 7, 1986, p. 13, and *Nihon kōgyō shimbun*, November 11, 1986, p. 17.

retirees. Rationalization, coupled with interest-rate liberalization, would allow the system's privatized successor to deploy the huge resources at its command at higher, more market-oriented rates of return.

Throughout the first half of the 1980s the Japanese government pursued a cautious hybrid of the first and second options. As lending rates plunged at the private banks during 1984–85, government financial institutions, in the face of rising domestic liquidity, did not follow suit. Instead they tried to expand lending volume at close to commercial rates by appealing to broader and less familiar constituencies. The Japan Development Bank (JDB), for example, started wooing small firms it had previously ignored—in stiff competition with the Hokkaidō-Tōhoku Development Corporation and other small-business institutions.[39] In mid-1982, the JDB also extended its first loans to a wholly foreign owned foreign firm, Fairchild Japan, for the construction of a ¥5.5 billion electronic components plant at Isahaya in Nagasaki Prefecture.[40] Government loans to foreign firms, which these companies value more for the mark of legitimacy in Japan than for economic reasons, increased steadily in subsequent years. Even the small and highly political People's Finance Corporation ultimately began lending to foreign businessmen. But the government banks (other than the Housing Loan Corporation) forced by their inefficient cost structure and lack of subsidization to lend at high rates, had an ever more difficult time finding Japanese customers.

The market-induced crisis of Japanese government finance can be seen graphically in the evolution of government-financed leasing programs during the first half of the 1980s. During the 1960s and 1970s, institutions such as the Japan Electronic Computer Corporation (JECC) played a key role in stimulating stable demand for domestically produced high-technology capital goods, even when the underlying market was volatile and the technology unproved. The value of lease contracts in Japan overall rose substantially during the 1982–85 period. Yet the value of lease contracts concluded by government financial institutions dropped dramatically from ¥6.3 billion in 1982 to *one-thirtieth* of that amount only three years later. This occurred despite extensive govern-

[39] *Nihon keizai shimbun*, August 21, 1984, p. 12.
[40] *Shukan tōyō keizai*, May 8, 1982, p. 15.

ment leasing programs in such high-growth sectors as computers, robotics, and medical equipment. The reason for this striking change was the declining price competitiveness of the government loans behind the public leasing program, as market interest rates available to competitors continued to decline.

The second possible strategy for the government financial institutions was to subsidize their credit. This would assure the credit's competitiveness with the private sector and enhance its effectiveness as a strategic and political tool. The lower the cost of government credit relative to market rates, the more attractive it became, of course, to prospective recipients. Under political pressure from the ruling Liberal Democratic Party (LDP), the MOF also embraced some credit subsidies during the early 1980s, particularly in housing and agriculture.

Support for government corporations in the national general account budget increased from ¥1.8 trillion to ¥2.56 trillion between fiscal 1978 and fiscal 1985. Of this, the proportion going to interest-rate subsidies at government financial institutions rose steadily from 11.7 percent to 21.8 percent of the total.[41] More than one fifth of all general account subsidies to government corporations—¥558.5 billion—was being devoted to interest-rate subsidies by 1985.[42]

Interest-rate subsidies were concentrated heavily in two areas: support for housing and support for agriculture. Housing alone in 1985 consumed ¥341.3 billion in interest-rate subsidies, up 19.2 percent from the previous year, stirring fears that it was becoming a "second JNR," in reference to the insolvent Japan National Railways. The press was particularly critical of the high proportion of high-income people borrowing for housing loans, noting how such activity was subverting the redistributive purposes of the programs.[43] Agricultural loan subsidies were also increasing faster than rice prices, which had been frozen in 1982 before beginning to decline five years later.

Despite rising subsidies and an aggressive if often unsystematic search for new customers, Japan's inefficient, high-cost government financial institutions were having trouble by the mid-1980s overcoming

[41]  Matsuda Osamu, "Kōteki kinyu no mondaiten" (Problems relating to government finance), *Senshu daigaku shakai kagaku nenpō*, no. 20, March 30, 1986, p. 132.
[42]  Ibid.
[43]  *Nihon keizai shimbun* (evening edition), February 17, 1984.

the deepening dilemma into which market forces newly prominent within the Japanese financial system had forced them. The proportion of unused FILP funds rolled over into future budgets rose from only 0.8 percent of the total FILP budget in 1981 to 10.6 percent by 1984—the second highest level since the founding of the program.[44] Yet rigid legislative floors on the cost of funds to the FILP from the Trust Fund Bureau, reinforced by the desire of party politicians to preserve a high return on the postal savings (which supplied the Trust Fund Bureau), made escape from the deepening dilemma impossible. The government financial institutions had plenty of money to lend but could not afford to lend it because of its high initial cost and their own high internal cost structure.

Japan's private banks, of course, saw the plight of the FILP as a golden opportunity to cripple what they had always considered an unfair, quasi-socialist competitor. The All Japan Bankers' Federation (Zenginkyō) and the more broadly based Federation of Business Organizations (Keidanren) launched strong attacks on the favored status of FILP. With the former head of the reform-oriented Administrative Management Agency, Nakasone Yasuhiro, in the prime minister's residence, they had more support than usual.

On December 5, 1986, in the face of escalating market and political pressures on both the government financial institutions and the postal savings program, the cabinet announced potentially far-reaching changes in the treatment of postal savings. Postal savings accounts were made taxable, as the private financial institutions had demanded, except in a restricted range of welfare cases. This measure would have the effect of slowing postal savings growth. At the same time, the Ministry of Post and Telecommunications (MPT) was accorded the right to deploy an increasing share of postal savings assets through independent management (jishū unyō), which would involve direct MPT borrowings from the Trust Fund Bureau. Starting with management of ¥2 trillion in fiscal 1987, drawn from a projected increase in funds available to the Trust Fund Bureau, funds under independent MPT management were to rise to ¥4 trillion annually by fiscal 1991, or a total of ¥15 trillion under independent management by that date. Funds under MPT management

[44] Unused funds were slightly higher in highly liquid 1978. See Ministry of Finance (Ōkurashō), *Zaisei kinyō tōkei geppō* (Fiscal and monetary statistics monthly), assorted issues.

in 1991 would equal the total assets in 1986 of Japan's largest life insurance company, Nihon Seimei.[45]

Aside from conceding a share of Trust Fund Bureau assets to the MPT for independent management, the Ministry of Finance also agreed to lend excess liquidity from the Trust Fund Bureau to developing nations. This helped to cut the surfeit of high-cost government funds without a domestic market, although at the cost of added subsidies to foreign borrowers. In March 1987 the MOF announced its intent to utilize ¥6 billion in FILP funds for fiscal 1987 and a total of ¥30 billion over three years to purchase yen-denominated World Bank bonds oriented toward assistance to Third World developing nations. The ministry would then donate them back to the World Bank gratis, as Japanese foreign aid. In ensuing years FILP funds became an ever larger share of Japan's foreign aid outlays, the largest in the world, totaling $11.3 billion by 1993.[46]

The early 1990s thus found Japan's postal savings program, its government financial institutions, and its private financial sector all in a state of momentous transition in response to the challenge from emerging market forces. The tension between economic forces and the preexisting institutional structure was far sharper than in the Anglo-Saxon world, where the logic of markets had been accepted earlier and more extensively. Institutions in traditionally control-oriented economies such as France faced some problems similar to those of Japan, but in attenuated form because capital surpluses were not accumulating or market interest rates declining as rapidly. Given differences in state structure and interest-group configurations between Japan and the major Western industrial nations, markets were assuming a different role in Japanese finance than they did in Anglo-Saxon or European financial systems. But market forces in Japan as elsewhere were sharply and insistently calling into question the ability of the state to systematically channel flows of credit toward public purposes. Even more than during the high-growth period, markets were strengthening the hand of the Japanese private sector in defining and determining the fate of public projects.

---

[45]   Nihon Seimei's total assets in 1986 were 5.6 trillion. See *Tokyo shimbun*, July 1, 1987, p. 12.
[46]   Keizai Kōhō Center, *Japan 1995: An International Comparison* (Tokyo: Keiza Kōhō Center, 1995), p. 54.

## The Political Dimension

The conventional wisdom of Japanese economic policy-making has long been that "politicians reign but bureaucrats rule."[47] Evidence from the industrial credit area suggests that this generalization needs some qualification. Chronic factionalism and a strong grassroots orientation, both stemming in large measure from Japan's unusual multimember district electoral system, have encouraged politicians to cultivate a small number of intense supporters in competition with other candidates of their own party. These endemic traits of Japanese politics inhibit Japanese politicians from playing a systematic policy-making role, even when they have the technical expertise to do so, and have instead forced them to focus on grassroots constituent support. But politics also compounds the problems of bureaucrats in pursuing strategic credit allocation by inspiring the creation of politically oriented government financial institutions, by skewing the allocation of government credit toward noncompetitive sectors, and by obstructing discreet business-bureaucratic efforts to cross-subsidize heavy industrial loans to large firms through the system of compensating balances.[48]

Politics has also played a crucial veto function in Japan, sustaining long-established and often obsolete regulatory patterns such as the differentiated structure of Japanese banking, controls on savings deposit rates, and the position of postal savings. For many years, politics has also helped sustain the privileged and immensely profitable position of banks in the Japanese political economy as a whole, while simultaneously providing gradually expanded opportunities to the securities industry. Although the Diet has only intermittently been the scene of major substantive decision, it has, after all, continually served as the locus of ultimate formal authority in Japan; its general concerns have defined the overall legal parameters within which bureaucracy and business have made the detailed, microlevel decisions. The role of politics, to be sure, has been more than simply static, interacting dynamically with the economic changes discussed above to produce new patterns of policy-making in the industrial-credit area across the 1970s, the 1980s, and the 1990s.

[47] See Chalmers Johnson, *MITI and the Japanese Miracle* (Stanford: Stanford University Press, 1982), chap. 1.
[48] For details see Calder, *Strategic Capitalism*, esp. pp. 134–73.

*Patterns of the High-Growth Period: Politics as Welfare*

The classic function of politics during the period of financial policy formation in the 1950s and 1960s was the same as during the prewar period: broadening access to capital for small business and agriculture.[49] Pressure from small businesses against the Yoshida government created the People's Finance Corporation (Kokumin Kinyū Kōko) amid the depression of 1949, diluting deflationary pressures against a politically strategic constituency through off-budget financing. The Small Business Finance Corporation followed in 1953, for similarly political reasons, as a Diet-initiated measure intended to insulate the financial needs of small businesses from competing industrial demands at the Japan Development Bank, through which many small firms had previously been funded.[50]

Similarly, the Environmental Sanitation Business Finance Corporation (Chinchō Eisei Kinyū Kōko) emerged in 1967 under the political auspices of Tanaka Kakuei, Secretary General of the ruling LDP, to provide funds for traditional Japanese inns (ryōkans), coffee shops, and bathhouses. Tanaka reportedly hammered out arrangements for this new institution in a single night of hard bargaining with officials of the Nihon Ryōkan Kumiai (Japan Innkeepers Association), not long before the 1967 general election. The new institution, which duplicated the functions of the two preexisting government corporations in the field, never even established independent credit verification facilities. But it provided an assured, independent source of credit for small businesses at the political grassroots. Such firms are strategic gathering spots in urban communities and potentially important locations for displaying posters and undertaking other sorts of subtle political activity.

---

[49]    Political initiative helped to create, for example, the Central Cooperative Bank for Agriculture and Forestry (Nōrin Chūō Kinkō) in 1923, five years after the Rice Riots of 1918, and the Bank for Commercial and Industrial Cooperatives (Shōkō Kumiai Chūō Kinkō) in 1936.

[50]    Both the Ministry of Finance and the Japan Bankers Association were initially opposed to the idea of an independent Small Business Financial Corporation, while MITI advocated the creation of a small business special account (*tokubetsu kaikei*), under its own control. The major support for the idea, which prevailed in the Diet when MITI and the MOF could not agree, came from the small-business-dominated Tokyo Chamber of Commerce and from the Japan Small Business Industrial Cooperative Association (Zenchūkyō), a major small-business pressure group. On the politics of the Small Business Finance Corporation's establishment, see Small Business Finance Corporation (Chūshō Kigyō Kinyū Kōko), *Chūshō kigyō kinyū kōko ni jyū nen shi* (A twenty-year history of the Smaller Business Finance Corporation) (Tokyo: Chūshō Kigyō Kinyū Kōko, 1974), pp. 65–81.

Their importance is magnified by Japan's very stringent legal restrictions on television and other conventional Western forms of campaign activity.

The Agriculture, Forestry, and Fishery Finance Corporation also emerged, albeit less dramatically, in response to interest-group pressure. When the Japan Development Bank was set up in 1951, agriculture was initially accorded only a special account within it. But in 1953, the Diet initiated legislation to establish a separate agricultural finance institution, so that agriculture would not be forced to compete directly for scarce government funds with the basic industries that were the JDB's fundamental clientele: a process of differentiation which closely paralleled—indeed, set the precedent for—small business finance.[51]

Just as the interest pressures of agriculture and various branches of small business resulted in the creation of specialized financial advocates, so also did the medical profession get its own specialized support body, with a budget insulated from broader competition for funds at the initial, MOF-dominated stage of budgeting.[52] As the 1961 White Paper on Welfare (Kōsei Hakusho) pointed out, doctors before 1960 had received limited loans from the two major government small-business finance bodies. But there was no recognition of the special needs of medical organizations, particularly the small hospitals and clinics so numerous in Japan.[53] Doctors desired a more responsive funding organization, and during a period of political turmoil in 1960 they secured Diet-sponsored legislation providing them with a privileged source of government funds, the Medical Care Facilities Finance Corporation (Ivyō Kinyū Kōko) which began operations in July 1962. Significantly the doctors received broad support from the Left as well as the Right for their demands—just as small business and agriculture had a decade earlier when they were successful in having captive government banks

---

[51]  See ibid., p. 75.

[52]  Establishing a relatively secure source of funding through an independent government finance body is tactically important for nonelite pressure groups because it strengthens them in the face of MOF pressures in the pre-MOF budget (*Ōkura Genan*) stage. That stage is, as Campbell points out, traditionally dominated by bureaucrats, in contrast to the highly political revival negotiations. See John Campbell, *Contemporary Japanese Budget Politics* (Berkeley: University of California Press, 1977).

[53]  Ministry of Health and Welfare (Kōseishō), *Kōsei hakusho* (White paper on welfare) (Tokyo: Ōkura Insatsu Kyoku, 1961), p. 328.

established on their behalf. At such points, party adherence was not yet set in stone.

Support for underdeveloped regions of Japan has been a traditional concern of the Japanese government since the Meiji Period. Special credit facilities for Hokkaidō and for Okinawa as well since its revision in 1972 can be explained on these grounds. But party politics has introduced important nuances into these programs. For example, the Hokkaidō Finance Corporation was founded in June 1956 to provide long-term development funds for Hokkaidō prefectures. A year later, seven Tōhoku prefectures (including Niigata, which had not been traditionally considered a part of Tōhoku) were added to its coverage, and it became the Hokkaidō Tōhoku Finance Corporation. Not coincidentally, Niigata was the home prefecture of the highly entrepreneurial future prime minister Tanaka Kakuei, who was very active during this period in promoting Niigata's interests.

## The Intensified Distributive Politics of the 1970s

During the early 1970s, party politics became increasingly important in inspiring major new programs within existing government financial institutions. Spiraling administrative costs and rising political resistance to the costly retirement benefits for the senior ex-bureaucrats who had directed these institutions reduced the chance of establishing new ones. But inefficient sectors of the economy experienced severe pressure in the face of protracted low growth and the credit restraint required to slow post–oil shock inflation. Small businesses did not enjoy the government assistance that agriculture received in the form of rice price supports, import quotas, and the nōkyō cooperative system. Small business bankruptcies rose steadily after 1973, even under the relatively loose credit conditions that prevailed once the inflation of 1972–74 had been subdued.

Reinforcing the motivation of conservative politicians to aid small business during the early 1970s in Tanaka Kakuei's Japan, as in Georges Pompidou's France, was the steadily rising political strength of the Left and the strategic position of small business as a swing constituency. This was dramatically apparent in the 1972 Japanese Lower House elections. Communist strength in the Diet nearly tripled from 14 to 38 seats, much of it on the strength of small business backing in Kyōto, Ōsaka, Tokyo, and Kanagawa prefectures. Membership in the Minshū Shōkō Kai (or Minshō Democratic Commercial Association) a small-business federation, associated with the Japan Communist Party, soared from 62,000 members in 1965 to 175,000 in 1971—about one-sixth of all Japanese small businesses were involved in the organization in some fashion.[54]

The LDP responded with a new program—the so-called no-collateral loan system (mutampo yūshi seido). This system entitled small businesses to borrow up to ¥5 million (around $20,000) in low-interest loans without mortgage or security. The only requirement was that applications be scrutinized by management advisors (keiei shidōin) affiliated with local branches of the conservative Japan Chamber of Commerce and Industry. Loans could be made for any purpose, so there were no clear strategic criteria applied. To the contrary, the system's purpose was purely political: drawing small businessmen away from the leftist Minshō. Government funds allocated to the no-collateral loan program soared from ¥30 billion in 1973 to ¥510 billion in 1978.[55] By the early 1980s, two of the four and one-half million Japanese small businessmen had ties to the no-collateral loan system and its conservatively oriented administration.[56] Even by its own calculations, membership in Minshō had not grown appreciably since the loan system was introduced in 1973.[57]

### Post–Oil Shock Consumer Activism

The Bankers' Kingdom, the Japanese financial system of the high-growth 1950s and 1960s, strongly subsidized big business borrowers at the expense of the individual depositor. The city banks did so by keeping the effective interest rates on loans relatively low to their preferred customers and offering only meager returns on individual deposits. The owners of the small financial institutions that supplied funds also benefited at the expense of depositors, since they provided funds to the call market at rates substantially above the rigidly controlled savings deposit

---

[54]  Hirose Michisada, *Hojokin to seiken tō* (Subsidies and the party in power) (Tokyo: Asahi Shimbun Sha, 1981), p. 42. On the broader political context, see Kent E. Calder, *Crisis and Compensation* (Princeton: Princeton University Press, 1988), chap. 2.

[55]  Hirose, *Hojokin to seiken tō*, pp. 44–45.

[56]  Ibid., p. 49.

[57]  According to unpublished figures supplied to the author, Minshō membership was about 300,000 in 1973 and 365,000 in 1983.

rates. Patrick calculates the gross redistributive effect from depositors to stockholders during the mid-1960s at around 1.3 to 2 percent of personal disposable income, a substantial sum.[58] Yet there was little overt political opposition to this transfer or to the relatively high profits of the banks throughout the high-growth period from 1955 to 1973.

Citizen activism on financial issues exploded into prominence in Japan during 1974–75 in one of the major postwar shifts in the political parameters of Japanese finance. Inflation was surging rapidly ahead of both wage increases and nominal increases in national savings following the oil shock, and the general public was angry. As the press prominently reported, the average Japanese household lost 12.7 percent of the value of its savings from the end of 1972 to the end of 1973 alone.[59] Yet the Japanese government, in sharp contrast to the policy responses of such other major industrialized nations as West Germany, made no upward adjustments in savings and other deposit rates to compensate.

The protest from the opposition and from citizens' groups was unprecedented and highly diverse. The Zensen Dōmei textile workers' union sued the government for losses from postal savings deposits, whose value had been badly eroded by inflation.[60] In November 1974 the Japan Consumers' Union began a campaign against the banks' practice, permitted by the MOF since 1950, of not paying interest on deposits under ¥1000, even though interest on housing loans was calculated to ¥100 increments. This long-standing practice, charged the union, generated an annual ¥5.8 billion in banking profits during the early 1970s. Union leaders confronted chairmen of the twelve major city banks and demanded to know how high deposit rates would be allowed to rise in compensation for inflation. Their protest was reinforced by a "one-yen deposit movement," which inundated many urban bank branches with minute, unprofitable accounts.

The Japan Socialist Party, together with the Kōmeitō (an opposition party with strong small-business ties), spearheaded criticism of LDP

---

[58]   Hugh Patrick, "Japan's Interest Rates and the 'Grey' Financial Market," *Pacific Affairs* 48 (fall–winter, 1965–66): 326–44.

[59]   See Furukawa Kazu, "Yokin meberi ni taisuru shomin no ronri" (The average person's reasoning about the erosion of savings by inflation), *Ekonomisuto*, November 5, 1974, p. 43.

[60]   Ibid., p. 42. See also Tsuruta Toshimasa, "Yokin meberi soshō to seifu no sekinin" (The savings erosion suit and the government's responsibility), *Ekonomisuto*, March 4, 1975.

inaction. They proposed to create a class of "small-scale accounts" (*koguchi yokin*) of up to ¥500,000, on which the banks would be required to pay 10-percent interest. A "welfare deposit" system was also proposed under which the elderly and single-mother families would also be accorded preferential rates to offset inflation.[61]

We have seen how agriculture and small business have often succeeded in implementing their financial proposals, particularly during periods of broad national political turbulence like the early 1970s. Consumer-oriented reforms have fared somewhat differently, as they did in this case. Although the banks consented to pay interest on small deposits—Chairman Sasaki of the Japan Bankers' Federation agreed to credit them on all amounts over 100 yen from August 1975—they made no substantive adjustment of deposit rates to compensate for inflation, and the proposal to establish preferential "welfare accounts" and "small-deposit accounts" died by the wayside. The heaviest political resistance to these innovations came from the small, consumer-oriented financial institutions, such as the consistently marginal and highly politicized credit associations (*shinyō kinko*),[62] founded through Liberal and Socialist Party intervention during 1950–51. Established members of the LDP "circle of compensation"[63] thus blocked the entry of new, consumer-oriented groups.

## Compensating Balances as a Political Issue

Controls, as economic theory so insistently suggests, invariably create their own distortions. A fundamental and repeatedly expressed demand of Japanese industrial strategists for many years after the war was to depress long-term interest rates below market levels. Such low-interest policies have both reduced the costs of capital-intensive industry and provided some allocative power to the banks and bureaucracy. These faced a heavy demand for low-cost capital and were obliged to impose a system of rationing. But interest-rate controls also intensified pressures on the lenders of low-interest funds to recoup income fore-

---

[61]  *Yomiuri shimbun*, February 23, 1975.

[62]  Ibid.

[63]  A "circle of compensation" is a group of individuals or organizations with reciprocal support obligations, usually of mixed political and economic character. See Calder, *Crisis and Compensation*, p. 160.

gone due to the controls, usually by collusively raising their noninterest income.

The most common means by which Japanese banks recouped profits lost to controls was through the system of compensating balances. When firms borrowed money from Japanese banks, they customarily redeposited a portion of it with the bank from which they borrowed, generally receiving only very low interest on these redeposits. Both large and small firms were subjected to this practice. Yet small firms, with little leverage in the financial world were generally forced to make proportionately high compensating balances. During the mid-1960s credit associations and mutual savings banks, which dealt primarily with small business, demanded compensating balances roughly four times as much as those charged by the city banks, which primarily funded large firms. Even in 1980 this differential continued to exist, although it had narrowed substantially.

Compensating balances bear relationships too complex and circumstantial in the vast world of borrowing and lending to be easily outlawed. And financial authorities, who must continually deal with the large banks, have had few incentives of their own to intervene. A continual bargaining process among business, bureaucracy, and politicians has produced few gestures at decisive control. So politicians—of the Democratic Socialist and Socialist Parties as well as the LDP—were given the chance to act alone to deal with the issue. Their leverage with big business and the state was enhanced, especially during the late 1960s and early 1970s, by the persuasive appeals that the Japan Communist Party was making to small-business voters.[64]

Compensating balances first arose as a major issue in 1948–49,[65] during a period of tight control on government finance introduced by the financial advisor of the Allied occupation forces, Joseph Dodge. The controls forced private firms to borrow more heavily from private banks, and encouraged the banks to demand a quid pro quo—compensating balances—in the emerging sellers' market for funds. At first the MOF objected strongly to the practice, which it declared illegal in

[64]    See Calder, *Crisis and Compensation*, chap. 7; and Ellis S. Krauss, "The Urban Strategy and Policy of the Japanese Communist Party: Kyoto," *Studies in Comparative Communism* 12, no. 4 (winter 1979): 322–50.

[65]    "Buzumi ryodate taiji ni kirifuda" (The trump card for destroying compensating balances), *Ekonomisuto*, June 23, 1964, p. 22.

March 1951.[66] But gradually the MOF, led particularly by its Banking Bureau, became more conciliatory to the banks and geared down to routine calls for bank "self-policing," ten of which were issued between 1949 and 1964.[67]

One high point of political concern and intervention came during the turbulent early 1960s. Following the Security Treaty crisis of 1960 and increasingly active Socialist and Communist efforts to organize small businesses, the conservative Ikeda government announced an extensive small-business policy, culminating in the Small Business Basic Law of 1963. Almost simultaneously its Income Doubling Plan and low interest-rate policy stimulated a capital-spending boom and capital shortage that gave financial institutions considerable leverage to demand compensating balances—particularly from small business.

During 1963–64 compensating balances became a major political issue, with Prime Minister Ikeda Hayato and BOJ governor Yamagiwa Masamichi promising to study the issue, and Minister of Finance Tanaka Kakuei appointing a special investigative commission. The Fair Trade Commission proposed that compensating balances be considered an antitrust question. The Finance Committee of the Diet demanded that compensating balances be phased out entirely by the banks within one year.[68] Under such pressure and faced by the prospect of the MOF losing its jurisdiction over the issue to the Fair Trade Commission, the MOF issued an administrative order (tsūtatsu) controlling compensating balances on June 25, 1964.[69]

The compensating balances question reappeared with each period of tight credit. Small business would mobilize politicians to put pressure on banks not to use the market power that credit shortages gave them to raise real interest rates. During 1974–75 the issue arose once more with the same force it had in 1948–49 and 1963–64. As in the other cases, major legislative initiative was taken by opposition parties with strong

[66]  Japan Bankers' Federation (Zenkoku Ginkō Kyokai), *Ginkō kyōkai ni jyū nen shi* (Twenty-year history of the Bankers' Association) (Tokyo: Zenkoku Ginkō Kyōkai, 1965), p. 492.
[67]  "Buzumi ryodate taiji ni kirifuda," p. 22.
[68]  Ibid., p. 23. On the political issue of compensating balances during 1963–64 more generally, see Inoue Kaoru, "Buzumi ryodate ni torikumu" (Wrestling with compensating balances), *Ekonomisuto*, December 3, 1963, pp. 52–55; and Oizumi Tsuneo, "Buzumi ryodate no jittai to kinō" (The reality and function of compensating balances), *Ekonomisuto*, January 14, 1964, pp. 40–43.
[69]  Japan Bankers' Federation, *Ginkō kyōkai ni jyū nen shi*, p. 445.

small-business ties, particularly the JSP, DSP, and Kōmeitō,[70] with tacit support from a Japan Communist Party continuously and scathingly critical of bankers' pressure on small business. The LDP, strongly connected to the banking world through Keidanren (Japan's preeminent big-business federation) and deriving much financial support from the large banks, rarely made such moves. But given the electoral significance of small business and a strong populist streak among party members who had not served in the bureaucracy, the LDP typically went along with the Diet rumblings against the commercial banks. Such political pressure may well have provided intermittent relief for small businesses.[71] But it did not generate structural changes in the Japanese financial system comparable to those that many of the policy innovations discussed above accomplished. The shifting political parameters of the 1970s effected no clear change in the political economy of the compensating balance system.

### Politics and the Business Mainstream

Party politicians have periodically intervened in the distribution of industrial credit to compensate nonelite groups disadvantaged by underlying economic trends. This pattern, an old one dating from before World War II, became more pronounced during the 1970s. It gained special force during the politically turbulent early 1970s as the demands of the disadvantaged gained particular resonance because of the ruling Liberal Democratic Party's precarious position in the Japanese political system.[72]

Beginning in the mid-1970s politics also became a vehicle for articulating some consumer interests in the financial sphere, although this has been a hesitant and underdeveloped process. During the

[70]  On April 4, 1974, for example, Suzuki Yasuo of the Kōmeitō demanded that the MOF use administrative guidance to prevent small businesses from being the principal victims of the restrictions on credit that followed the oil shock. See *Asahi shimbun*, April 5, 1974.

[71]  After opposition pressure, Finance Minister Ōhira Masayoshi announced on February 21, 1975, in the Lower House Budget Committee that the MOF Banking Bureau Director General would issue a directive to all financial institutions to refrain from demands for compensating balances. See *Asahi shimbun*, February 22, 1975.

[72]  For a broader treatment of linkages to the political process, see Calder, *Crisis and Compensation*, chap. 2.

1980s transnational politics also began influencing the configuration of Japanese credit flows and the structure of the financial system, reflecting growing global economic interdependence and particularly intensified economic relations between the U.S. and Japan. How this new phenomenon of transnational politics helped accelerate the liberalization of Japanese finance will be considered in this chapter's conclusion.

Perhaps the most important—and most obscure—impact of politics on the configuration of Japanese domestic industrial credit has been its role in shaping the position of banking, securities, and postal savings in the financial system as a whole. The essential features of the Bankers' Kingdom system of industrial credit allocation were virtually all in place by the end of the Allied occupation in April 1952. Domestic politics within Japan had relatively little to do with creating the structure itself, which was more an outgrowth of wartime mobilization. But politics clearly played an important if unobtrusive role in sustaining a bank-centered financial and industrial system once that system was established.

Among the salient realities in the politics of Japanese finance has long been the strong support that the banks—particularly the large money-center banks—provide to the ruling Liberal Democratic Party as an institution. The All Japan Bankers' Federation (Zenginkyō), embracing both large banks and small, was a major driving force behind the creation in 1961 of the Kokumin Kyōkai (literally, The People's Association), Keidanren's mechanism for efficiently funding the LDP without provoking competition within the business world for its favors. Together with steel and electric power, banking was one of the three traditional funding mainstays (*Gosanke:* literally "honorable three families") of the LDP throughout the high-growth period. Its standard assessed share of Kokumin Kyōkai political contributions in early 1974, for example, was reportedly 16.7 percent of the total for the business world as a whole, compared to 8.3 percent for steel, 7.6 percent for electric power, and sharply less for other sectors.[73]

---

[73] The electronics industry, for example, was assessed 4.9 percent of total business contributions, construction and automobiles 4.5 percent each, private railways 4.3 percent, and securities 3.6 percent, according to *Asahi shimbun* calculations reportedly leaked from confidential Kokumin Kyōkai sources. See Asahi Shimbun Keizai Bu, *Ginkō* (Banks) (Tokyo: Asahi Shimbun Sha, 1976), pp. 152–53.

The large city banks provided by far the largest share of their industry's standard contributions to the Kokumin Kyōkai, with the sixteen members of the Tokyo Association of Banks, representing the largest banks in Japan, providing three-quarters of the total for all banks or 12 percent of all contributions to the LDP in early 1974. The regional banks provided 2.4 percent of national business support, the trust banks 1.0 percent, and the mutual savings banks 1.3 percent.[74] From the late 1970s on, however, the relative share of the city banks fell and that of the local banks rose,[75] reflecting changes in both relative profitability and in perceived interests as the banking sector confronted financial liberalization.

The banks, particularly the large city banks, also lent and donated substantial sums to the LDP directly. In October 1974, for example, nine major city banks (Dai Ichi Kangyō, Fuji, Sumitomo, Mitsubishi, Sanwa, Mitsui, Tōkai, Taiyō Kobe, and Daiwa) had ¥9.935 billion in loans outstanding to the LDP without collateral and at interest rates between 9 and 9.5 percent, which was quite low in the context of the times. In 1972 city bank lending to the LDP had been ¥6 billion.[76] Banking support appears to have played a crucial role in both the general election of December 1972 and the Upper House election of mid-1974, both presided over by former prime minister Tanaka Kakuei.

Despite their heavy political contributions, the large banks received mixed treatment at the hands both of the ruling LDP and the financial bureaucracy. To be sure, the MOF regulatory policies assured great profits for the city banks under the Bankers' Kingdom regime. But in many ways the smaller banks were treated even better, despite their significantly smaller political contributions. Despite heavy funds demand, for example, the access of the city banks to new funding sources was strictly limited; regional banks during the period from 1955 to 1973 were allowed to expand their branching network three times as rapidly as the city banks, despite their being less called upon for loans.

The MOF's regulatory decisions after 1973 progressively curtailed the lending prerogatives of private banks in such areas as compensating balances in order to support industry. National policy meanwhile allowed

---

[74]    Ibid., p. 152.
[75]    Gerald L. Curtis, *The Japanese Way of Politics* (New York: Columbia University Press, 1988), pp. 183–84.
[76]    Asahi Shimbun Keizai Bu, *Ginkō*, pp. 150–51.

postal savings to expand at the expense of large banks. Particularly since the early 1970s, a number of pressure groups, many of them from outside the financial sector entirely, have joined the commercial banks in political struggles related to selective credit policy.

Throughout the postwar period, large banks have been presented with a classic free-rider problem in their relationship to the Japanese political process. Together with the equally risk-averse and heavily regulated steel and electric power industries, they have maintained a broad, pervasive interest in the stability of the prevailing political and economic arrangements, safeguarded until 1993 by a continuous one-party conservative government. Other elements in the business world, including the securities and construction sectors, shared this interest in political stability, but they had fewer incentives to provide strong financial backing to the LDP as an institution. The Gosanke were already fulfilling that function eminently well. These free-riding sectors concentrated on cultivating individual factions and politicians rather than the LDP as a party, always intervening pragmatically and strategically to secure distributive benefits for themselves. The large banks, in contrast, sustained a more comprehensive but vaguer structure of conservative dominance, which yielded them progressively less direct benefit.

Seen in comparative context, Japan's securities industry exhibited unusual influence in financial policy-making during the 1980s—an influence that helps explain why Japanese financial liberalization diverged from that of other strongly bureaucratic states. In France, for example, the *agents de change* who serve as brokers on the Bourse have traditionally been pawns of bureaucratic power, and during the late 1980s they gradually lost their role in the French financial system.[77] They had little relationship to politics, having failed to develop the reciprocal ties that might have sustained them in the face of growing pressures for deregulation.

In sharp contrast to this situation, brokerage houses in Japan steadily increased their role in both the Japanese national and the international financial systems. Indeed, by the late 1980s they were the most affluent and rapidly growing financial intermediaries in Japan. And their mete-

---

[77] Financial reform plans of the mid-1980s were for the monopoly of *agents de change* on brokerage transactions on the Bourse to disappear by January 1, 1992. See Philip G. Cerny, "The 'Little Big Bang' in Paris: Financial Market Deregulation in a Dirigiste System," *European Journal of Political Research* 19, no. 1 (1988).

oric rise in profitability and economic influence was deeply rooted in the political system. The support that party politics gave to the Japanese securities industry before the collapse of LDP rule in 1993, particularly during the financial bubble of the late 1980s, is probably the single most important political influence on the Japanese financial system since World War II.

The relationship of the securities industry to conservative politics in Japan goes back to the early aftermath of World War II. Early Occupation regulatory policy tended to favor banking, a favoritism reinforced by General MacArthur's personal bias against securities. Within the Ministry of Finance the supporters of banking held preeminence over those of the securities industry, partly because of the much greater age and size of the MOF's Banking Bureau compared to its Securities Bureau. As an outsider during the Bankers' Kingdom period, the securities industry was forced to appeal to politics, and did so, not always successfully, for redress of its mounting grievances over the orientation of the financial system.

Among the earliest political associates of the securities industry was Ikeda Hayato, who repeatedly obtained much of his faction's political funding from Nomura Securities, the largest of Japan's securities firms. Another supporter was Tanaka Kakuei, Finance Minister from 1962 to 1965, who pressured Bank of Japan officials into granting a special emergency loan to the nearly bankrupt Yamaichi Securities in 1965— the only such special loan extended by the BOJ to a nonbanking institution in its history, before or since.[78] The number of politicians close to the securities industry increased particularly quickly after 1975, when changes in the Japanese campaign financing law placed constraints on direct donations by individual corporations and made stock manipulations increasingly important as a source of campaign funds. The dynamics of manipulation became publicly known during the recruit scandal, in which special shares were provided to key politicians at below-market prices. The scandal forced the resignation of Prime Minister Takeshita Noboru, one of the strongest supporters of the securities industry in the political world, in the spring of 1989. Other dynamics surfaced in the ongoing financial scandals of the early 1990s.

---

[78]    On the details, see Kusano Atsushi, *Shōwa yon jyū nen go gatsu ni jyū hachi nichi* (May 28, 1965) (Tokyo: Nihon Keizai Shimbun Sha, 1986).

The scandals of the early 1990s, coupled with the collapse of Japan's financial bubble and of its conservative ruling party, undermined the role of the securities industry in Japan's broader political economy. One major beneficiary was the bureaucracy, which then moved the economy toward the reregulation noted earlier. But given long-run trends toward the internationalization and liberalization of the Japanese economy, together with a revival of conservative political fortunes after mid-1994, the prospects for a resurgence in the influence of securities within the Japanese financial system remain good.

Fiscal deficits and excess corporate liquidity were, to be sure, the central factors driving the liberalization of Japanese finance during the 1970s, 1980s, and early 1990s. But politics has profoundly influenced that transformation, particularly in defining the rights and responsibilities of the massive postal savings fund in the emerging market-oriented financial system. It was LDP politicians, for example, who obtained for the Ministry of Post and Telecommunications the right, beginning in July 1987, to manage a ¥15 trillion share of postal savings funds independently of the Ministry of Finance by 1991, with investment fees going to the major securities companies.[79] Politicians, whose strength in policy processes grew slowly but steadily during the late 1980s, helped to produce a financial system in which the securities industry held unusual and rapidly rising influence. Politics in this sense played a major role in producing the gradual divergence of the Japanese financial system from the French model during the post-1975 decade, calling into question John Zysman's argument for Japanese-French similarity.[80]

As suggested earlier, the relationship of politics to Japanese financial liberalization abruptly shifted with the collapse of LDP one-party rule in mid-1993. The ensuing political confusion, which produced four prime ministers and three major shifts in ruling coalitions in 1993 and 1994 alone, temporarily arrested the rise of political influence in financial policy making. It also weakened the securities industry and strengthened the bureaucracy. Financial scandals that led to resignation of CEOs at two of the largest four securities firms (Nomura and Daiwa), together with the collapse of the 1980s financial bubble, contributed to

---

[79] *Tokyo shimbun,* July 1, 1987.
[80] On the argument for similarity in the Japanese and the French financial systems, see John Zysman, *Governments, Markets, and Growth* (Ithaca: Cornell University Press, 1983), pp. 99–169, 234–51.

the ascendancy of the bureaucracy and exacerbated the crisis in the alliance between politics and securities. Yet as a new conservative coalition emerged in 1994–95, headed first by the unlikely Socialist prime minister, Murayama Tomiichi, and then by the veteran LDP politician Hashimoto Ryutaro, signs of earlier patterns of the 1980s reappeared.

## The Emergence of Trans-National Financial Politics

Closely related to the rising influence of banking and the securities industry and the corresponding decline of the state in the Japanese political economy—indeed, a primary cause of both—has been the rapid intensification of Japanese financial ties with other parts of the world. In 1970 the Euromarket, for example, provided less than 2 percent of Japanese corporate financing; by 1984 this figure had risen to 36.2 percent, including nearly 52 percent of all corporate bond issues.[81] In 1970 Japanese capital outflows were virtually nil; the country had been in chronic balance of payments deficit throughout the postwar period. By 1988, however, these outflows had risen to over $130 billion annually, largely mediated by Japanese financial institutions.[82]

In 1990 fresh capital outflows fell to under $40 billion a year,[83] and by 1994 they actually reversed to inflows, as Japanese banks repatriated funds to Japan after the bubble's collapse. The remaining $500 billion stock of Japanese offshore portfolio investment testifies to a heavy and enduring financial interdependence between Japan and the broader world, however, as do the heavy Japanese corporate financing undertaken in offshore capital markets and the huge volume of short-term cross-border flows in increasingly integrated global capital markets. Accompanying this development, Japanese banks and securities firms grew to become the largest in the world, although with very different strategic concerns than during the high-growth era of the 1950s and 1960s.[84]

---

[81]   Ichikawa Nobuyuki, "Kigyō kinyū no kōzō henka wa doko made susunde iru no ka?", *Kinyū zaisei jijō*, December 8, 1986, pp. 34–39.

[82]   *Nomura Investment Review*, April, 1991.

[83]   Ibid.

[84]   In 1990, for example, the five largest banks in the world in terms of total assets were all Japanese. See JETRO, *Nippon 1992: Business Facts and Figures* (Tokyo: JETRO, 1992), p. 94.

Although the dominant Japanese financial institutions, huge in international terms, had grown increasingly mobile in their global operations by the mid-1980s, the Ministry of Finance continued to retain remarkably tight controls over their expansion into new business areas. The segmented character of the Japanese domestic financial system, purposely maintained by the MOF, kept commercial banks out of trust banking at home and out of most underwriting transactions both at home and overseas. The conservative character of the MOF regulation also inhibited the emergence of important new instruments in the Tokyo financial market, such as commercial paper and bankers' acceptances, while suppressing the free flow of investment capital from Japanese insurance firms to all corners of the world.

In the globalized financial system that was rapidly emerging during the 1980s, actors in many nations had a stake in the evolution of the Japanese industrial-credit system, which had conventionally been a concern of the Japanese alone. In the United States, for example, the Semiconductor Industry Association and the National Association of Manufacturers began, from the early 1980s on, to complain bitterly that government restrictions within Japan kept interest rates low for key industrial sectors and the yen chronically and artificially weak.[85] Foreign banks and securities companies, together with U.S., British, and German financial authorities among others, made increasingly insistent demands for change in the Japanese financial structure. These demands were given ever greater credence by the rapid advances of Japanese firms into overseas financial markets.

Within Japan itself, major interests were divided on the propriety of financial liberalization, giving foreign pressure a potentially decisive role in propelling and structuring the process. Broadly speaking, elements traditionally benefiting from the traditional, administratively enforced segmentation within the Japanese domestic financial system, such as the trust and long-term credit banking sectors, opposed liberalization. Their reservations were evident in the controversies of 1982–86

---

[85]   See, for example, Semiconductor Industry Association, *The Effect of Government Targeting on World Semiconductor Competition* (Cupertino, Calif.: Semiconductor Industry Association, 1980); and Chase Financial Policy, *The U.S. and Japanese Semiconductor Industries: A Financial Comparison* (New York: Chase Manhattan Bank, 1980).

over the International Banking Facility and the liberalization of trust banking, and Euroyen underwriting.[86] On the other side, favoring liberalization, were multinational firms desiring more flexible, lower-cost access to credit, together with some commercial banks and securities firms. Japanese Dietmen occasionally became involved, when, for example, they pressed for a Tokyo International Banking Facility beneficial to the small regional banks with which many provincial Dietmen were affiliated.[87]

Ultimately, however, it was transnational politics that inspired change: establishment of the Japan Offshore Market International Banking Facility (December 1986), the admission of foreign firms to the trust banking business (1984) and to the Tokyo Stock Exchange (June 1985), the gradual liberalization of Euroyen underwriting and issuing (after 1984), and the expansion of foreign activities in insurance and pension-fund management (especially in 1994–95). Through mechanisms such as the U.S.-Japan Yen-Dollar Committee of 1983–84, and the U.S.-Japan Framework Talks of 1993–95, as well as more ad hoc threats and demands for reciprocity, foreign financial authorities impacted decisively on the domestic Japanese liberalization debate then under way.

The persisting segmentation of the financial system and the still underdeveloped state of retail financial services within Japan suggest that foreign pressure has not effected a total transformation of the Japanese financial system by any means. Domestic interest groups and bureaucratic institutional concerns have continued to impede the liberalization process significantly.[88] But where domestic support for change exists, transnational politics, combining domestic interest-group representation and foreign pressure, has recently become an important new ingredient in the Japanese financial policy equation. This trend has significant long-term implications not only for Japan but for a much broader world now critically reliant on the efficient flow of capital from a nation that within a generation has become its largest capital exporter.

[86] On the politics of these liberalization controversies, see Frances McCall Rosenbluth, *Financial Politics in Contemporary Japan* (Ithaca: Cornell University Press, 1989), pp. 50–95.
[87] On December 29, 1984, for example, fifty-three LDP politicians formed the Dietmen's League for the Promotion of an International Market (Kokusai Shijō Ikusei Giin Renmei), which pressed for creation of an offshore banking facility in Tokyo that would afford smaller banks new access to international finance. The group was apparently significant in the final establishment of the Japan offshore market in December 1986. See ibid., pp. 84–88.
[88] Ibid., pp. 94–95.

# Slouching toward the Market: The Politics of Financial Liberalization in South Korea

MEREDITH WOO-CUMINGS

In the late 1970s the South Korean government made a pledge to loosen its grip on the nation's financial market.[1] The path of liberalization since then has been tentative and halting, taking two steps forward and one step back. As of 1996 the Korean government has yet to complete the final step toward interest rate deregulation and other reform measures. Impatient at the pace of reform, the U.S. Treasury Department has often protested, threatening to unleash retaliation against South Korea for keeping its market relatively closed to U.S. financial institutions and investors.

The truth, though, is that Koreans have crawled a long distance toward liberalization since the early 1980s. The government has sold, over the years, all the city banks it used to own; it has opened the hermetically sealed Korean financial market, allowing outside firms to come in and inside firms to go out to raise capital where they pleased; it created a vibrant stock market out of nearly nothing; and it did all that by gradually transferring to the market its prerogative in setting financial prices. If the pace of this transformation seems infuriatingly slow to interested outsiders, it is only because of the enormous economic and political stakes that financial liberalization entails in Korea.

Financial liberalization in the Korean context does not simply mean greater efficiency in allocating credit. I will show in this chapter that it

[1] The Bank of Korea traces the beginning of financial liberalization to the introduction of commercial paper at unregulated rates in June of 1981. *Financial Liberalization and Internationalization in Korea* (Seoul: Bank of Korea, 1994), p. 3.

also marks a historical eclipse of a developmental political economic regime that engineered one of the world's fastest growth programs. I have argued elsewhere that the interventionist power of the Korean state—to structure and restructure industries, to force sectoral mobility, and to make and break the firm—derived from its ubiquitous control of the flow of capital.[2] In relinquishing its control over banking and finance, the Korean state is now forced to redefine its relationship to the economy and society: it is little wonder, then, that this "reform from above" is slow and deliberate.

In this chapter I seek to explain why the Korean state has promoted financial liberalization despite its obvious drawbacks for the regime. This requires an understanding of the political economy of Korean development, which had its genesis in the colonial period (1910–45) but which achieved its full elaboration only in the 1970s. We need to know why the Korean state opted for the kind of political economy it did for the major part of this century. This requires some familiarity with the global political circumstances that the Koreans found themselves in, with the developmental model most available to them, and with the method they used to implement it. I shall show that although the political economy of rapid development eventually fell of its own weight, the collapse was brought on by a shift in global politics and hegemonic economic policies, which have always determined the broad parameters of Korean action. If the importance of global political economy is more pronounced in the Korean instance than in the four other cases included in this volume, this is doubtlessly because of the strategic importance of Korea in the heyday of the cold war.

## State and Finance in Korean Industrialization

The political economy of South Korea's development in the last quarter century was characterized by the allocation of domestic and a vast quantity of foreign capital by the state to rising industries and firms; in the process the state created an impressive constellation of industrial firms, which in turn provided political support for the state. The Korean

---

[2] Jung-en Woo (Meredith Woo-Cumings), *Race to the Swift: State and Finance in Korean Industrialization* (New York: Columbia University Press, 1991).

economy's relative openness to the outside world (in contrast to Latin America's ill-fated import-substituting pattern), combined with its remarkable insulation from shocks generated by the global economy, gave the state a dynamic, pivotal role in moving from mendicant to world-competitive status. The centrality of the state could never be understood without grasping the political logic of Korea's financial structure. This will become more apparent when we look at the categories of financial mobilization and allocation, and their social consequences. By *mobilization* I mean the gathering together of foreign and domestic resources by the state. The Korean manner of mobilizing foreign savings to finance industrialization was unique, notably in comparison with that of Japan (which did not rely on foreign savings) and Latin America (which relied on different sources of foreign savings). By *allocation* I mean the modalities by which the state directs these resources in terms of its own goals, which in the Korean case did not always correspond to the conventional wisdom on economic development. By *social consequences* I refer to the state's capacity to restructure society and to resist or insulate itself from domestic social forces. In the Korean context, this meant the creation of a spectrum of concentrated well-capitalized industrial firms, which ultimately hamstrung the state in spite of its economic powers.

## Mobilization of Financial Resources and State Power

No consideration of the relative autonomy of the Korean state can proceed without mention of its position as a security state in the global system. Whether we speak of Japanese industrialization in Korea in the 1930s and 1940s or the postwar development of Korea, security concerns have always justified the logic of industrialization and dictated the pattern of industrial financing. What is unique about the Korean case is the role of outside guarantors like the United States and Japan who, intent on preventing South Korea from being another domino, have opened up a realm of opportunity for Korean action. This security environment has brought a shower of benefits in the form of bilateral aid or multilateral loans, and it has enhanced Korea's maneuverability by, for example, justifying in security terms its development of heavy industrial capacity in the 1970s. Because of the strategic location of Korea, the United States has historically been willing to pump financial resources into the country. Koreans first used munificent bilateral aid to build a social basis of support for a strong state in the 1950s; later, multilateral lending was used to finance ambitious developmental projects. Sources of funding have important political implications. Here the effect was to augment state power.

In Latin America, by contrast, the source of funding was usually multinational corporations. Foreign capital, possessing its own investment and market goals, bypassed the state and emerged as a formidable domestic force which left the state hamstrung. In Korea the opposite occurred: state power increased and foreign influence shrank. It seems as though a generation of scholars who have taken dependency theory as their focus have given us a parochial, limited theory, one that cannot explain how Korea, or for that matter Taiwan, has "triumphed" over dependency.

The Japanese state achieved a great deal of autonomy, it is true, without resorting to foreign loans. But this is an exception that proves the rule. As Kent Calder argues in this volume, it was the vast pool of private funds—postal savings, for instance, accounting for more than 30 percent of total savings deposits—that enabled the Japanese bureaucracy to avoid dependence on private banks and other financial institutions while promoting strategic industrial programs. In the Japanese case as in Korea, in other words, the source of savings that finances industrialization has a great deal of influence on the state's autonomy.

The Korean financial structure, along with the external source of finance, also helped to cement a social coalition. Again there was a dialectic—in this case between the state and business. In a nation with a dearth of accumulated capital, business has had to rely on credits from banks that were controlled and, until recently, owned by the state. Since Korean firms are highly leveraged, much more so than in Mexico or Brazil, business has had to maintain good relations with the state so as to avert the possibility of a severance of credit. Public records show remarkable expenditures not found in Western corporate experience. Glancing at the annual reports of firms listed on the Seoul Stock Exchange, one comes upon an entry called "voluntary contribution" to the government. Typically the voluntary contribution of big business amounts to some 22 percent of corporate net profit, taking third place only after the firm's operating and financial costs.[3]

---

[3]  *Maeil kyôngje shinmun*, March 12, 1985.

State mobilization of credit on preferential terms used to drive down bank interest rates, which had a dire effect on household savings, causing them to flee mostly into an unregulated financial market, called the "curb." Channeling resources from the curb into institutionalized financial intermediaries without altering the interest structure would have proved too taxing for the state. Thus it is no coincidence that the first and major economic decree of the *yushin* state—the bureaucratic authoritarian structure which prevailed in the 1970s—was a moratorium on corporate debt to the curb, intended to coerce curb investors into placing savings in banks. The state and business were the beneficiaries, and the casualties were the citizens who had stayed away from the banks. This type of decree—and many were to follow—is highly typical of the economic policies of an authoritarian state with the financial structure we are describing.

*Allocation of Finance, State Interventionism, and the Industrialization of Korea*

Contrary to what liberal economists may say in their panegyrics about Korea's open economy and its pursuit of comparative advantage, Korea has maintained a strong import-substitution regime for target industries and consumer goods. Its industrial policies in the 1970s hardly conformed to comparative advantage and international competitiveness. Instead, the 1970s were marked by the Korean state's conscious attempt to protect infant industries—the second or "deepening" phase of import substitution—and to enhance military preparedness by investing in heavy industries. Notwithstanding considerable protest from international development agencies, the Korean state has heavily intervened in the financial allocation process to direct resources into heavy industry sectors. It provided incentives in the form of "policy loans" and interest rate and other subsidies, and it showed a willingness to share the risk of default with firms that were willing to conform to state policies. The state eventually did become concerned about international competitiveness and industrial transformation, but for reasons that were primarily political and security oriented. Korea's economic nationalism coincided with the observation that the United States was declining as a hegemonic power: the Nixon Doctrine, the first major troop withdrawals, and the fall of Vietnam. President Carter's threat to withdraw the remaining ground troops from Korea, his human rights salvos, and "Koreagate" further provided the impetus and context for Korea to push for heavy industrialization and national self-sufficiency. Investment in heavy industries, often implemented without regard to actual or future demand or the international market situation, resulted predictably in waste, idle capacity and overall inefficiency, producing a storm of protest from international agencies and economists.

Yet, it often happens that considerations of efficiency loom large only in the minds of economists; rarely, if ever, do they command priority in the national economic policies of any nation. The top priority, as Susan Strange argues, is national efficacy.[4] Such was the case historically in European continental and Japanese "late" industrialization. (The lack of external security concerns may partially explain why in Latin America this convulsive élan—a spurt of industrialization geared toward the production of capital goods—did not take place with the same intensity and compression.) Investment in projects with long gestation periods, and with an uncertain future market to boot, cannot be undertaken by the private sector, unless, of course, the state is willing to shoulder the risk or provide significant subsidies.

The argument here is that the credit-based financial structure made possible the upward mobility of the industrial sector. In this kind of structure, according to John Zysman, firms rely on bank credit—to the extent that the banks are the main suppliers—for raising finance beyond retained earnings.[5] The banks may be either autonomous, as in Germany, or dependent on the state, as in East Asian countries such as Japan, Taiwan, and Korea. The Korean banking system has exhibited the most extreme case of dependence on the state. Unlike the privately owned Japanese banks, identified by T. J. Pempel as "the most centralized and controllable in the industrialized world,"[6] the Korean banks did not enjoy even limited autonomy with respect to the criteria of lending and response to non-performing loans. Nor were the Korean banks "pawn-shops" with high collateral requirements, as in the case of Taiwan.

---

[4] Susan Strange, "Protectionism and World Politics," *International Organization* 39, no. 2 (1985): 233–69.

[5] John Zysman, *Governments, Markets, and Growth* (Ithaca: Cornell University Press, 1983).

[6] T. J. Pempel, "Japanese Foreign Economic Policy," in Peter Katzenstein, ed., *Between Power and Plenty* (Madison: University of Wisconsin Press, 1978).

The advantage of the credit-based system is that the state can exert influence over the economy's investment pattern and guide sectoral mobility. Another element strengthening state influence is the highly leveraged nature of business firms, which is a logical consequence of state-mobilized credit. When compared with Brazil or Mexico in the 1970s, where the debt-equity ratio of firms averaged 100 to 120 percent, Korea showed a rate of 300 to 400 percent in the same time period, and Taiwan 160 to 200 percent. Under these conditions, even small changes in the discount rate or in concessional credit rates between sectors can have dramatic effects on resource allocation, because the effect of such changes on a firm's cash flow position is much greater than where firms have lower debt-equity ratios. The Korean firms would therefore exhibit a high propensity to conform to the macroeconomic policy goals of the state.

On top of this basic financial structure, the Korean state erected a complex incentive structure to facilitate sectoral mobility. Policy loans are a good example. At the end of 1981 there were some 221 types of policy loans among a total of 298 types of bank loans.[7] Policy loans are those earmarked for specific sectors or industries at lower rates than the already highly subsidized bank loans. Banks, which have no voice in their allocation, have to accommodate these loans irrespective of their portfolio strategies. In fact, in a milieu where real interest rates are negative, inflation being higher than interest rates, and where the state exercises control over all allocation decisions, every institutional loan might well be considered a policy loan. With this mechanism, the state can give large manufacturers greater access to bank loans than small and medium manufacturers; or the state can push the export sector rather than the domestic market, or give higher priority to heavy industry than to light manufacturing.

So far, we have only discussed the advantages of the Korean variant of the credit-based system. But the Korean financial system was also intrinsically unstable. Three reasons may be identified, two of which arose directly out of the incentive system of the financial structure, while the third was due to the structural condition of Korea's open economy. First, the incentive of a negative interest rate (a virtual interest rate

---

[7]   Kim Byôungju and Pak Yôngch'ôl, *Hanguk kyôngje wa kûmyung* (Seoul: Pakyôngsa, 1984).

subsidy) was so attractive that those firms with access to the loan window tended to resist going public, preferring to remain highly leveraged. But then bankruptcy was a perennial threat, since highly leveraged firms are vulnerable to declines in current earnings to below the level required by debt repayment. (Debt repayment is a fixed cost whereas payments on equity vary as do profits.) Banks often ended up carrying a large number of nonperforming loans, and if these were incurred by mammoth firms, known as the *chaebol* in Korea, the state often had no choice but to bail them out through loans from the Bank of Korea, which in turn fueled inflation. (A *chaebol* is a family-owned and -managed group of companies that exercise monopolistic or oligopolistic control in product lines and industries, isomorphic to the Japanese *shinko zaibatsu*, the new zaibatsu, of the pre-war era.)

Second, since this system was perennially in a situation of what Theodore Lowi calls the "state of permanent receivership," whereby any institution large enough to be a significant factor in the community shall have its stability underwritten (the system promotes bankruptcy, but the state cannot let big firms go bankrupt),[8] it was in the interest of the firms to expand and to become so large that the possibility of bankruptcy posed a threat. While the state was chary of the expansion mania of firms, once credit was allocated it was difficult to track down the actual use of the funds since various bookkeeping devices could hide it. The excessive concern of the chaebol with expansion rather than with the soundness of their financial base thus bred instability for the Korean financial system.

The third point is that since Korea has a small domestic market and relies more extensively on exports (more so than, say, Japan) Korean firms were tested in the fires of international competition and were more vulnerable to external shocks. A major slowdown in the global economy could shake the domestic economy from the bottom up. Firms would collapse like card castles, as they did in the 1970s, creating instability in the financial system.

Thus, state interventionism in the market was necessarily ambiguous. The state could achieve its goal by manipulating the financial structure, but once it did so it had to socialize the risk, either through inflationary refinancing of the nonperforming loans to bail out the firms (a mone-

---

[8]   Theodore Lowi, *The End of Liberalism* (New York: Norton, 1979).

tary response) or through expansion of the state's equity share in the banks so as to write off the bad loans (essentially a fiscal response). The former was a form of indirect taxation on the populace, and the latter, direct.

## Social Consequences: State Finance and the Rise of Big Business

In referring to the state in Korea, scholars have used various adjectives ranging from interventionist, discretionary, or (wrongly, since it confuses Korea with Japan) guiding. Lately, descriptive phrases such as "senior partner" or "Korea Inc." have circulated. The silent counterpart of this concern with the state, however, is the absence of any countervailing social power. Korea's historical development corresponds to Barrington Moore's third path to modernity: China's. All other things being equal, the weakness of the bourgeois impulse, in Korea as in China, should have led to a peasant revolution. This did not occur in Korea for reasons that need not concern us here.[9] Capitalist development in such a social milieu, however, comes to resemble capitalism without the capitalist class or, in Gerschenkron's terms, a striking substitution of the state for the "natural" historical process of development. The Korean state has met comparatively little resistance in transforming the industrial structure of the nation because domestic resistance has been feeble. Not only that, whatever powerful groups exist today in Korea—mostly the chaebol—had to be built by the state. As such, the historical mission of the Korean state has been not so much one of reproducing social relations, as state theorists argue, but *producing* them: aborting labor organizations through repression and nurturing big business by supplying financial resources.

While Latin American and two East Asian countries (Korea and Taiwan) all share experiences both of colonialism and phases of import-substitution industrialization, the differing nature, duration, and intensity of the colonial and import-substitution phases made the social consequences radically different. Under Japanese colonialism, domestic capital was given neither the time nor the space to develop, though this

---

[9]   Barrington Moore, *Social Origins of Dictatorship and Democracy* (Boston: Beacon Press, 1981). The suppression of peasants in the 1945–47 period is documented in Bruce Cumings, *The Origins of the Korea War*, vol. 1 (Princeton: Princeton University Press, 1979).

is true of Korea, more so than of Taiwan. Colonialism deepened the weaknesses of the Korean bourgeoisie, placing practical and even legal impediments in the way of commercial and industrial investment, preserving landed capital as the main arena of business, and thereby locking Korea's bourgeoisie to the land and to its relative backwardness as a class. Thus in the two Asian countries, but especially in Korea, powerful agrarian export interests did not emerge to play havoc with the state's industrialization attempt, nor did a protected domestic sector militate against the attempt to turn the economic structure toward the export of manufactured goods. This opened more space for state autonomy and made transitions from one industrial phase to another more fluid. But perhaps the most important product of this historical development has been the modal type of capitalist firm in Korea: the chaebol. Three of these (Hyundai, Daewoo and Samsung) have been included in the top fifty corporations in the world for some time, and the founder of Hyundai was ranked by *Forbes* as one of the ten wealthiest men in the world in 1995. The top twenty chaebol, it is estimated, accounted for fully one-third of Korea's GDP in the late 1970s and account for as much today. Ostensibly, therefore, they bring a powerful force of concentration into the economic realm and thus constitute a formidable competitor to the state. In reality they are creations—productions and not reproductions—of the state and the Korean financial structure. This is true to the point where one wonders whether an important distinction exists in Korea between public and private and between the state and civil society. Most of the chaebol already existed as firms in the immediate postwar period, but they were small enterprises milling rice or repairing automobiles. Daewoo did not even appear until the late 1960s. The others did not grow into large enterprises until the 1970s; thus, the conglomerates are a very recent phenomenon. Furthermore the characteristic of the big chaebol groups is their concentration in heavy manufacturing; by definition, they could not exist before the "deepening" of the early 1970s. Our argument about the Korean financial system, financial policies, and the role of the state would lead us to predict precisely such an outcome. Interest rate subsidies, preferential lending, and other such devices have been the energy fueling the growth of these firms.

The liberalization agenda of the 1980s has introduced many changes into this picture, as we shall now see. After discussing some of the economic problems that surfaced at the end of the 1970s and set the stage for Korea's economic restructuring—considered to be most successful by the World Bank and the IMF[10]—we shall attempt to understand the paradox of hegemonic influences within the country; market pressures that have both combined and clashed with the traditional support for dictatorship. In the end, global capitalism won over national capitalism, and economics took command over politics, such that by 1989 Korea found itself not only with a more liberal and open market but—its political counterpart—a state that was less interventionist, more hesitant to resort to force, and often stiff-armed by the growing power of the moneyed class. The final portion of this chapter focuses on the domestic origins of the turn toward the market, on the Rashomon-like Korean state, on the chaebol, and on the popular opposition to economic liberalization's political impact, chiefly in the financial realm.

### The Politics of Financial Liberalization

*The Crisis of 1979–80*

The era of heavy industrialization (1971–79) ended with a bang in 1979. President Park Chung Hee (1961–79), who had led the postwar boom, was assassinated by his henchman, inflation was at the decade's highest, the current account deficit had tripled, and the GNP growth rate had slowed from over 10 percent to 6.5 percent before nose-diving to a dismal –5.2 percent in 1980—a cataclysmic figure in the Korean context. Riots spread like wildfire in the summer of 1979, led by outraged female workers in, significantly, the textile sector—still the largest earner of foreign currency but crippled by the rising exchange rate, ignored by policy makers, and rapidly losing what export competitiveness it once had.[11]

The crisis in 1979–80, termed "the sternest test since the end of the Korean War" by *The Wall Street Journal*, was really a conflation of three

---

[10] See Bijan Aghevli and Jorge Marquez-Ruarte, "A Case of Successful Adjustment: Korea's Experience during 1980–1984," IMF Occasional Paper, June 1985, p. 1; *Korea: Managing the Industrial Transition*, vol. 1 (Washington, D.C.: World Bank, 1986), pp. v–xiv; *The World Development Report 1989* (Washington, D.C.: World Bank, 1989), p. 127.

[11] In August 1979 women textile workers who were laid off and chased out of their company dormitories appealed for help at the opposition party headquarters. They were subsequently raided by about a thousand riot police. *New York Times*, August 11 and 14, 1979.

phenomena. The first was that some of the heavy industries built in the 1970s, just coming on stream, were severely hit in the global recession of the early 1980s, which created great excess capacity in machine building, construction, and most critically, in shipbuilding. In hard times, this looked like a stupid waste, another example of Korean recklessness. But the truth was that it also held out the promise of rapid recovery with an upturn in the global economy. Fruits of the forced march in the 1970s would be reaped not in 1980 but a few years later. In this respect, the Korean situation was not unlike that of Brazil in the first half of the 1980s: recovery was less a result of routine market reaction to "maxidevaluation" than to the maturing of the ultimate stage of import-substituting industrialization.[12]

So the Koreans did what was rational under the circumstances. They girded their loins and, biding their time, sought to bolster the competitiveness of their heavy industries. They did this in a Korean-style *pan y palo* of "industrial reorganization," which meant resuscitation through monetary infusion of those heavy industrial firms likely to be competitive in the world market and mergers for the less likely. The winnowing worked because the state controlled all industrial credit.[13]

The second problem fueling the 1979–80 debacle was inflation. The source of this inflation was the foreign sector: massive infusion of foreign capital into heavy industries, strong exports, a huge liquidity flood from the Middle East construction boom (and related to it, wage increases at home). The last point merits some explanation. In the early 1970s, the Korean government began pushing hard for construction contracts in the Middle East. It formed an overseas construction corpo-

---

[12] Albert O. Hirschman, "The Political Economy of Latin American Development: Seven Exercises in Retrospection," Paper for the Eighth International Congress of the Latin American Studies Association, Boston, October 23–25, 1986. The term "maxidevaluation" was coined to refer to the large Brazilian devaluation of the early 1980s.

[13] Hyundai, Daewoo, and Samsung were ordered to give up the production of power generating and heavy construction equipment and merge into Korea Heavy Industries and Construction (KHIC). Saehan Motors was ordered merged with Hyundai in 1980 so that there would be only two makers of passenger cars that would be internationally competitive (Daewoo and Hyundai). Kia and Dong-a were merged into a monopoly on trucks and buses. Production of marine diesel engines over 6,000 horsepower became the exclusive right of Hyundai and KHIC; those below 6,000 horsepower were the right of Ssangyong, which had taken over a subsidiary of Daewoo. The heavy electric subsidiaries of Ssangyong and Kolon were merged with Hyosong. Production of electronic switching systems became a duopoly of Samsung and Lucky-Goldstar. Copper refining became a monopoly of Korea Mining and Refining Co. and so on. *Chugan maekyông*, March 14, 1985, pp. 21–22.

ration with equity ownership of twenty-five construction firms and subsidized it with export loans and a 50 percent corporate tax reduction.[14]
By 1978 Koreans were receiving $15 billion in contracts for Middle
East construction. This massive export of labor fueled inflation in two
ways. First, the influx of money sent home by overseas workers helped
push up prices, much as Spanish gold helped produce European inflation in the 16th century. On top of the already high level of domestic
liquidity, the money supply, broadly defined, jumped by 40 percent
without a corresponding increase in domestic production.[15] Second, the
exodus of skilled labor put pressure on wages, such that raiding and out-
bidding for workers became a common practice. In fact, a perusal of
macroeconomic indicators for the two decades prior to 1984 reveals that
real wages were running ahead of increases in productivity during the
1977–79 period, something that had never happened before. Labor's
share of national income also recorded a stunning increase, reaching a
peak of 51.2 percent in 1978.[16]

Most important, however, the crisis of 1979–80 reflected a global
economic malaise that depressed demand yet saw interest rates and oil
prices shoot up. The price of oil leaped from $13 per barrel in 1978 to
$36 in 1981, which meant that Koreans, who had been paying $2.2 billion for oil in 1978, now found themselves footing a $6.5 billion bill in
1981. The burden of interest payments on Korea's external debt may be
judged from the fact that LIBOR jumped from 8.8 percent in 1978 to
16.8 percent in 1981, which for Korea translated into payments of $900
million in 1978 and $3.5 billion in 1981, a fourfold jump.[17]

Koreans responded to external shock exactly the same way they did
during the first oil crisis: they absorbed the full shock through devalua-

[14]  Chungwhahak kongôp ch'ujin uiwônhoe kihoekdan, *Hanguk kongôpwha paljôn e kwan-
han chosa yôngu* (A study of industrial progress in Korea), vol. 3 (Seoul, 1979), p. 456.
[15]  *Far Eastern Economic Review,* April 13, 1979, p. 47.
[16]  In 1981, however, real wages actually fell by 1 percent while labor productivity leaped by
18 percent. The annual increase in labor productivity for 1980–84 averaged 12.1 percent and
the average increase in real wages straggled at only 3.1 percent: a precipitous drop indeed from
15.8 percent in 1977–79. Such a productivity increase might have been obtained through uti-
lization of excess capacity in the early 1980s, but wage restraint was an artifact of sheer terror that, by contrast, made even the Yushin years appear like halcyon days. Chungwhahak
kongôp ch'ujin uiwônhoe kihoekdan, p. 276.
[17]  Economic Planning Board of ROK, *Ôichae paeksô* (White paper on foreign debt) (Seoul:
Economic Planning Board, 1985), p. 6. LIBOR refers to the London interbank offer rate,
which is applied to interest rates in the Eurodollar market. Lenders offer loans at some margin
or "spread" above LIBOR, which floats up and down according to market conditions.

tion, higher exports, and more borrowing. The Korean external debt, which stood at $20.3 billion in 1979, snowballed to $40 billion in 1983 and to $46.7 billion by 1985.[18] At the end of 1980, Korea was the developing world's second largest borrower after Brazil and Asia's biggest, and also one of the riskiest: *Euromoney*'s country risk rating ranked Korea 35th out of 67, trailing far behind Taiwan (19th), Mexico (21st), Brazil (23rd), and the Philippines (24th).[19] This bad report card was, however, no deterrence to international bankers, who clamored to lend to Korea at attractive terms, so that even in the midst of this crisis Korea had no difficulty raising more than $6 billion, more than half of that in long term loans.[20] Part of the reason was the backing that the United States and Japan extended to Korea in the pivotal year 1980.

The 1979–80 economic crisis—caused by excess industrial capacity in a period of global economic recession, inflation through income transfers from abroad, and a series of external shocks—was a temporary crisis. It was easily addressed with the tools and habits of this flawed economy: industrial reorganization by fiat, labor repression, foreign loans to ride out the bad times, and waiting—waiting for the end of the global recession so that factories could run at full capacity, as they eventually did. Why, then, was there such eagerness to unlearn the past, to do away with the program of heavy industrialization, to "liberalize" the economy, to adjust it "structurally"? Why were policy makers, who for so long had resisted the sagacious advice of international agencies and domestic economists, suddenly all ears?

The reasons for this turnaround were deeply political and ideological, as well as economic.

### Antinomies of Hegemonic Influence

The era of heavy industrialization ended because it was a success and not, as it is widely believed, because it failed. It was dismantled because its mission was largely completed, its raison d'être voided, and not because economic "reformers" willed it. The Big Push of the 1970s,

---

[18]  Ibid., p. 2.
[19]  *Euromoney*, October 1980. Credit worthiness is calculated by factoring in the country's natural, human, and financial resource bases, its economic policy, and the balance of payment outlook. For an explanation of country risk ranking, see *Euromoney*, April 1979, pp. 135–59.
[20]  *Wall Street Journal*, May 2, 1980; *New York Times*, April 14, 1980.

which originated in response to the Nixon Doctrine and culminated during Carter's human rights crusade, was a reaction to the vicissitudes of "big power politics," as President Park Chung Hee often put it. So its demise should not be so surprising, given the volte-face in Carter's policy toward East Asia and Korea, made perfectly clear in 1979 when Carter reneged on his pledge to pull all U.S. troops and nuclear weapons out of Korea.

This new policy toward East Asia, inaugurated during the Carter administration and consolidated in the Reagan era, sought to counter the Soviets in the Far East through economic and security ties between the United States, on the one hand, and Japan, Korea, and the People's Republic of China on the other. Much more problematic was the effort to promote ties among these Asian nations themselves. The logic of this sort of regional consolidation led to the swift U.S. embrace and support of the new dictatorship in Korea. The Japanese were no less forthcoming in this, infusing, at American prodding, billions of dollars in financial aid to the new regime.

This happy *ménage à trois* ultimately came to an unhappy end, however. The reason, to anticipate our argument, was the antinomy of politics and economics in Reagan's foreign policy, the ultimate incommensurability between its intense patronage of a strong Korean state—more intense than under any other American administration—and an economic ideology bent on denying and eradicating the economic functions of that very state. In a way, this was an old conundrum in American foreign policy, and it was usually resolved with politics taking command—at least in the heyday of the Pax Americana. But the 1980s version was different: this time the American economic agenda arrived with fangs, in the form, first, of structural monetarism, propagated by Stanford economists and applied earlier in the southern cone of Latin America,[21] and second, of unrelenting pressure to pry open Korea's market to American imports and financial institutions. This commingling of rightwing political orthodoxy and militant monetarism led to an unfore-

---

[21]  For works on Latin American experiments with structural monetarism, see Alejandro Foxley, *Latin American Experiments in Neo-Conservative Economics* (Berkeley: University of California Press, 1983); Vittorio Corbo and Jaime de Melo, "Liberalization with Stabilization in the Southern Cone of Latin America," *World Development* 13, no. 8 (1985): 863–66; and Carlos Diaz-Alejandro, "Good-Bye Financial Repression, Hello Financial Crash," *Journal of Development Economics* 19, nos. 1–2 (1985): 1–24.

seen and unintended result, at least from the Korean perspective: a "structural" adjustment and liberalization program that chipped away at the state's many prerogatives and ultimately created what Alfred Stepan calls—in the Chilean instance—a "small state, strong state."[22] This set the stage for change in the political regime toward the end of the 1980s, and it explains why the United States and the Korean haute bourgeoisie were content to sit on the sidelines and watch the military regime collapse. But to understand how all this came to be, we have to go back more than a decade.

Nixon pulled a division out of Korea in 1971 because the American troop commitment—intended to act as a tripwire in the event of war—stood in the way of his "grand design": a more flexible competition with the Soviets based on an offshore naval nuclear strategy that would avoid American involvement in risky regional conflicts.[23] Carter sought to complete Nixon's Korean agenda, but was motivated by different concerns. He wanted to give Korea a slap on the wrist for its human rights abuses, and his trilateralist view stressed not containment but economic interdependence, diplomacy, and arms control.

Research based on interviews with officials in the Carter administration found, however, that Carter's Korean policy was fiercely resisted and eventually subverted through the concerted effort of officials in the State Department and, predictably, the U.S. Army.[24] The U.S. Defense Intelligence Agency's dramatic upward assessment of the number of North Korean tanks, made in 1976 and confirmed by the CIA in 1977, became grist for the mill of opponents of Carter's Korean agenda. In 1978 the House Armed Services Committee issued a comprehensive attack on the policy, and by January 1979 the Senate was overwhelm-

---

[22]    Alfred Stepan, "State Power and the Strength of Civil Society in the Southern Cone of Latin America," in Peter Evans, Dietrich Rueschemeyer, and Theda Skocpol, eds., *Bringing the State Back In* (New York: Cambridge University Press, 1985).

[23]    For an excellent analysis of Richard Nixon's foreign policy, see Franz Schurmann, *The Grand Design: The Foreign Politics of Richard Nixon* (Berkeley: Institute of International Studies, University of California at Berkeley, 1987).

[24]    Richard Holbrook, Assistant Secretary of State for East Asian and Pacific Affairs, leading a pack including Morton Abramowitz and Michael Armacost from the Pentagon and Leslie Gelb from the State Department, successfully persuaded Senators Sam Nunn, John Glenn, and Gary Hart, who in turn brought over powerful Democratic party military reformers to oppose Carter's policy. See Peter Hayes, *Pacific Powderkeg: American Nuclear Dilemmas in Korea* (Lexington, Mass: Lexington Books, 1991), chap. 5.

ingly in favor of dropping withdrawals.[25] The Carter agenda was, for all practical purposes, dead.

By early 1979 Park Chung Hee was a dictator who had come in from the cold. A year later the United States was extending hospitality to another general, releasing at his request troops from the combined U.S.–South Korea Command for use in the Kwangju massacre. Soon afterwards the head of the combined forces was publicly endorsing the coup d'état.[26] This shift in the U.S. policy came about because of the reconfiguration of regional security, which now included the People's Republic of China. The new security map, which both required and reinforced the stability and security of South Korea, showed a triangulation of East Asia into two zones. Security relations between the United States and China, on the one hand, and the United States and Japan, on the other, defined two sides of the first triangle, of which Sino-Japanese economic relations formed the third side. A foreign policy cause célèbre in the Carter administration, this triangle was in place by 1978.[27] The second zone is less well known: a triangle of U.S.–South Korean and U.S.-Japanese security relationships, joined by security cooperation between South Korea and Japan, mediated by the United States. These two triangles, which shared a common U.S.-Japanese security base, linked Japanese and Chinese security dependence on the United States to the fate of its ally South Korea.[28] Thus in 1980 Secretary of Defense Harold Brown asked the directors of Japan's Self-Defense Agency for a

---

[25]   House Committee on Armed Forces, *Impact of Intelligence Reassessment on Withdrawal of U.S. Troops from Korea* (Washington, D.C.: GPO, 1977); House Committee on Armed Forces, *Review of the Policy Decision to Withdraw United States Ground Forces from Korea* (Washington, D.C.: GPO, 1977); Senate Committee on Foreign Relations, *U.S. Troop Withdrawal from the Republic of Korea: A Report to the Committee on Foreign Relations by Senators Hubert Humphrey and John Glenn* (Washington, D.C.: GPO, 1978).

[26]   The Pentagon disclosed that South Korea requested that some of its ground forces—rear echelon units—be released from the combined U.S.–South Korea Command for use in crowd control and security work, which was granted by General John A. Wickam, Jr. See *New York Times*, May 23, 1980. General Chun Doo Hwan also requisitioned front-line forces under General Wickam's control, a hanging offense in any other military command structure. *New York Times*, June 13, 1980. In early August 1980, General John Wickam, Jr., stated that "provided that [Chun Doo Hwan] demonstrates over time a broad base of support from the Korean people and does not jeopardize the security of the situation here, we will support him, because that, of course, is what we think the Korean people want." *New York Times*, August 3, 1980.

[27]   For U.S. security relations with China, see Bruce Cumings, "Chinatown: Foreign Policy and Elite Realignment," in Thomas Ferguson and Joel Rogers, eds., *The Hidden Election: Politics and Economics in the 1980 Presidential Campaign* (New York: Pantheon, 1981).

[28]   Hayes, *Pacific Powderkeg*, chap. 11.

loan for Korea's military modernization efforts.[29] But it really was Reagan, with his global strategy that emphasized confrontation with the Soviets and greater defense contributions by allies, who designated Korea's demilitarized zone as the Asian equivalent of the European central front and thus explicitly coupled the security of Korea with that of Japan.

As soon as Reagan entered office, he chose Chun Doo Hwan to be the first foreign head of state to visit Washington, sold him thirty-six F-16 jet fighters and related equipment for $900 million, and had Secretary of Defense Weinberger resume U.S.–South Korea security meetings and promise sophisticated weapons and economic concessions. Simultaneously, Weinberger was calling on Japan to do its part in the "common defense" and in the "rational division of burdens," which was to be part and parcel of a new global (not Eurocentric) strategy.[30]

All of this could not have been more opportune and fortuitous for a fledgling Korean regime grappling with an economic crisis, massive popular disaffection, and to top it off, a disastrous harvest. Thus the Korean government, encouraged and emboldened by the United States, presented Japan with a request for $10 billion in aid and loans over a five-year period starting in 1982. In the end, Korea received $4 billion from Japan, consisting of $1.85 billion in governmental loans and $2.15 billion in loans from Japan's Export-Import (EXIM) Bank, most of that in suppliers' credit to be paid over seven years starting in 1983.[31] This loan represented nearly 13 percent of Korea's net external debt, more than 5 percent of the GNP and almost a fifth of total investment in 1983.

This Japanese aid, a particularly dramatic example of the linkage between security and development finance, was by no means exceptional in the early 1980s. The chairman of the U.S. EXIM bank traveled to Korea in the thick of the economic crisis, sending a signal to American and Western European banks that Korea, the EXIM's largest market at $3.1 billion in loans outstanding, was sound enough to be

---

[29] Chong-sik Lee, *Japan and Korea: The Political Dimension* (Stanford: Hoover Institute Press, 1980), p. 106.

[30] *New York Times*, February 1, March 27, April 12, 29, and 30, May 1, August 12, 1981.

[31] Details of the aid negotiation, both from the Japanese and the Korean side, are contained in a doctoral dissertation by Kim Hosup, "Policy Making of Japanese Official Development Assistance to the Republic of Korea, 1965–1983," Ph.D. diss., University of Michigan, 1986.

granted more loans.[32] Japanese bankers, while not eager to increase their exposure in Korea, were also busy making loans, as one banker put it, "for reasons of politics."[33] These were followed by highly visible visits by Nobusuke Kishi, David Rockefeller, and William Spenser. Soon foreign banks were competing to make loans to Korea at the best available terms.[34]

Korea's foreign guarantors helped the Chun Doo Hwan regime weather the storm that threatened to undo the coup, and they gave the regime a new claim to legitimacy, since Chun clearly saw eye to eye with Reagan, Suzuki, and later Nakasone. But that was only half the story of Korea's critical turn in foreign relations; the other half was, for the Korean president, much less happy. Taking back with one hand what it gave with the other, America pummeled Korea to open its markets to American goods.

Protectionist retaliation was not a threat that a trading nation like Korea could take lightly. The share of exports subject to import restrictions in industrialized countries had already increased from 32.3 percent in 1981 to 42.9 percent of Korea's total exports in 1982, and the number of Korean cases brought under antidumping and countervailing charges jumped from 13 in 1981 to 23 in 1983 and 30 in 1984. The volume of Korean exports subject to antidumping measures—which are really a form of protectionism directed against the poorer nations— rose from 8.2 percent of Korea's total exports to 12.4 percent in 1983 and 17.9 percent in 1984. The new regime in Korea moved swiftly to accommodate American wishes. This meant dismantling the program of heavy industrialization, a consequence of which had been a three-fold increase in the estimated effective rate of protection for all industries between 1968 and 1978.[35] Import restrictions on steel products, machinery, petrochemicals, and shipbuilding had to be rapidly

[32]  John Moore, Jr., the chairman of the U.S. EXIM Bank, arrived in Korea in June 1980 to discuss the Korean request for an additional $630 million in EXIM loans to cover fourteen projects. Richard Holbrook gave a personal clearance for this travel, which came soon after the Kwangju incident. *New York Times*, June 3, 1980.

[33]  *Euromoney*, July 1980, pp. 107–8.

[34]  For Kishi's visit, see *Korea Herald*, September 2, 1980; for Rockefeller's and Spenser's visits, *New York Times*, September 22, 1980; for competition among foreign banks for the Korean market, see *Wall Street Journal*, March 20, 1981.

[35]  Larry Westphal and Kim, "Industrial Policy and Development," quoted in *Korea: Managing the Industrial Transition*, p. 58.

scrapped, and the sector that had received the most protection in the 1970s, agriculture, was pried open to receive American rice, wheat, grains, and tobacco. Pressure on consumer goods was also applied across the board.[36]

The Korean government began shifting large numbers of items from its import restriction list to its "automatic approval list," so that the latter, which had included 68.6 percent of imported goods categories in 1980, covered 74.5 percent in 1981, 87.7 percent in 1985, and by the end of the decade, nearly 100 percent of the total imported goods category. The tariff structure, while less important than quantitative restrictions as a protection device, also saw an overhaul that included phased general reductions in tariff levels and changes aimed at producing greater uniformity among these levels. So, in terms of tariff reduction, the average tariff rate, which in 1982 was 31.7 percent, came down to 23.7 percent in 1983, 21.9 percent in 1984, and 18 percent in 1988. Tariffs above 50 percent, which had been slapped on 15.5 percent of all imports in 1983, were imposed on only 5.5 percent in the following year. Even tariffs over 30 percent became a rarity by 1988.[37]

Trade liberalization stirred up nationalist resentment and anti-Americanism. For some, like farmers, it was simply a matter of livelihood. In protest they herded cows into downtown Seoul, not unlike Americans who smashed Japanese cars in public. But for others, like students, the trade issue was another humiliating symbol of Korea's lackey status, a reminder that the state, ruthless at home, was feckless abroad. This bitterness, combined with the suspicion that the United States was standing in the way of Korean unification—and judging from the Kwangju massacre, Korean democratization as well—propelled students into a replay of the sort of anti-Americanism that might have been found in Latin America two decades earlier.

Even so, the concession on import liberalization was not as problematic as that on finance, nor did it have as profound an impact on the state, the economy, and society. As Rudiger Dornbusch put it, importing alfalfa might be far less costly and far more salubrious than

---

[36] The proportion of iron and steel products on the restricted list jumped from 28 percent in 1967 to 75 percent in 1978 (on an items basis) and from 35 percent to 91 percent (on a value basis). Similar patterns were discernible in petrochemicals and machinery, which nearly doubled from 34 percent to 61 percent between 1968 and 1978. Ibid., p. 59.

[37] Ibid., pp. 68–77.

giving in on the issue of financial reform.[38] The idea of financial liberalization was nothing new to Korea: practically everyone who had been opposed to the regime had advocated it in one way or another. In the 1950s American economic advisors like Arthur Bloomfield advocated the independence of the state's financial apparatus in order to curtail the inflation resulting from government deficit spending. Kim Dae Jung—Korea's most prominent opposition figure—made passionate pleas for financial liberalization in the 1960s as a way of cutting the knot that tied the state to the chaebol. In the late 1960s a change was made to the interest rate structure. It was a lackadaisical attempt at financial reform and was dropped entirely by the early 1970s.

In the 1980s, however, financial liberalization came as part and parcel of the long stabilization mentioned earlier, and this time there was nothing lackadaisical about it. Korea, like the southern cone of Latin America, experimented with what came to be known as "structural monetarism." In a curious parallel to the Keynesian way of thinking, this new creed insisted that fundamental economic changes were needed in order to cope with symptoms or ills such as inflation. It distinguished itself from the monetarism of the 1950s and 1960s, which had offered a sort of a quick fix for the economy using instruments such as control of the money supply, reduction of the government deficit, exchange rate devaluation, freeing of prices, and elimination of subsidies. But the new monetarism was also a radical repudiation of Keynesianism in that it sought economic redemption through "modernization," which meant developing the domestic capital market and deepening domestic ties with international financial institutions. It was also inexorably free-market, probusiness and anti–big state.[39]

This new evangelism hit Latin America before it did Korea, and the result there had been disastrous, a fulfillment of the worst possible fears regarding financial liberalization. In Chile and Argentina, high interest rates (leading to high capital costs, which, according to the structural monetarist or debt-intermediation view, are necessary to encourage savings and ensure allocative efficiency) choked businesses and precipitated the collapse of the financial sector, already burdened by a large

---

[38] *Business Korea*, October 1986, p. 25.
[39] Foxley, *Latin American Experiments*, chaps. 1–2.

number of bad loans. Internationalization of finance led not to competition but to capital flight, and privatization led not to efficient allocation of resources but to the conglomerate control of banks, the resources of which were used to buy up firms that were being privatized. In the end, both Chile and Argentina had to bail out their banks and reimpose control over the financial sector.[40]

The lessons of Latin America were not lost on Korea, but they stimulated rather than dampened enthusiasm for financial liberalization. Having blamed the failure in Latin America on inadequate preparation for financial liberalization, some money doctors were now scalpel-happy to find a country that seemed ready for it, a country without inflation of Latin America's caliber, without serious fiscal deficits, and with an external sector that was relatively open.[41] The fact that Korea had already begun to liberalize imports, both to soak up inflation and to placate America, also obviated all the hand wringing about the correct sequencing of liberalization, i.e., whether liberalization should be simultaneous in both capital and commodity markets or not, and if not, which market should be liberalized first and which would be more responsive to liberalization in the other.[42]

The quest to liberalize Korean finance was carried out by transnational elites who served as economic technocrats in ministries or research outfits like the Korean Development Institute (KDI). Often they held Ph.D.'s in economics from the United States (in the case of the KDI, all thirty-five members held U.S. degrees), and they all professed allegiance to the goal of liberalization. The ideological osmosis could

---

[40]  See Corbo and de Melo, "Liberalization with Stabilization"; Diaz-Alejandro, "Good-Bye Financial Repression"; Julio Galvez and James Tybout, "Microeconomic Adjustment in Chile during 1977–1981: The Importance of Being a *Grupo*," *World Development* 13, no. 8 (1985): 969–94.

[41]  For the cause of the failure of the financial liberalization attempt in Chile and Argentina, see Ronald McKinnon, "The Order of Economic Liberalization: Lessons from Chile and Argentina," in Karl Brunner, ed., *Economic Policy in a World of Change* (Amsterdam: North-Holland, 1982); *Korea: Managing the Industrial Transition*, vol. 2, pp. 82–83.

[42]  Ronald McKinnon, for example, hypothesizes that control over public finances is a necessary condition before trade can be liberalized, and it should be followed first by the liberalization of domestic markets and then by the removal of exchange controls on the capital account of the balance of payment. McKinnon, "Order of Economic Liberalization," pp. 159–86. On the other hand, if the lessons of Chile and Argentina were that these governments had a "credibility problem," one might argue for a blitzkrieg in the liberalization attempt. See David Stockman, "Comment";  Ronald McKinnon, "Reply to Stockman"; and Jacob A. Frenkel, "A Comment," in Brunner, *Economic Policy in a World of Change*.

not have been more complete.[43] This was in great contrast with the past, when economic architects were men who had been educated under the Japanese, who had cut their financial teeth in Japanese banks in colonial Korea, and who looked to Japan for guidance.[44] Another difference was that Korea's new presidents in the 1980s were by their own admission tabulae rasae in economics, and for that reason venerated this discipline and gave the technocrats great freedom to make policy. The climate was very different from that which prevailed under Park Chung Hee, a homespun economist with a fierce contempt for transnational ivory-tower thinkers. Chun Doo Hwan, parroting his American-educated policy makers, pledged in his 1980 inaugural address that economic liberalization would henceforth be the aim of the new republic; and Roh Tae Woo imparted the wisdom that while the supreme leader could "never be too knowledgeable" in political affairs, in affairs of economics it was "better to know less."[45] But the affairs of politics and economics were not so readily separable.

## Economics Takes Command

Repression of finance, we have argued in this chapter, gave strength to the state in Korea. Throughout its history, the state insulated its small financial market from the world, negotiated and brokered the flow of foreign capital, prohibited capital flight, and in so doing avoided some of the worst tribulations of dependency. Within this hermetic domain, the state owned all banking institutions and set financial prices, usually so low that money was transferred from savers to investors—mostly the chaebol. This arrangement was terribly irrational from the perspective of allocative efficiency, as it prompted

[43] These technocratic elites included men like Kim Chae-ik, a Stanford Ph.D. who, after a brief duty at the Economic Planning Board, became Chun Doo Hwan's economic Svengali. Other experts on finance were Shin Pyong-hyon, Kim Man-je, Sakong Il, Kim Ki-hwan, and Pak Yong-chol, all with American Ph.D.'s. For the backgrounds of economic technocrats in the Fifth Republic, see "Che 5 kongwhakuk ui pawŏ eritudŭl" (Power elites in the Fifth Republic), *Shindonga*, October 1983 and November 1983; "Sowi sŏganghakpa kyongje kanryo ui kwao" (Errors of the Sogang school economic bureaucrats), *Shindonga*, August 1985; "Hanguk ŭi kisulgwallyo" (Korea's technocrats), *Ikonomistu*, April, 1984.

[44] This was particularly true of men like T'ae Wan-sôn, Kim Yong-ju, and Chang Ki-yông. See Karl Moskowitz, "Current Assets: The Employees of Japanese Banks in Colonial Korea," Ph.D. diss., Harvard University, 1979, pp. 356–72.

[45] *Maeil kyôngje shinmum*, March 25, 1985.

investors to produce at a loss whatever pleased the government, simply to receive financing. But efficiency itself was never a virtue in Korea. Koreans wanted industrialization, and they got it by giving cheap money to the chaebol, forcing them to build industries and to export more, and threatening to withdraw the honey pot if they failed. This is how the state in Korea became "Brumairean," in Marxist terms, and came to be called Korea Inc. The two images are merely two different sides of the same coin.

Financial liberalization meant the end of all that. It meant that Korea's financial market would be *internationalized* and not protected: foreigners would enter into banking, insurance, and capital markets in competition with domestic institutions, granted as a quid pro quo for Korea's entry into foreign financial markets. To compete at the world level, Korean financial firms had to behave like capitalists and not bureaucrats, think profit and not control; and this meant the *privatization* of banks. But since banks cannot thrive in situations of financial repression, finance would have to be *deregulated*, ceilings on interest rates lifted, the practice of policy loans abolished, and returns on financial assets allowed to increase so that saving and lending would be profitable. The high cost of capital thus issued would lead the chaebol to find other sources of financing, and this, combined with a surplus in the current account that had been growing since 1985, would result in the blossoming of the capital market. Thus, internationalization, privatization, financial deregulation and the development of capital markets were all inseparable parts of financial liberalization. The implication of these changes for the state was colossal.

The state had many reasons to liberalize finance despite its many political drawbacks, but the most important one was its desire to reduce the burden of socializing risk—the problem of default—in a system where the state, as owner of the banks, was the creditor. This desire turned into an imperative as the number of nonperforming loans skyrocketed in the 1980s, making extremely credible the threat of massive financial collapse.

Giving up economic control—and the political rents that accrued from it—has not been easy for the state. Financial liberalization in Korea has been a protracted process, and a decade after the initial salvo of economic liberalization and after many speeches and pledges, it still remains incomplete. It is a struggle that has locked foreigners in with the Korean state and the chaebol all pushing and elbowing to get the most out of the reforms.

For foreigners—mostly Americans—financial liberalization has meant internationalization, especially desirable since the U.S. banks in Seoul were making money hand over fist; in 1980 the Bank of America, Citibank, Chase Manhattan, Manufacturers' Hanover, and Lloyd Bank recorded returns on capital that were as high as 359 percent.[46] And profits kept rising. In 1984 foreign banks saw a 26.6 percent increase in net profits from the year before. Their net profits were almost equal to those of Korean banks.[47]

For foreign banks, operating in Korea was all gravy since it was virtually risk free. In addition to the guarantee on a given margin, exchange risk was eliminated by the swap facility, and default risk was reduced by a payment guarantee, either from a domestic bank or from the principal firm of the chaebol group, and by the freedom, denied to domestic banks, to lend to credit-worthy firms only. More American and European banks therefore clamored to get into the Korean market, and the existing ones demanded more freedom to expand their operations. The Reagan administration put considerable pressure on the Korean government on behalf of these banks.

Senator E. J. "Jake" Garn, who was one of the authors of the proposed bill linking the permission for a foreign country's bank to operate in the United States with that country's treatment of American banks, visited Korea in the fall of 1983 and demanded the easing of restrictions for American banks operating in Seoul. Donald Regan was reported to have demanded "equal treatment" for American financial institutions doing domestic business in Korea.[48] The Reagan administration's insistence on a financial open door grew even more vociferous as years went by. By the end of 1993, the number of foreign banks in Korea nearly doubled, from forty branches in 1981 to seventy-three.

Americans, of course, did not really want their banks to be treated equally with Korean ones—not as long as Korean banks were saddled with their policy loans and other allocation orders from higher up. What an open door meant was an equal opportunity to benefit from munifi-

---

[46] *New York Times*, April 14, 1980.
[47] *Maeil kyongje shinmun*, March 15, 1985.
[48] *Business Korea*, June 1984, p. 35.

cent banking policies like receiving the Bank of Korea's rediscount on export loans, and the freedom to play possum when it came to making politically imperative but economically nonlucrative loans. By 1985 Americans got what they demanded by and large: permission to expand their working capital, to venture into trust banking, to join the National Bank Association and the Clearing House, and most important, to receive the Bank of Korea (BOK) rediscount on export loans. (In 1985, commercial banks charged 10 percent interest on export financing, 70 percent of which was rediscounted at the BOK at a 5 percent interest rate; this 5 percent margin made export financing extremely lucrative.) Preferential treatment and exemption from compulsory lending did not last, however: the government of Korea lowered the guaranteed yield and reduced the ceiling on swap facilities (in 1985 and 1987, respectively), imposed a loan quota for small enterprises (1985), and abolished corporate tax exemptions for interest income deriving from foreign currency loans (1989).[49]

Insurance was another market that was pried open through U.S. pressure. Life insurance, which in Korea works like time deposits, was enormously lucrative and strictly off-limits for foreign firms. The situation came under investigation for possible violation of Section 301 of the U.S. Trade Act, so Koreans had to open up life insurance to American participation, lest America retaliate by restricting Korean commodity exports.[50]

Koreans have been extremely wary, however, of opening up the stock market, which has been undergoing explosive growth since 1985. The short-term reasons for this reluctance were the concern that the low price of Korean stocks would result in the shift of substantial rents to foreigners and the fear of a massive inflow of short-term foreign capital atop a large current account surplus. But the fundamental question was one of foreign control of Korean industries—hardly an idle concern in an era when big New York financial firms were making extraordinary profits by orchestrating hostile takeovers. Foreigners therefore were allowed only indirect investment through mutual funds like the Korea

---

[49]    *Financial Liberalization and Internationalization in Korea*, p. 17.
[50]    Yoonje Cho, "Liberalization of Korea's Financial Market in the 1980s," paper presented at the East Rock Institute Conference on Dynamics of United States–Korea Trade Relations, Yale University, November 10–12, 1988, p. 30. Nonlife insurance has been partially open to foreign participation since 1968.

Fund and the Korea Europe Fund.[51] This restriction was eventually lifted in 1992 after repeated delays; even so, direct investment by an individual nonresident remains subject to a limit of 3 percent of a company's total outstanding shares. Moreover, no more than 10 percent of a company's shares may be owned by nonresidents. By the end of 1993, net stock investment funds worth $7.8 billion had flowed into the domestic stock market from abroad.[52]

The loss of a tight grip on the money supply, because of either foreign capital inflow or domestic capital outflow (increasingly encouraged in Korea after 1985 to soak up the trade surplus), can be traumatic for any interventionist state, whether it be Japan, France, or the most extreme example, Korea. But as Michael Loriaux shows with regard to the French experience of financial liberalization in the 1980s, the world market does place effective limits on the power of the state. At the end of this century, in an era of unprecedented bourgeois supremacy, economics has taken command.

The global financial market knocking at Korea's door defined another agenda for the state: privatization. In theory, nothing really doomed state-owned banking enterprises to mediocrity or left them unable to compete at the world level; but neither were there compelling reasons to keep banks nationalized once they were transformed from vehicles of industrial policy to lucrative capitalist outfits. Such a transformation was the chaebol's preferred interpretation of financial liberalization, and it deeply troubled the state.

The fear was not unwarranted: privatization in the southern cone of Latin America had its conglomerates running amok, buying up banks to buy up other enterprises, stacking up loan portfolios with loans made out to affiliated firms, and sending interest rates skyrocketing with "false demands" caused by rolling over debts of related firms. Pell-mell deregulation created a situation in which Chilean and Argentine *grupos* amassed enormous profits while contributing to the collapse of the financial sectors in these countries.[53] It was entirely possible that Korea's chaebol, with their egregious financial structure

---

[51] The Korea Fund issues equity shares to American and other foreign investors to finance the purchase of Korean stocks; it is listed on the New York Stock Exchange. The Korea Europe Fund is based in London and serves European investors.

[52] *Financial Liberalization and Internationalization in Korea*, p. 23.

[53] Galvez and Tybout, "Microeconomic Adjustment in Chile."

and insatiable appetite for expansion, might be tempted to use newly acquired banks to finance their own expansion and to deny credit to competitors. Public opinion, to the extent that it mattered, was also against the chaebol's acquisition of the nation's city banks. All three parliamentary opposition parties denounced the favoritism shown to the chaebol and called for an end to chaebol domination of the economy.

The move toward privatization was therefore extremely cautious. Before the state proceeded to sell its bank shares, it tried to tackle the problem of nonperforming loans. It called upon the chaebol to put their financial houses in order by selling off all non-business-related land and affiliate enterprises defined as "nonmainstream," i.e., enterprises in which the group had no competitive edge.[54] Paralleling this financial surveillance, the Economic Planning Board launched a campaign—the Fair Trade Act—to prohibit the chaebol from monopolizing markets. These measures probably created more sound and fury than anything else, but they did signal to the chaebol that acquisition of finance capital was not going to be as easy as in the past.

Divestiture by city banks of government-owned stocks began in 1981 (one city bank had already been privatized in 1978), and by 1983 all of Korea's five city banks were privatized. This privatization was, however, in name only. Catch-as-catch-can restrictions were inserted to prevent chaebol control of the banks. A 10 percent ceiling was imposed on the shares a single individual could procure. Ceilings were also imposed on the loans and loan guarantees extended to the chaebol. The chaebol tried to beat the system by purchasing stocks in more than one bank, and did succeed in procuring sizable participations, though they did not succeed in duplicating the structural links with banks that characterized the Japanese *zaibatsu*. Management of the city banks continued to be the prerogative of the state, which often used the rapidly rotating bank presidencies as political sinecures. The introduction in 1993 of a more transparent system for nominating bank presidents helped impart some managerial autonomy to the banks, but state inter-

---

[54] Business groups with loans outstanding over a certain ceiling, encompassing 1,217 firms owned by thirty or more of the largest chaebol groups, were ordered to sell their non-business-related landholdings to improve their financial structure. The twenty largest chaebol groups were also required to streamline their business and concentrate on what they do best. *Donga ilbo*, October 25, 1980.

ference continues to be legitimized as a check on the influence of chaebol stockholders.[55]

Deregulation of interest rates, which started in 1981, has had a long and tortuous history in Korea. During most of the 1980s the state retained the right to set financial prices, but successfully controlled inflation and set high real deposit rates that more closely approximated market prices in what some scholars have called "de facto financial liberalization."[56] As can be seen in Table 3.1, the real bank deposit rates have steadily increased, especially since the 1970s, although they did not rise quite as high as curb rates, which incorporated high-risk premiums. Loan rates, which had been negative in real terms throughout the 1970s, also became positive starting in 1981. Table 3.2 shows that by 1982 inflation was slowed to a 7.6 percent level, which translates into a real interest rate of 2.4 percent for general bank loans; when inflation dropped to 3 percent, the real interest rate leaped to 7 percent. Also noteworthy is the fact that by 1982, the Korean government did away with special rates for major policy loans (export, MIPF, and NIF loans). From then on, the rates on all bank loans became uniform at around 10 percent.

It was only toward the end of 1988 that the government launched a comprehensive program of interest deregulation—only to backtrack when macroeconomic conditions proved unfavorable. Finally, a revised plan in 1991 called for a multistage deregulation whereby the short-term lending rates of banks and nonbank financial intermediaries would be liberalized. This was successfully completed by 1993. The second stage in the following year deregulated all lending rates of financial institutions, save for those financed by BOK rediscounts, as well as rates on long-term deposits. The third and fourth stages, to be completed by 1997, would see deregulation of all remaining interest rates, barring any sharp downturn in economic conditions.[57]

Policy regarding nonbank financial intermediaries (NBFI) provided another route to de facto liberalization. The most important of these NBFIs are investment and finance companies dealing in short-term commercial papers, and life insurance companies and investment trust

---

[55] *Financial Liberalization and Internationalization in Korea*, p. 7.
[56] Yoon Je Cho and David Cole, "The Role of the Financial Sector in Korea's Structural Adjustment," Paper for the World Bank, undated.
[57] *Financial Liberalization and Internationalization in Korea*, pp. 38–39.

*Table 3.1.* Bank deposit and curb market rates

| Year | Inflation (GNP deflator) | Bank deposit | | Curb market | |
|------|------|------|------|------|------|
| | | Nominal | Real | Nominal | Real |
| 1972 | 16.2 | 15.0 | −1.0 | 39.0 | 19.7 |
| 1973 | 13.4 | 12.0 | −1.2 | 33.3 | 17.5 |
| 1974 | 29.5 | 14.8 | −11.4 | 40.6 | 8.5 |
| 1975 | 25.7 | 15.0 | −8.5 | 41.3 | 12.4 |
| 1976 | 20.7 | 15.5 | −4.3 | 40.5 | 16.4 |
| 1977 | 15.7 | 15.8 | 0.1 | 38.1 | 19.4 |
| 1978 | 21.9 | 16.7 | −4.3 | 41.2 | 15.8 |
| 1979 | 21.3 | 18.6 | −2.2 | 42.4 | 17.4 |
| 1980 | 25.6 | 22.9 | −2.2 | 45.0 | 15.4 |
| 1981 | 15.9 | 19.3 | 2.9 | 35.3 | 16.7 |
| 1982 | 7.1 | 11.0 | 3.6 | 30.6 | 22.8 |
| 1983 | 2.9 | 8.0 | 5.0 | 25.8 | 22.3 |
| 1984 | 3.9 | 9.0 | 4.9 | 24.7 | 20.0 |
| 1985 | 3.8 | 10.0 | 6.0 | 24.0 | 19.5 |
| 1986 | 2.7 | 10.0 | 7.1 | 23.1 | 22.0 |

*Source:* Bank of Korea.

companies, both of which attract longer-term funds for investment in corporate bonds or for direct loans to business. Established in the early 1970s, the NBFIs had been given permission to pay higher interest rates on deposits in order to soak up funds from the curb. With financial liberalization, the state accelerated deregulation of the NBFIs by allowing private ownership and greater flexibility in interest rates and management, lifting ceilings on commercial paper and unsecured corporate bonds that NBFIs deal in, removing the burden of making policy loans, relaxing entry barriers, and permitting a wide variety of financial services. As a result the business of NBFIs soared in the 1980s, with the number of investment and finance companies jumping from 20 in 1980 to 32 in 1987 and the number of mutual savings and finance companies from 191 in 1980 to 239 in 1984. The share of NBFI deposits as a percentage of the total, less than 20 percent in 1975, climbed to 30.1 percent in 1980, 45.5 percent in 1984, and 51.3 percent by 1987, when more deposits headed to the NBFIs than to the banks.[58]

From the statist perspective the relaxation of control over the NBFIs was ingenious, for it eased the pressure on the country's financial jugular without relinquishing state surveillance of the financial system: money fed into the NBFI probably flowed out of the curb anyway. In

[58]   Cho, "Liberalization of Korea's Financial Market," pp. 9, 10, 13.

*Table 3.2.* Interest rates on various loans

| Year | Curb market | Corporate bond | Bank loans | | | | GNP deflator |
|------|-------------|----------------|---------|--------|--------|--------|--------|
| | | | General | Export | MIPF[a] | NIF[b] | |
| 1973 | 33.3 | — | 15.5 | 7.0 | 10.0 | — | 13.40 |
| 1974 | 40.56 | — | 15.1 | 9.0 | 12.0 | 12.0 | 29.54 |
| 1975 | 41.31 | 20.1 | 15.5 | 9.0 | 12.0 | 12.0 | 25.73 |
| 1976 | 40.47 | 20.4 | 17.0 | 8.0 | 13.0 | 14.0 | 20.73 |
| 1977 | 38.07 | 20.1 | 15.0 | 8.0 | 13.0 | 14.0 | 15.67 |
| 1978 | 41.22 | 21.1 | 18.5 | 9.0 | 15.0 | 16.0 | 21.39 |
| 1979 | 42.39 | 26.7 | 18.5 | 9.0 | 15.0 | 16.0 | 21.20 |
| 1980 | 44.94 | 30.1 | 24.5 | 15.0 | 20.0 | 22.0 | 25.6 |
| 1981 | 35.25 | 24.2 | 17.5 | 15.0 | 11.0 | 16.5 | 15.9 |
| 1982 | 33.12 | 17.3 | 10.0 | 10.0 | 10.0 | 10.0 | 7.6 |
| 1983 | 25.77 | 14.2 | 10.0 | 10.0 | 10.0 | 10.0 | 3.0 |
| 1984 | 24.84 | 14.1 | 10–11.5 | 10.0 | 10–11.5 | 10–11.5 | 3.9 |
| 1985 | 24.0 | 14.2 | 10–11.5 | 10.0 | 10–11.5 | 10–11.5 | 3.8 |
| 1986 | 23.1 | 12.8 | 10–11.5 | 10.0 | 10–11.5 | 10–11.5 | 2.22 |

*Source:* Bank of Korea.
[a]  MIPF: Machinery Industry Promotion Fund.
[b]  NIF: National Investment Fund.

other words, the uncontrolled, unofficial financial market was becoming supplanted by a more deregulated but official financial market. The state killed two birds with one stone.

This sort of liberalization was riddled with problems for the chaebol. The chaebol got their first taste of owning finance capital when they acquired NBFIs and limited portions of bank shares; but their rewards paled because they had to meet the higher cost of capital as interest rates rose. Rates were, to be sure, still lower than the would-be market rate, but even a small rise was immediately translated into a major burden, since more than a quarter of the cost of manufacturing in Korean firms, it was estimated, was financial cost. The Federation of Korean Industrialists, representing more than three hundred big enterprises, lobbied hard to keep the lid on interest rates, but the heyday of the chaebol was rapidly coming to a close.

The chaebol, however, did not wish to go on record as having stood in the way of laissez-faire finance, if this was to be the wave of the future. So the Federation of Korean Industrialists touted and defended liberalization—but wanted it to happen with all deliberate speed (to borrow a vexing and useful phrase from America's desegregation rulings). The chaebol

endorsement was not entirely insincere, however; Korea's haute bourgeoisie did in fact possess reasons for wanting to get the state out of its
hair.

One reason was that the cost of currying favor with the state to obtain
financing was getting out of hand. A convenient measure, if incomplete,
of the chaebol's propitiatory offerings to the state comes from entries in
corporate ledgers under "secondary tax" (*chunjose*). This includes various fees and dues paid out by corporations (*kongkwase*), corporate
social expenditures (*sahoejôk ômmu kwangge piyông*), and, most illus-
trative, "contributions" (*kibukum*).[59] The last category is widely understood as a financial forced draft that is accorded in order to stay on the
good side of the state. In 1983 it constituted some 0.85 percent of corporate value added, which was 2.4 times higher than a similar entity in
Japan, pegged at 0.35 percent. It has increased by an average of 45.3
percent each year since 1976. The total secondary tax in 1983 was 7.79
percent of corporate value added, which was higher than the primary
corporate tax, worth 5.21 percent of value added. In terms of total sales
volume, secondary taxation was equivalent to 1.37 percent of total sales,
versus 1.03 percent for tax payment. The total levy imposed on firms
listed on the Seoul Stock Exchange amounted to 22 percent of their net
profits in 1985. Some firms reportedly had to make their "contributions" even as they verged on bankruptcy.[60]

These expenditures were by no means as corrupt, extortionary, or
substantial as the so-called "political contributions," however. The full
extent of the latter may never be known, but a glimpse of the kind of
greasing performed by Korea Inc. was provided by the extraordinary
investigation into financial misconduct under the Chun regime
(1980–87). At a hearing in the democratically elected parliament, the
founder of the Hyundai group admitted to donating close to $2.5 mil-

---

[59]  Dues and fees include payments to various business associations, the Red Cross, a multitude of state-sponsored efforts (to promote exports, job training, road pavement, traffic safety,
thrift, etc.), various user fees, and medical and fire insurance. Social corporate expenditures do
not go for local development, as might be expected from the Japanese practice, but to
employee relations. "Contributions" include those for victims of flood and other natural dis-
asters, various social projects organized by the state, the Red Cross, national defense, the
Korean equivalent of the USO, anticommunist leagues, welfare organizations, sports organizations, sports- and education-related funds, subway construction, etc. About forty different
activities appear under the contributions category. *Donga ilbo*, October 22, 1984.
[60]  *Maeil kyongje shinmun*, March 11, 1985.

lion to the Ilhae Foundation, a personal "think tank" for the president, and making donations to the political party coffers "always in the amount asked." Groups like Daelim, Shindonga, P'ungsan, and Koryo likewise made hefty donations to Ilhae, for which they were alleged to have received not only bank financing but lucrative concessions. Those who did not make satisfactory donations ended up staring into the corporate abyss of credit severance. Yang Chong-mo, the founder of the Kukje group (Korea's seventh-largest conglomerate, which had capsized in the early 1980s) bitterly complained that the destruction of Kukje was caused by his slow compliance with the government's request for donations. These examples are only the tip of the iceberg, but they are highly suggestive of the operational method of the patronage network found in Korea Inc., which is far more arbitrary and jagged than that found in Japan Inc. In the Korean instance, a racketeering state had become the flip side of the benign developmentalist state.[61]

Another reason for the growing state-chaebol discord, probably vastly more important than the resentment over state racketeering, had to do with the regulations and restrictions that the state imposed on the chaebol. Thus, in the 1980s, the bigwigs of the Federation of Korean Industrialists bewailed the state's microeconomic interventions, which were of course made possible by dangling the carrot of bank credit. In one revelatory meeting with the nation's top economic bureaucrats, Korea's richest industrialists accused the government of a multitude of sins: not providing adequate business financing while frequently ordering corporate restructuring; causing an industrial downturn through financial mismanagement; hanging an albatross from the nation's industrial neck by maintaining a mediocre financial system; creating instability and corporate default through arbitrary standards and whimsical decrees; and refusing to privatize banks in the true sense of the word.[62] Other signs of discord in the 1980s included resentment over quantitative ceilings imposed on loans to the chaebol and the adoption of an

---

[61] Examples of such corruption abound: Daelim was said to have received hefty bank financing for a corporate takeover as a reward for making large political contributions. For similiar contributions, the Shindonga Group was allowed to take over Chônnam University and Poongsan was awarded the right to issue coins for the Asian Games and the 1988 Olympics. *Chosun ilbo*, November 12, 1988.

[62] *Donga ilbo*, March 9, 1985.

arbitarily defined "healthy" debt-equity ratio for determining whether firms were eligible for bank loans.[63] To cap it all, Chông Chu-yong, the patriarch of Hyundai and Korea's most influential industrialist (and a presidential contender in 1992), made a public plea for ending state interventionism, eliminating secondary taxation, and granting full autonomy to the financial sector.[64]

Such confidence and independence as the chaebol came to express in the late 1980s would not have been possible had the securities and stock markets not taken off in the 1980s and become important sources of chaebol financing. The number of companies listed on the Seoul Stock Exchange increased from 352 firms at the beginning of the decade to 523 as of May 1989; listed capital shot up from 2.4 trillion won in 1980 to 13.7 trillion won in May 1989, which is more than a fivefold increase; total market value increased twenty-eight times in the same period; and the composite price index, at 100 in January 1980, was at 932.76 by May of 1989. The greatest spurt occurred between 1985 and 1988, when the total market value was multiplied by a factor of almost ten and the composite price index by almost six. The size of this bustling stock market is brought home when we consider total market value as a ratio of GNP, which was only 9 percent at the end of 1985 but 56.6 percent three years later. In terms of market capitalization, the Korean stock market became the ninth largest in the world in 1990, and according to some estimates, could easily grow to become the fourth largest by the turn of the century.[65]

Growing corporate reliance on the equity market and nonbank intermediaries overdetermined the political position of the chaebol. They no longer had much need for the state to run interference on their behalf. Additionally, there was always the danger that the state could just as easily use its muscle to shield other interests, such as the long-neglected medium-sized industries, and dump the chaebol as socially undesirable. Chông Chu-yong worried aloud if the state might not be tempted to confiscate chaebol property outright.[66] In an age of deepening finance and maturing capitalism, the chaebol grew suspicious of a capricious political order that so casually mixed benevolence with terror. They came to

---

[63]  *Maeil kyôngje shinmun*, March 1 and 9, 1985.
[64]  *Maeil kyôngje shinmun*, April 15, 1985.
[65]  *Wall Street Journal*, January 27, 1989; *New York Times*, April 30, 1990.
[66]  *Chosun ilbo*, November 2, 1988, and December 19, 1988.

desire greater stability and the rule of law, even if that meant liberal democracy. Thus Ku Cha-kyong, the head of the Federation for Korean Industrialists, pledged to put an end to chaebol contributions to political parties and to "nonparliamentary forces" that did not respect the principles of the free market or the rules of liberal democracy.

The Korea Inc. phenomenon derived from the state's adroit exploitation of its geopolitical situation, its control and manipulation of financial policies for industrialization, and in the process, its creation of a constellation of industrialists known as the chaebol. The 1980s marked the slow beginning of the end of the Korean variant of late industrialization, effectively closing the era of rapid development fired by the security concerns of the 1970s. The interpretation of Korea's financial liberalization in this chapter differs from the conventional one, which assumes that liberalization was part of an economic modernization or a correction of the "mistakes" of the heavy industrialization on the 1970s.

I have argued that financial liberalization in Korea was triggered by a much larger global process—and that this is not surprising since the course of the Korean political economy is critically influenced by events that occur in New York and Washington, the epicenters of world capitalism and politics. The story of the 1980s and the early 1990s, then, is less a story of Korea "reforming" after behaving badly in the past than of adjusting to new realities in Washington.

That, however, required a reshaping of Korea's political economy. America's laissez-faire world often meant protectionism at home and free trade abroad for the United States. In this world a strong and interventionist state like Korea, from the U.S. perspective, had no place. The liberalization of Korea's import market provides a well-known instance of successful application of U.S. pressure. But finance is the stuff that power is made of, and the attempt to liberalize finance in Korea—more than ten years in the making and still not complete—has precipitated a silent revolution. That revolution has surreptitiously altered the relationship between state and society.

# CHAPTER FOUR

# Capital Mobility and
# Mexican Financial Liberalization

SYLVIA MAXFIELD

The diversity among countries liberalizing their financial poli-cies in the 1980s and 1990s can be taken as evidence of strong interna-tional pressures to deregulate.[1] Yet the thesis of internationally induced policy convergence is controversial, even in the case of financial policy. As is so often noted, there are cross-national differences in the way international pressures are filtered through domestic political processes and institutions. Countries vary in their overall vulnerability or sensi-tivity to international pressures for financial deregulation. So do the specific channels through which international pressure operates. For example, international geopolitical or security concerns made the Korean government especially vulnerable to U.S. pressures for financial liberalization. In contrast, a balance of payment deficit and a general financial crisis made Mexican leaders sensitive to the need to adopt policies that would induce foreign creditors and investors to commit resources to the country.

Countries also begin financial liberalization from different starting points; some embark on liberalization with no financial markets to speak of, while others need merely to deregulate interest rates or lift minor restrictions on exchange convertibility. As is evident in the cases

[1] Portions of this chapter draw on material from Stephan Haggard and Sylvia Maxfield, "The Political Economy of Financial Internationalization in the Developing World," *International Organization* 62 (1996): 1; and Sylvia Maxfield, "The Politics of Mexican Financial Policy," in Stephen Haggard, Chung Lee, and Sylvia Maxfield, eds., *The Politics of Finance in Developing Countries* (Ithaca: Cornell University Press, 1993).

discussed in this book, financial liberalization encompasses exchange convertibility and financial institution ownership as well as interest rate regulations and credit controls. The politics of deregulation may vary depending on which aspects of liberalization are most important in a given national context.

For example, although one of the general factors contributing to liberalization of credit allocation and interest rate controls is the diversity of industry financing sources, the specific nature of diversification shapes how lobbying efforts of industrialists will influence the politics of financial liberalization. Alternative financing sources will lessen the opposition to reduction of subsidized credit coming from industrialists. Yet alternatives to government-controlled bank financing can come from internal funds as corporate profits rise, or from international sources or domestic nonbank sources. Where alternative industrial financing is in part international, as in Korea and Japan, industrialists may begin to have a stake in another kind of financial liberalization: deregulation of international financial transactions. To the extent that diversification of industry financing comes from the rise of a nonbank financial market, as has occurred to varying degrees in all five cases examined in this volume, the interests of nonbank financial institutions such as securities firms become increasingly important in understanding the politics of financial liberalization.

An important part of the liberalization story in Japan and Korea, from the perspective of interest group politics, involves banks that, although protected by restrictions on international financial operations, ceased to oppose deregulation in this arena as they gained the ability to raise and lend funds abroad. In Mexico, in contrast, the advantages of lowered entry and exit barriers were not as clear to domestic banks, and they opposed deregulations that would open them to greater international competition.

Just as the impact of international forces varies depending on the interests of particular groups in domestic society, it differs according to the interests of governments and the priorities of politicians. For example, a broadening of banks' legally sanctioned participation in financial markets is often the result of government efforts to strengthen commercial banks for reasons partially independent from the banks' lobbying efforts. Although, according to the state-centric argument, the government's fiscal concerns may provide the overall incentive for financial liberalization, the motives of specific governments vary. The French government in the 1960s sought to increase the attraction of banks to investors in order to expand the pool from which government-directed financing could be drawn. The Mexican government in the 1980s aimed to strengthen the nationalized banks to make them attractive to private sector buyers, expecting a fiscal boost from the privatization. The Korean government sought deregulations that would strengthen the banks in order to reduce the fiscal liability associated with government control of the banking sector.

Similarly, in other instances where government fiscal goals and the interests of societal groups converge, the implications for the politics of financial liberalization will vary. In Japan, the government's refinancing needs forced it to pay attention to the preferences of the large city banks for liberalized international financial transactions. In Mexico, politicians' commitment to resolving the nation's fiscal crisis mandated attention to the policy preferences of potential creditors and investors.

Government interest in financial liberalization may also be a function of commitment to monetary as well as fiscal goals. Financial liberalization is often linked to controlling inflation, but a commitment to control inflation may have different motives. In France credit allocation and interest rate controls were reduced because they contributed to inflation, which jeopardized the government's commitment to exchange rate stability and the European Monetary System. In Mexico, although financial liberalization was not directly linked to fighting inflation, it was part of a broad policy package designed to show a commitment to keeping inflation low and making Mexico safe for new investors and creditors.

Even if one concedes that different countries will converge in the medium-to-long run (say, twenty years), the speed and course of financial liberalization will still vary. This is nowhere more apparent than in the Mexican case discussed in this chapter. Here, within a ten-year period, we see a unique pattern of financial policy change from bank nationalization, decreed because of frustration with the loss of national autonomy resulting from international financial integration, to rapid and far-reaching financial liberalization. Although other Latin American countries also liberalized their financial systems, Mexico's deregulation was exceptional (Table 4.1).

*Table 4.1.* Mexican bank privatization in
Latin American perspective (private bank
assets/total bank assets)

|           | 1984      | 1994     |
|-----------|-----------|----------|
| Argentina | 57.5%     | 52%      |
| Brazil    | 20.49%[a] | 56.7%[b] |
| Chile     | 45.3%     | 83.8%    |
| Colombia  | 50%       | 74%      |
| Mexico    | 0         | 100%     |

*Source:* Data supplied by Morgan Stanley.
[a] 1979.
[b] 1993.

Mexico's abrupt about-face in policy and its rapid commitment to financial liberalization were the product of the severe economic crisis the country experienced after the debt boom of the 1980s turned to bust. They were also due to Mexican political leaders' near-fanatical commitment to reshaping the economic and political environment facing potential investors and creditors. Mexican policymakers moved forward with financial liberalization with the hope that it would lead to a strategic exchange: policy commitments would be made to those who could mobilize finance and investment, and they in turn would provide new resources for the national economy.

A financial crisis most frequently produces a desire to increase credibility with potential creditors, but it can also engender an anticreditor backlash, depending on the strategic concerns of political leaders. These strategic concerns will be partly shaped by the severity of the economic situation and the importance of a healthy economy to politicians' electoral prospects. Nonetheless, politicians may perceive different ways out of economic difficulty and may believe that nationalistic or antibusiness measures may win them support in the short run. Rarely, however, are politicians able to sustain an anticreditor strategy in the context of deep fiscal difficulties or balance of payments problems.

The Mexican bank nationalization, which created a very negative impression among potential investors and creditors, resulted from the frustration with international financial pressures felt by José López Portillo, an outgoing president with no reelection possibilities and little to lose by alienating business. López Portillo's successors understood, however, that

*Table 4.2.* Mexican exchange rate and international account balances

|  | Exchange rate (new pesos per SDR[a]) | Trade balance ($ million) | Overall balance |
|---|---|---|---|
| 1987 | 3.1 | 7,189 | 4,134 |
| 1988 | 3.1 | 274 | −10,062 |
| 1989 | 3.5 | −2,596 | −211 |
| 1990 | 4.2 | −4,433 | 2,218 |
| 1991 | 4.4 | −11,329 | 7,793 |
| 1992 | 4.3 | −20,677 | 7,793 |
| 1993 | 4.3 | −18,891 | 1,745 |

*Source:* International Monetary Fund, *International Financial Statistics* (Washington, D.C.: International Monetary Fund, 1994).
[a]  Special Drawing Rights.

sustained economic recovery from the nation's fiscal and balance of payments crisis would require reestablishing Mexico's investment and creditworthiness. An explanation of the country's policy of rapid deregulation thus lies in the nation's severe economic crisis of the 1980s and the decision of political leaders to respond with a broad program of institutional and policy change that would limit the state's involvement in the economy.

In the Mexican case, the changes in financial policy and institutions were state centered; they were part of a government initiative aimed at creating credibility in the eyes of potential investors and creditors. The primary concern of high-level state officials was Mexico's need for private funds to finance a massive reorientation of the economy toward diversified export-led growth. (Data indicative of Mexico's need for international finance are presented in Table 4.2.)

Reprivatizing the nation's banks, for example, required a constitutional change and was meant to signal the government's commitment to private property. As one banking industry magazine noted, "There is no better proof that Mexico's reformers mean business than the speed with which they have moved the country's banks onto the auction block."[2] Although this chapter primarily makes the state-centered argument that business pressure is internalized by government actors who then initiate changes, in a few aspects of the financial liberalization process we see the direct impact of bankers' interests.

---

[2]  Ann Dugan, "Investing in Mexico: Under the Hammer," *Euromoney*, special supplement, December 1990, p. 14.

## History of Financial Regulation

Financial liberalization in the Mexican case centers primarily on ownership issues, including foreign entry and the deregulation of interest rates and credit allocation. Although establishing currency convertibility is an important part of financial liberalization in some countries, Mexico has a long history of relatively liberal currency exchange policies. This contrasts with a relatively extensive program, dating to the 1940s, of state guidance in establishing the cost and distribution of credit throughout the domestic economy. Ownership rules have also been relatively restrictive. Foreign ownership of Mexican financial institutions has been strictly limited since the 1940s, and in 1982 virtually all commercial banks were taken over by the state. The following section briefly reviews the history of financial regulation in Mexico prior to the liberalization moves of the late 1980s.

Three aspects of financial regulation concern us: rules for currency exchange, ownership of financial institutions, and credit allocation. Mexico's long-standing commitment to a liberal currency exchange policy reflects its early concern for creating and maintaining confidence in Mexican government policy in order to minimize capital flight. This motive for adopting and maintaining liberal exchange rate rules was later echoed in the decision to liberalize in other areas of financial policy. The policy of regulating credit allocation began as a compromise strategy for inflation control in a populist political context. Protecting domestic banks from foreign ownership or competition was part of the government's commitment to the growth of private banking. Rapid development of private banking was a cornerstone of the government's system of noninflationary government finance.

The brief history presented here suggests that Mexico's commitment to financial liberalization has had a long past, although it has occasionally been interrupted or constrained by populist appeals. Since the 1930s, the rationale behind Mexico's exceptionally liberal exchange control regime has been to attract and keep capital in a country where the 2,000 mile border with the United States caused an intense fear of capital flight. Paradoxically, both credit control and private bank protection also reflected Mexico's financial technocrats' commitment to economic orthodoxy, which these technocrats have been more or less successful in imposing depending on the nation's need for creditworthiness. The debt bust and balance of payments crisis that the bust created gave the proponents of economic orthodoxy leverage in the 1980s, just as it had in the 1920s and 1950s.

## Exchange Convertibility

Mexico has had a long-standing commitment to free exchange convertibility and a unilateral peg of the peso to the dollar. This historical commitment to a principle of international financial liberalism—freedom to convert currency—was not matched in other areas of international financial transactions or domestic financial regulation. The combination of free convertibility, the unilateral, but unsustainable peg to the dollar, and other restrictions on international capital mobility created cycles of external shock and domestic policy error leading to creeping peso depreciation, speculative attacks on the currency, and recession-inducing devaluation.

The commitment to convertibility grew out of intractable problems with capital flight and financial instability. These in turn were related to the long border with the United States, impossible for Mexico to monitor, and the lack of government policy credibility. The commitment to currency convertibility dates to the 1920s, when gold, silver, pesos, paper pesos, and dollars all circulated within the Mexican financial system. Gold and dollars were the preferred store of value, and both of them, with the help of Mexican banks, flowed out of the national financial system at any sign of political or policy instability.

In the 1920s Mexico was heavily indebted to international banks (mostly in New York) and was struggling to make minimal debt service payments in order to win renewed access to international credit markets. In 1930, convinced that it was impossible to arrest capital outflows through legal or administrative actions, government policymakers decided that the massive speculative capital flows and the balance of payments instability could be stopped only through a government guarantee of convertibility. Negotiations with international creditors led to the provisional return to Mexico of a recent debt service payment to be deposited with the U.S. National City Bank as part of a fund that would back "healthy" demand for currency exchange.

In a foreshadowing of its later commitment to other aspects of financial liberalization, the government brought forward a liberal currency exchange policy, under the assumption that credibility was important to prevent capital flight and maintain a healthy balance of payments. As one historian concludes, creating a U.S. bank fund to back demand for peso-dollar exchange and prevent currency speculation "linked foreign debt with the exchange problem [and] balance of payments equilibrium. . . . It was a way of arresting lack of confidence . . . and lack of foreign capital."[3]

Although this guarantee of free convertibility did not entirely put an end to capital flight or the lack of confidence in government policy, the lesson that capital controls are basically ineffective appears to have been indelibly etched in the minds of Mexican policymakers. Within a few years, the populist economic program of President Cárdenas caused the financial system to become increasingly dollarized. The peso, which had been fixed at 3.6 pesos to the dollar in 1933, became overvalued. There was no official prohibition at the time on opening dollar-denominated and fully convertible accounts with Mexican banks. Between 1934 and 1937 dollar deposits relative to total demand deposits reached levels they would not reach again until the 1982 Mexican financial crisis. Nonetheless, Cárdenas resisted curtailing currency convertibility. The central bank director argued that exchange controls would hurt international trade and could never be effectively and efficiently administered without compromising democracy in Mexico.[4] Perhaps more sanguine about Mexican democracy, in his final decision to reject currency controls Cárdenas merely cited the impossibility of effectively administering them given Mexico's long border with the United States and its relatively limited state administrative capacity.[5]

In the absence of exchange controls, Cárdenas's 1938 nationalization of the oil industry induced a speculative crisis and forced a devaluation

---

[3] Ricardo Torres Gaytán, *Un siglo de devaluaciones del peso mexicano* (Mexico City: Siglo XXI, 1980), p. 184. On financial policies in this era see also Eduardo Turrent Diaz, *História del Banco de México*, vol. 1 (Mexico City: Banco de México, 1982).

[4] "The establishment of exchange controls," the central bank's 1938 annual report states, "would require a series of coercive and restrictive international trade measures, that, in addition to hurting our relations with other countries, presuppose close vigilance of all operations including the private life of the individual, which is incompatible with the general ideology of a democratic country." Quoted in Sylvia Maxfield, *Governing Capital* (Ithaca: Cornell University Press, 1990), p. 72.

[5] Guillermo Ortiz Martínez, "La dolarización en México: Causas y consecuencias," Banco de México, Serie de Documentos, vol. 40 (1980).

of the peso. After a short period of managed floating, the government returned to a fixed exchange regime disrupted only by speculation-forced devaluations in 1949 and 1953.[6]

In 1955 Mexico entered an exceptional period of exchange rate stability; the peso remained at the same fixed rate, 12.5 to the dollar, until 1976. During this time the freedom to convert pesos into dollars came to be seen as a popular right in Mexico. Some observers believe that the peso had become dangerously overvalued as early as the late 1960s. Nonetheless, inflation accelerated extremely rapidly in Mexico in the 1970s, and although Mexican president Echeverría swore he would "defend the peso like a dog," the accumulated overvaluation led to speculation and then to devaluation in 1976. After this adjustment, the Mexican government returned again to a fixed exchange rate regime.

Discovery and pumping of vast oil reserves in Mexico, combined with excess liquidity in the international banking system, led to a huge inflow of foreign exchange. When this bonanza dried up in 1981, speculation against the peso intensified. In February 1982 the central bank had to withdraw from the exchange market, having drawn down reserves dangerously in the previous months' efforts to support the fixed exchange rate. In August 1982 the government announced a dual exchange rate system composed of a free market rate and a preferential, government managed rate for specified transactions. Downward pressure on the peso continued, culminating in September 1982 with the sudden nationalization of domestic banks and the imposition of exchange controls. The government restricted the transfer of funds outside Mexico and placed tight limits on the amount of foreign exchange that could be acquired for international travel. Proceeds from exports had to be repatriated and sold immediately to the banks, and dollars for imports were rationed.[7] When dollar-denominated accounts were declared inconvertible, broader exchange controls imposed and Mexico's banks nationalized in 1982, indignant Mexicans referred to the transformation of Mexdollars into "ex-dollars." The president of an autonomous Mexican business association (as opposed to one of the state corporatist associations) declared that the right to exchange pesos

---

6    Gaytán, *Un siglo de devaluaciones.*
7    Carlos Tello, *La nacionalización de la banca en México* (Mexico City: Siglo XXI, 1984).

into dollars and to export them, "a form of protection and defense of savings," had been violated.[8]

## Extent of Foreign and Private Ownership

The commitment to free currency convertibility was not accompanied by a liberal policy on foreign entry into the domestic financial market. The interests of the financial sector and of the government itself dictated a protectionist policy. From 1924 until 1941 branches of foreign banks were allowed to conduct banking and credit services in Mexico only with permission of the Finance Ministry. They were prohibited from engaging in bond issues. A number of foreign banks left Mexico in 1936 when legal changes required all banks to affiliate with the new central bank, the Banco de México. In 1941 foreign bank activities were further curtailed. From then until greater restrictions were imposed in the 1970s, the combination of operational limitations and Ministry of Finance refusal to grant new entry authorizations significantly reduced the foreign bank presence in Mexico. Legislation enacted in 1973 expressly forbade the establishment of foreign bank branches but permitted the operation of foreign bank representative offices. The one foreign bank branch active in Mexico at the time, Citibank, was allowed to keep its license. Representative offices were essentially prohibited from engaging in any form of financial intermediation.[9]

This protection corresponded to the preferences of Mexican private banks. Uncompetitive by international standards they enjoyed a regulatory environment that made their operations highly profitable. Closure also reflected the motivations of the Mexican government. It facilitated efforts to control a small portion of domestic bank lending for industrial and agricultural policy reasons. Perhaps more important, the Mexican government financed state-led industrial growth in the 1950s and 1960s through reserve requirements on private domestic banks. Banks accepted these reserve requirements in return for a government financial policy regime including protection from competi-

---

[8]   Quoted in Maxfield, *Governing Capital*, p. 75.

[9]   Francisco Borja Martinez, *El nuevo sistema financiero mexicano* (Mexico City: Fondo de Cultura Económica, 1991); José Manuel Quijano, "Finanzas Latinoamericanas y Banca Extranjera," in J. Quijano, H. Sánchez, and F. Antia, eds., *Finanzas, desarollo económico y penetración extranjera* (Puebla: Universidad Autónoma de Puebla, 1985).

tion, which allowed them to compensate for the costs of the reserve requirements.

Mexican government hesitancy to allow foreign ownership of Mexican financial institutions followed in part from a commitment to encouraging the growth of private domestic financial institutions. From 1930 until 1954 public financial institutions accounted for a continually growing majority of resources flowing through the national financial system. But in the 1960s, nurtured by government policy, private financial institutions slowly began to catch up with public bank growth. In 1963 the resources of private investment banks (*financieras*) surpassed those of the public development bank Nafinsa for the first time since the latter's founding in the 1940s. Public bank resources fell as a proportion of the system's total resources from 57 percent a year on the average from 1949 to 1958, to 43 percent from 1965 to 1970. Private bank resources rose concomitantly.[10]

The policy of supporting development of private financial institutions was abruptly reversed in September 1982 when Mexican president José López Portillo expropriated the nation's private banks. The decision was made in frustration over rising capital flight and the declining capacity of the state to induce and guide industrial investment. Economic advisers sympathetic to national populist ideals linked the decline to the accumulation of wealth and power by conglomerates of banks and industry. The rising fortunes of private conglomerates were in turn seen as partly facilitated by growing international financial integration. Nationalization was a belated effort to implement policies that would be popular among peasants, workers, and owners of small and medium businesses, in part because it would help direct the allocation of financial resources away from private oligopolies.

The bank nationalization reflected the power of the Mexican presidency, which gave López Portillo the option of making a populist appeal to restore his positive place in Mexican history after several years of gross economic mismanagement. López Portillo knew that nationalization, a slap in the face not only to bankers but all private wealth holders, would not be acceptable to the financial technocrats. He developed the plan in secret, announcing it to his cabinet only twelve hours before

[10]    María Elena Cardero, *Patrón monetario y acumulación en México* (Mexico City: Siglo XXI, 1984), pp. 101, 103.

his address to the nation. He asked for the resignations of anyone object-
ing. The head of the central bank, Miguel Mancera, did resign. Finance
Minister Silva Herzog, then deeply involved in Mexico's international
debt renegotiation, also tendered his resignation; but López Portillo
refused to accept it because Mexico's economic future depended on the
course of debt renegotiations. Herzog did, however, manage to extract a
promise of measures that would effectively weaken implementation of
the nationalization.[11]

*Interest Rate and Credit Allocation Controls*

Bank nationalization also reflected a long-standing division within
the Mexican government between those in favor of state control of
financial markets to support activist credit policy and those who viewed
state financial control as tolerable only insofar as it contributed to inflation control.

Beginning in the 1940s the Mexican government added several tools
of selective credit allocation to those already in use, which primarily
involved differential rediscounting, that is, the extension of credit to private banks by the central bank at interest rates that varied according to
the private banks' areas of activity. By imposing differential requirements based on a private bank's liability and asset structures, the central
bank could encourage or discourage specific types of bank activity. The
central bank had three types of reserve requirements which it used to
regulate private bank lending: cash reserve requirements, securities
reserve requirements, and a directed credit requirement, referred to as a
*cajón*. *Cajones* (boxes) are quotas for loans to specific types of borrowers that banks had to fill. The central bank enjoyed the power to raise
the maximum reserve requirement to 100 percent of any increase in liabilities. Marginal reserve requirements were adjusted more than thirty
times between 1950 and 1970.

From 1940 through 1970 the primary motivating factor for the central bank's credit control program was minimizing inflation's impact on
the Mexican economy. This goal conflicted to some extent with those of
government agencies such as the Ministry of Agriculture or the
Ministry of National Patrimony, which backed the program for more

[11]   Maxfield, *Governing Capital*, chap. 5.

heterodox reasons. They wanted a tool of intervention that would support specific geographic or sectoral activities and would increase their ability to respond to "populist" political pressures.

In some ways credit allocation and interest rate controls were a second-best tool, which the central bank chose because the populist political milieu and the relationship between the central bank, the industrial development bank, and private banks ruled out their preferred policies.

In its effort to mitigate the inflationary impact of World War II on the Mexican economy, the Banco de México's first choice would have been to develop the central bank's capacity for open market operations. But the industrial development bank Nafinsa insisted that the stock market was under its jurisdiction and that any issues, like its own Certificados de Participación, needed to carry a repurchase guarantee. The Banco de México was not willing to make such a guarantee on government issues and Nafinsa's staunch commitment to its guarantee policy virtually closed off the option of open market operations.

Constraints on the central bank's policy options also derived from its relationship with the private banks. Nafinsa policy aside, the Banco de México knew from earlier experience that the private banks were extremely reluctant to hold government paper. Because the major banks were relatively liquid, the central bank could also not count on effectively using the rediscounting tool to regulate credit expansion and the money supply. The Banco de México had few options other than to turn to credit control instruments linked to reserve and portfolio requirements. Although not pleased, the bankers agreed to selective reserve and portfolio requirements provided they were granted certain privileges: freedom to oligopolize the unregulated portion of the market, which involved charging very high fee-inclusive interest rates in the 30 percent of the commercial bank loan market that was not government controlled; freedom to own investment banks (the financieras), which were unregulated and highly profitable despite the fact that the banking system was supposed to be specialized; and largesse to partially comply with sectoral lending requirements by lending to industries to which the banks were linked through ownership or management.

The selective credit control program was tremendously effective from the point of view of achieving the goal of noninflationary government finance. The high reserve requirements with selective exemptions provided resources that could be employed by the government without great risk of inflation. The program was not effective as a subsidy to small-scale agriculture or industry, however. The Banco de México was willing to tolerate only limited compliance with sectoral lending requirements in return for acceptance of very high reserve requirements. Nevertheless, because the selective credit program could be presented as a populist measure, the government gained some much-needed political support, which might not have been forthcoming for a more orthodox inflation-fighting program.

## Financial Liberalization

The trend toward financial liberalization began with the partial reprivatization of the commercial banks shortly after their nationalization in 1982. This took the form of an almost immediate reversal of the September 1982 exchange controls and, beginning in 1986, a reduction in the provision of preferential credit through public development banks.[12] The period of extensive liberalization, which began in 1988, included freeing interest rates, lifting credit controls and reserve requirements on private banks, shrinking the size of public development banks, and fully reprivatizing the commercial banks. Each instance of liberalization—the reversal of the 1982 foreign exchange control and nationalization decree, the decontrol of credit allocation, and the decision to allow foreigners to establish or buy into existing private banks— reflects the indirect influence of domestic and international creditors and investors; and each reflects, too, the power of those within the ruling party who were interested in catering to creditors and investors as part of a strategy for maximizing their tenure in government. In the case of foreign entry and interest rate deregulation, the direct influence of

---

[12] Between 1982 and 1986 preferential credit distributed through public development banks and *fideicomisos* amounted to 4 percent of the GDP on the average. It went down to 1.7 percent in 1987 according to Dwight S. Brothers, "Financial Sector Planning and Mexico's New Development Strategy" (paper presented at a conference on Mexico's Search for a New Development Strategy, sponsored by the Economic Growth Center of Yale University, New Haven, Conn., April, 1989), pp. 13–14. This reduction was achieved in part through reductions in the rate of subsidy provided by the loans. One important goal was to try to simplify the subsidy rate schedule by equalizing rates for the many different loan categories (e.g., small farmers, small businessmen, exporters). The rates were also indexed to the weighted average cost of deposits.

private bankers is evident, as one would expect in a traditional rent-seeking or regulatory "capture" model.

### Reversing the September 1982 Decree

Several factors led to the rapid repeal of exchange controls in 1982. First was the lame-duck status of the López Portillo administration and the knowledge that the incoming president, Miguel de la Madrid, opposed the policy, as did many Mexicans, and fully intended to remove the controls as rapidly as possible. Furthermore, the International Monetary Fund expected Mexico to end exchange controls as part of the Standby Loan negotiation, which was of key importance in the successful renegotiation of Mexico's debt to private international creditors. Reversal of the prohibition on banks offering dollar-denominated time deposits was delayed longer than reversal of exchange controls. But in August 1989 the Finance Ministry reverted to the pre-1982 decree policy of allowing dollar-denominated time deposits in commercial banks.

Although the bank nationalization was not immediately reversed, as were exchange controls, its potential impact was constrained by several decisions regarding interpretation of the decree. For example, Carlos Tello, appointed central bank director at the time of the September 1 decree, decided immediately that the government should relinquish control of nonbank stocks owned by the nationalized banks. This was done in order to placate the private bankers and minimize divisiveness within the ruling party.

The de la Madrid administration extended the scope of returned stocks to include those of nonbank financial institutions. Capitalizing on the exclusion of these institutions from the nationalization decree and the growing inefficiency of the nationalized banks, private entrepreneurs spurred the development of a nonbank parallel financial market, which grew dramatically and diverted resources from the nationalized banks. During the second half of the 1980s former bankers as well as new entrepreneurs profited hugely from ownership of insurance companies, stock brokerages, leasing firms, and warehousing concerns.

Limited divestiture of bank stock into private hands beginning in 1987 and regulatory changes in 1989 paved the way for full bank reprivatization in 1991 and 1992. Limited divestiture helped strengthen bank capitalization. Legislation of March and August 1989, discussed in more detail below, involved sufficient deregulation of interest rates, credit allocation guidelines, and reserve requirements to increase the prospects for bank profitability significantly.[13] In December 1989, legislation increased the administrative independence of bank management, encouraged the conglomeration of nonbank financial enterprises, strengthened bank supervision and capitalization, and allowed minority foreign investment in banks and financial groups.

This spate of legislation immediately caused speculation that full privatization of the banks might be on the horizon. Few expected it to be announced so quickly, however.[14] Most observers expected President Salinas (1988–94) to wait until after the 1991 midterm elections to take the seemingly politically risky step of reprivatizing banks nationalized in the name of national populism only eight years before. Nevertheless, on May 2, 1990, the Mexican president sent Congress legislation mandating sale of the government's 66 percent holding in the nation's eighteen commercial banks.

The legislation Salinas sent to the Mexican Congress to permit reprivatization involved amending the constitutional provision, dating to 1982, categorizing commercial banking as a nationally strategic industry and reserving it for state control. It was the first time since the 1917 revolution that the Mexican government proposed a constitutional change to reduce the size of the state. Because it was a constitutional amendment, the legislation needed to pass the national legislature with a two-thirds majority and a simple majority in thirty-one state legislatures. The Partido Revolucionario Institucional (PRI), holding only 263 of 500 seats in the Mexican congress, needed to find allies in order to secure the bill's passage. Salinas counted on, and received, the support of the Partido de Acción Nacional (PAN) deputies, who held the largest single block of minority party seats.[15]

[13]  At the end of 1990 Mexican bank capitalization averaged close to 8 percent. "Suddenly, This Summer," *The Banker* 141, no. 782 (April 1991).

[14]  "Aspe wants more efficient banks," *Latin American Weekly Report*, August 17, 1989, p. 11; "Mexico," *Business Latin America*, January 8, 1990, p. 8.

[15]  There was some opposition within the PAN to supporting the bank reprivatization legislation. In August 1989, after rancorous debate, the PAN made the fateful decision to support the PRI's proposed electoral law. The law drew a fine line between opening up the electoral system and guaranteeing PRI dominance and therefore limited the PAN's political potential. The party became bitterly divided over the decision to support the PRI legislation, and some feared

The banking legislation passed in July 1990 permitted 100 percent private ownership of all Mexico's commercial banks with certain restrictions.[16] To prevent concentration of ownership, which was seen as one of the problems originally leading to nationalization, the law prevented individuals from owning more than 5 percent of any single bank's stock, or 10 percent with a special dispensation from the Ministry of Finance. Institutional investors were authorized to hold up to 15 percent. The legislation encouraged the formation of financial holding companies whose percentage ownership was unlimited. It permitted up to 30 percent foreign ownership. The legislation encouraged the trend toward "multiple" or "universal" banking, legally initiated in the 1970s. While the number of commercial banks in Mexico fell from forty-one (the number of banks nationalized in 1982) to eighteen (the number put up for sale in 1990), further concentration was considered necessary in order to prepare Mexican banks to compete directly with foreign ones. The legislation foresaw the opening of new branch offices of foreign financial enterprises; these would perform banking functions with nonresidents but could not participate in financial intermediation in national financial markets without special authorization from the Finance Ministry.[17]

---

further upheaval resulting from support of the nationalization. Furthermore, PAN deputies, together with those of leftwing minority parties, were on "legislative strike" to protest the government's refusal to investigate allegations of fraud at the government fishing industry bank (Banpesca). Nevertheless, the bill passed, although with a relatively high number of abstentions, after the PRI conceded to PAN demands that the legislation be amended to limit concentration of bank ownership by individuals.

[16]    The constitutional reforms were published in the *Diario Oficial*, June 27, 1990. The two new laws, the Law of Credit Institutions and the Law to Regulate Financial Groups, and the reforms and additions to the Stock Market Law were published in the *Diario Oficial*, July 18, 1990. The details of the legislation and the government's interpretation and rationale are presented in Secretaría de Hacienda y Credito Publico, "La nueva banca y las agrupaciones financieras en México," mimeographed, August 1990.

[17]    U.S. commercial banks had long had "representative offices" in Mexico, which are legally limited to performing advisory services and assisting nonresidents. The scope of such activity has been quite broad. As of late 1990, several U.S. investment banks had set up, or were arranging to set up, Mexican offices, hoping to compensate for declining business in the United States with fees from Mexican incorporated firms desirous of floating bonds and selling stocks abroad. Among these were Merrill Lynch; Bear, Stearns; and Goldman, Sachs. Goldman won the highly desirable contract of helping the Mexican government sell the state telephone company. That job itself was not highly profitable, but it gave Goldman an inside line on the lucrative business of floating telephone company bonds in foreign markets. The group of banks contained institutions of different size, scope, and regional base. The composition of these packages may have reflected bidders' preferences.

The July 1990 legislation also sought to establish a transparent and fair process for auctioning state banks. To avoid charges of government collusion with favored entrepreneurs, pains were taken to devise a corruption-proof sales procedure. A "Bank Disincorporation Committee" was established, composed of the undersecretary for credit of the Finance Ministry and three other Finance Ministry officials, the director of the central bank, the president of the National Banking Commission, and two other Finance Ministry nominees. This committee, assisted by external auditors, was charged with determining the value of eighteen "packages" of state-held banks and reviewing the qualifications of potential bidders.[18] Guidelines for bidder qualification included financial soundness and financial industry experience. Legal procedure for sale provided for secret auctioning and acceptance of the highest bid.

In September 1990 the Bank Disincorporation Committee began evaluating and then registering potential buyers.[19] Bidders fell into three groups: owners of Mexico City brokerages (these had mushroomed as the parallel, private financial market boomed in the aftermath of the bank nationalization), Monterrey financial or industrial groups, and former bank owners. Foreign interest was scarce; U.S. banks in particular counted on the North American Free Trade Agreement to allow them entry in their own right. The first group of banks offered for sale included three of the multiregional banks: Banca Cremi, Multibanco Mercantil, and Banpais. These banks and four other multiregional banks operated in more than one of Mexico's states but not in all. Operating in the entire country were the nation's largest banks, called the Big Six: Banamex, Bancomer, Serfin, Somex, Comermex, and Banco Internacional. Prior to sale, these six accounted for 83 percent of the total value of the banking sector in Mexico.[20] The first of the Big Six to be sold was the Banco Nacional de México in August 1991, followed by Bancomer in October.[21] The banks on average sold for 3.07 times their

---

[18]  McKinsey and Booz Allen were hired to do the evaluations. Banks also had to do their own evaluations as well. "Mexican Bank Privatisation," *The Economist*, March 9, 1991, p. 81.

[19]  For detail on the sale process see: Rebecca Hovey, "The Mexican Bank Privatization and the Realignment of Industry and Finance" (paper prepared for the meeting of the Eastern Economic Association, Boston, Mass., March, 1994).

[20]  "Suddenly, This Summer," p. 27.

[21]  The financial details of bank reprivatization are summarized in Stefano Natella and Justin Manson, *The Mexican Banking System* (New York: Equity Research Department, CS First Boston, May 1991).

book value, compared with an average of 2.2 times the book value for sales of U.S. banks between 1987 and 1992.[22]

The push for privatization was primarily motivated by the government, acting independently of direct private sector pressure. The bank sale contributed $12.5 billion to government coffers.[23] Private sector pressure was indirect, reflecting the "structural power of capital," that is, the ability of private actors to invest or lend capital, shape public economic well-being, and thereby affect the political fortunes of government leaders.[24] Salinas's motive for privatization was part of his larger economic plan to restore Mexican growth with new inflows of foreign capital. This was not lost on one of the most influential reporters of Mexican business conditions, who explicitly linked the bank privatization with the government's intent to entice flight capital back into the country.[25] In fact, the bank sale was one of a series of moves—including unilateral trade liberalization, removal of restrictions on foreign direct investment, and promotion of a free trade agreement with the United States—that were designed to create foreign and domestic capitalist confidence in Mexico's economic future. Privatization was perhaps the most effective way to reassure foreign and domestic investors of Mexico's security, maintain the flow of foreign capital into the country, and keep domestic interest rates low.[26]

*Deregulation of Credit Allocation and Interest Rates*

The first in a series of rapid changes in policies governing interest rates and credit allocation came in October 1988. Banks were allowed,

---

[22]   Carlos Elizondo, "The Making of a New Alliance: the Privatization of the Banks in Mexico" (paper presented at the seventeenth international congress of the Latin American Studies Association, Los Angeles, September, 1992), p. 12. There has been considerable debate over why the banks commanded such inflated prices. See Hovey, "Mexican Bank Reprivatization," and Peter M. Garber and Steven R. Weisbrod, "Opening the Financial Services Market in Mexico," in Peter Garber, ed., *The Mexico-U.S. Free Trade Agreement* (Cambridge: MIT Press, 1993).

[23]   *U.S.-Mexico Free Trade Reporter*, July 13, 1992, p. 8.

[24]   Charles Lindblom, "The Market as Prison," *Journal of Politics* 44 (May 1982); Adam Pzeworski and Michael Wallerstein, "Structural Dependence of the State on Capital," *American Political Science Review* 82 (March 1988).

[25]   Damian Fraser, "Cash Returns to Mexico's Coffers," *Financial Times*, August 29, 1991, p. 23.

[26]   This inflow and the lowering of domestic interest rates it permitted allowed the Mexican government to begin reducing its internal debt—which had become even more worrisome to many potential investors than the external debt.

for the first time, to issue bankers' acceptances, short-term letters of credit (three months or less) issued at a discount by a nonfinancial private enterprise and guaranteed by a financial institution. These letters of credit are also known as commercial paper. In the aftermath of the bank nationalization a large, unofficial, commercial paper market dominated by stock brokerages had developed. Investment in commercial paper allowed the stock brokerages to offer returns on their mutual funds that were relatively high compared with bank deposit rates. Giving banks access to the commercial paper market was an important step in increasing the profitability of the commercial banks and making them potentially viable private properties. Deregulation in this arena was therefore partially motivated by a commitment to bank reprivatization.

In March 1989 Guillermo Ortiz, the undersecretary of finance, announced the government's intention to liberalize interest rates and stop financing public debt through reserve requirements on the commercial banks. Reserve requirements were reduced to 30 percent from 90 percent effective April 3, 1989. Interest rate liberalization was delayed until May 1, because the commercial banks claimed they needed time to prepare for the increased competition for deposits that would result.[27] Deregulation of deposit rates significantly reduced the spread between active and passive rates. The March 1989 legislation also eliminated most requirements for special credits to "priority" sectors.

Further financial liberalization came in August 1989. At this point the government significantly reduced the legally mandated reserve requirements. The result was a large increase in credit available to the private sector. A third package of financial reforms was announced in December 1989. This legislation divided bank capital into three kinds of stock. These changes in share ownership guidelines were significant because they allowed for foreigners to own up to 34 percent of voting stock and increased the percentage of shares any single company or individual could own from 1 percent to 5 percent. The December 1989 financial policy changes also allowed for banks to invest in nonbank financial enterprises. These policy changes also permitted foreigners to own up to 49 percent of insurance, financial leasing and bonding companies, bonded warehouses, and investment societies. Foreigners had previously

---

[27] "Mexico Plans Industrial and Financial Reform," *Business Latin America*, March 27, 1989, pp. 89–90; "Mexico," *Business Latin America*, April 24, 1989, p. 128.

been prohibited from owning such operations, and they continued, after this legislation, to be excluded from owning brokerages.[28] This legislation also explicitly freed bank boards from Finance Ministry supervision over a variety of managerial decisions ranging from opening and closing branches to installing computer systems.[29] Perhaps the most significant policy change for the future bank privatization was a provision in the December 1989 legislation allowing for formation of nonbank financial holding companies. This allowed for the creation of financial conglomerates potentially in a position to buy banks as they came up for sale.

Finally, reserve requirements for commercial banks were eliminated entirely in September 1991. The earliest of the wave of reforms that led to this elimination was directly linked to 1988–89 negotiations between Mexico and the International Monetary Fund. The terms of Mexico's letter of intent to the IMF were crucial because the resulting IMF loan would lay the basis for new funding from the World Bank, rescheduling with the Paris Club, and ultimately the outline of a full-scale debt rescheduling.[30]

There was virtually no public opposition to deregulation of credit allocation and interest rates or to bank privatization. Leadership of the Mexican labor federation, the Congreso de Trabajadores Mexicanos (CTM), supported financial liberalization as reflected in the bank privatization. Government officials, the CTM leadership, and the president of the Senate spoke in support of the constitutional measure paving the way for bank privatization on the grounds that "times have changed" since the nationalization of 1982. Former president Luis Echeverría, who had foreshadowed López Portillo's 1982 bank nationalization with his own brand of end-of-term populism, heralded the legislation mandating private bank ownership as born of the "profound nationalism that has been the hallmark of the current administration."[31] The only public opposition to the reprivatization came from leftwing congressional representatives and the architect of the bank nationalization, Carlos Tello.

Lack of opposition to liberalization and reprivatization reflects both the technocratic nature of financial decision making and the distribution of costs and benefits among social groups with different organizational

---

[28]    "Suddenly, This Summer," pp. 22–23.
[29]    "Aperture of Opportunity," *The Banker* 140, no. 770 (April 1990): 53.
[30]    "Tomorrow Is Another Day," *The Banker* 139, no. 765 (November 1989): 101.
[31]    "Eight Years On, Denationalisation," *Latin American Weekly Report*, May 17, 1990, p. 4.

capacities and kinds of policy influence. The bank nationalization had originally been decided and implemented by President López Portillo and a small circle of advisors. Little effort was made to involve potential supporters of the move at any stage in the policy process. The decision was made, and then, as one former Mexican financial official put it vividly, "se lo pintaron de color populista" (they painted it a populist color). The privatization decision was made similarly. After the decision was taken, the PRI made an effort to present it in the media in the most populist light possible. The party took out a newspaper advertisement stating that the move was part of Salinas's "project of nationalist and popular modernization," and government publications of the bill were prefaced with similar language.[32] A poll conducted for *La Jornada*, then the only Mexican daily not subsidized by the government, found the day after the privatization bill went to Congress that 34.5 percent had not heard about it, 29.9 percent were strongly in favor, and 20.3 percent mildly so.

Those who stood to lose directly from the cutoff of subsidized credit from the commercial banks were relatively few. Although intended to benefit small and medium-sized entrepreneurs and certain sectors of the economy, selective credit programs were never particularly effective in channeling private bank credit to socially prescribed ends. The nationalization also did little to improve the allocation of credit to small and medium-sized industrialists and other targeted groups. The cutback of subsidized credit allocated through the public development banks such as Nafinsa was more likely to be felt directly, but collective protest was limited due to the diversity of the beneficiaries and the rise of the new targeted state aid program, Pronasol. Large-scale industrialists had ceased to rely heavily on "internal" financing, as they had in the 1960s, but in seeking external financing they shifted more toward the stock market and stock brokerages than to loans from domestic banks.

## Liberalization of Exchange Rate Administration

Although the exchange controls brusquely imposed in September 1982 were quickly removed, the Mexican government continued its policy of administering the peso's exchange rate. The Mexican government finally broke with the fixed exchange rate regime in late 1991. It intro-

[32] Ibid.

duced a target zone, designed to increase the market's role in setting the peso's exchange value within a relatively wide but firmly bounded exchange rate band. Although denied publicly, central bank officials from both the United States and Mexico had begun earlier that year to probe the possibility of a monetary agreement involving a bilaterally negotiated currency band, or target zone, within which the peso-dollar exchange rate would be set by market conditions. At its outer limits the band would be backed by currency swaps or reserve-sharing agreements and by occasional summits, like those among the G-7 countries, between the two nations' central banks.

Federal Reserve economists advocated a change in the Mexican exchange rate regime to protect U.S.-Mexican trade and Mexican growth in general. Congressional representatives in the United States also grew increasingly concerned about the impact of exchange rates on their constituents' potential benefit from the North American Free Trade Agreement.[33] The Mexican central bank sent a study mission to Europe to gather information on European exchange policies and monetary integration. The goal was to formulate a report, based on European experiences, about the likely impact on Mexico of regional monetary integration. After carefully evaluating the Spanish case in particular, Mexican central bankers came to believe that a bilateral target zone would be advantageous. When support for this idea seemed to wane within the U.S. Federal Reserve system, Mexican central bankers discussed linking Mexican concessions on opening the financial sector in the NAFTA negotiations to U.S. support for a bilateral or multilateral exchange rate agreement.[34] But in November 1991 the Banco de México decided to move ahead unilaterally, liberalizing control of the peso exchange rate within a target zone. The Banco de México decreased the rate of preannounced crawling devaluation in the purchase price of pesos and stipulated a freeze in the sale price. This widened the "bid-ask" spread in the interbank peso market. The strong positive market reaction to the move, evident in a nominal peso appre-

[33]  House Committee on Small Business, *Hearings on NAFTA and Peso Devaluation: A Problem for U.S. Exporters?* Statement of Representative John J. LaFalce, May 20, 1993; Richard Lawrence, "Exchange Rate Policy Urged as One of NAFTA Side Deals," *Journal of Commerce,* May 21, 1993.
[34]  Patricia Armendáriz, "Zonas de paridad cambiaria: El caso Europea y una propuesta para México" (Mexico City: October 1991, mimeographed).

ciation within the target zone, encouraged the Bank of Mexico to widen the band even further in March 1992. At this time the Banco de México admitted publicly to the change in exchange rate policy. The band has been steadily widened.[35]

What lies behind this decision to liberalize exchange rate administration? The answer lies in the incentives for Mexican business and the Mexican government that growing regional economic integration created. For businesses the target-zone exchange rate makes the exchange rate risk associated with investments a function of market conditions rather than (possibly) capricious government action. It facilitates the development of a peso futures market through which regionally operating businesses can try to cover their exchange risk. By reducing the potential effects of arbitrary government decisions on businesses investing in the country, the government hoped to increase Mexico's attractiveness as a business site.

Although U.S. central bankers refused to pursue a formal monetary and exchange rate arrangement to help back the peso target zone, their response to pressure on the peso in the aftermath of the assassination of Mexican presidential candidate Colosio, in March 1994, suggests that a de facto agreement exists. U.S. authorities contributed billions of dollars to help keep the peso's value within the target zone and limit investor fear and capital flight from Mexico. Such de facto multilateralism in exchange rate matters adds tremendous credibility to the new exchange rate regime, because it suggests that Mexico will not have to bear the burden of unexpected market shocks alone. U.S. motivations are similar to those of the Mexican government: to protect regionally exposed businesses. The extent of U.S. investment in Mexican securities is great; the United States intervened not only as a friend to Mexico but because a peso free fall would have severely harmed major U.S. institutional investors.

### Foreign Ownership

The final aspect of Mexican financial liberalization involves the relaxation of restrictions on foreign ownership of Mexican banks. The

---

[35] Raul A. Feliz and John H. Welch, "The Credibility and Performance of Unilateral Target Zones: A Comparison of the Mexican and Chilean Cases" (paper prepared for the 68th annual international conference of the Western Economic Association, Lake Tahoe, June 1993).

first significant relaxation came in 1992 when the Mexican Congress approved legislation creating special "L" bank shares with limited voting rights. When added to foreigners' ability to own "C" and "B" shares, the creation of "L" shares opened the possibility for foreigners to own bank equity equal to 79 percent of total voting capital or 60 percent of total voting and limited vote capital.[36]

Further relaxation of barriers to foreign entry into the Mexican financial services sector came with the ratification of the North American Free Trade Agreement. Potential profits from growing trade, corporate finance, and retail banking spurred U.S. bankers to seek a rapid opening of the Mexican banking industry to U.S. bank branches under NAFTA terms.[37] But the Mexican Finance Ministry, seeking to limit the impact of U.S. bank competition on the Mexican banking sector, drove a hard bargain. Even though Mexican banks' operating efficiency was steadily improving, new private sector owners of Mexico's largest commercial banks were not anxious to face foreign competition.[38]

Mexican bank opposition to financial services liberalization was first clearly articulated to the United States in a series of private sector talks in November 1991 between the U.S. Coalition of Service Industries (CSI), the U.S. Industry Sector Advisory Committee, and the Mexican Business Coordinating Council (COECE).[39] In addition to U.S. industry associations, two geographically concentrated banking groups also had a strong interest in the substantial liberalization of

---

[36] "Mexico Eases Laws on Foreign Investment," *Financial Times*, May 28, 1992, p. 32.

[37] A Mexican Budget and Planning Ministry estimate places the profitability of banking in Mexico at three times that in the United States or Canada. See Elizondo, "Making of a New Alliance." For another assessment of opportunities for foreign banks in Mexico see "U.S-Mexican Free Trade: What's in It for Banks?" *ABA Banking Journal*, September 1991, p. 80.

[38] Operating efficiency, defined as administrative expenses expressed as a percentage of net revenues, improved from 72% in 1991 to 59% in 1993. Some have suggested that the government was hesitant to yield to U.S. pressure on the financial services portion of the NAFTA agreement until all the banks were sold. Carlos Viana has compared the evolution of prices paid for banks with the chronology of NAFTA negotiations on financial services. He found that the highest price, 5.4 times book value, was paid just after a draft of the financial services section of NAFTA was leaked that indicated that Mexico would not yield to U.S. demands. The lowest price, 2.8 times book value, was paid when it was apparent that Mexico would make many concessions to the United States on financial services. Carlos Viana, "The Political Economy of Freeing Trade in Financial Services" (Yale University, Fall 1993, mimeographed).

[39] Members of the CSI are the American Bankers Association, American International Group, American Express, Beneficial Management Corporation, Citicorp/Citibank, Dean Witter Reynolds, Financial Services Council, Ford Financial Services Group, Investment Company Institute, and the Securities Industry Association.

the Mexican financial services industry: money-center banks in New York and California interested in wholesale banking in Mexico and U.S.-Mexico border banks interested in the Mexican retail banking market. Mexican bankers, alleging that U.S. financial regulations were the real obstacle to financial services liberalization, argued against U.S. banks' preferences for 100 percent foreign ownership of bank branches and suggested partial foreign ownership of bank subsidiaries instead. (The distinction is significant because subsidiaries have to be individually capitalized while branches do not; capitalization substantially raises the entry cost for foreign banks.) The U.S. banks stood firm in the five demands they had made to the U.S. negotiating team: branch access, access to credit card business, permission to engage in investment banking business, and fair regulation of cross-border activities.

In December 1991 the Mexican government gave negotiators a draft of its position on financial services, which reflected the interests of the new private bank owners. The Mexicans would initially allow only 0.5 percent of the total financial industry capital to be in foreign hands; but this percentage would rise slowly to a 5 percent ceiling in 2010. No foreigners would be permitted in top management positions in bank subsidiaries, and special approval would be required to open more than one subsidiary branch. The CSI sent a letter to top Bush administration officials expressing their dismay at the Mexican proposal. The Mexicans backed down somewhat during February 1992 negotiations in Dallas, raising the permanent ceiling on foreign ownership to 12 percent of the total financial industry capital and moving the date forward to 2002. The U.S. banks were still disappointed. Negotiations appeared to be at an impasse, with the Mexicans linking further concessions in financial services to U.S. concessions in agriculture. COECE even proposed that these two sectors be excluded from NAFTA.

In the end U.S. banks had to settle for authorization to open subsidiaries rather than branches in Mexico. The agreement also limited individual foreign banks to 1.5 percent of the bank market during a six-year phase-in period. During this period the total combined foreign market share in banking, measured as the percentage of authorized foreign capital to total aggregate capital of all banks in Mexico, could rise from 8 percent in 1994, the first year of the phase-in, to 15 percent in 1999.

For four years after the phase-in period Mexico would reserve the right to impose a three-year freeze on the foreign market share, should it exceed 25 percent.[40] Similar provisions apply to foreign entry in the securities and insurance industries.

The primary motive for allowing foreign entry into Mexican financial markets was, once again, the Mexican government's belief that it would facilitate capital inflow and forestall capital flight. As one trade journal noted in discussing the rationale for foreign participation, "The [Mexican] government wants to forge international links and create fresh channels for capital entering the country."[41] For Mexican banks, long protected by government from foreign competition, the prospect of foreign banks operating in Mexico was threatening. In this instance of financial liberalization we see that investors and creditors exerted an indirect "structural" influence on the government in its search to solve a liquid and fixed capital shortage; and we see evidence that the interests of those regulated, Mexico's commercial bankers, directly shaped the liberalization process. Although the bankers' interests influenced the exact nature of liberalization as it progressed, the initiative for liberalization came from the state.

Even though the terms of the final agreement fell short of the U.S. banks' desires, many are in 1995 planning their entry into the Mexican market. Mexican guidelines for establishing subsidiaries were published in the spring of 1994, and with encouragement from the Mexican government between twelve and twenty-four U.S. banks have made plans to apply for licenses to open subsidiaries in Mexico. Some banks, including J. P. Morgan and Chemical Banking Corporation, were considering applying for licenses to set up securities affiliates.[42] Most U.S. banks planned to stick to wholesale banking activities, i.e., selling services to topflight Mexican companies, other financial institutions, multinational subsidiaries and the Mexican government. Mexican banks were hopeful that this would leave them free to expand and profit from the booming Mexican retail banking market. As the data in Table 4.3 show, Mexico remains relatively "underbanked."

[40]  *North American Free Trade Agreement Text: Final Version* (Chicago: Commerce Clearing House, 1994), September 6, 1992, chap. 14, Financial Services.

[41]  *Euromoney*, September 1990, p. 164.

[42]  Sam Zuckerman, "Trade Pact Positions U.S. Banks for Key Role in Mexico's Future," *The American Banker*, April 8, 1994.

Table 4.3. Scope for Mexican Bank expansion (total loans/GDP, year-end 1993)

| Country | Percent |
|---------|---------|
| Brazil | 21% |
| Mexico | 32% |
| Chile | 65% |
| U.S. | 81% |
| Canada | 82% |
| Germany | 105% |
| U.K. | 115% |

*Source:* Data provided by Morgan Stanley.

The Mexican financial liberalization process also highlights one of the key reasons for policy convergence. The growing mobility of capital makes governments that are intent on attracting and keeping credit and investment at least partially subject to the policy preferences of those institutions that control financial resources. Governments are increasingly guided in their financial policy choices by the belief that potential investors and creditors look to institutional and policy changes for signs of government credibility and commitment to the preservation of an environment that is favorable to capital.

# CHAPTER FIVE

# Socialist Monetarism and Financial Liberalization in France

MICHAEL LORIAUX

In 1981, François Mitterrand was elected to the presidency of France on a platform that called for extensive nationalization of industrial and financial firms and a reinvigoration of the state's interventionist role in economic affairs. In 1990, the *Financial Times* awarded François Mitterrand its prize for the year's "Best Monetarist." In the intervening decade, the government abolished the selective credit controls that had given the state extensive influence over the allocation of credit by banks, it created a money market that was made to function much like its liberal American and British counterparts, it established a financial futures market to rival that of Chicago, it abolished exchange controls, it cut back dramatically on the allocation of loan subsidies to industry (including export industries) by public and semipublic financial institutions, and all the while it encouraged one of the most dramatic bull markets ever to hit the Paris stock exchange.

What happened? Why would one of the most interventionist of the advanced industrialized democracies, under a Socialist government, embrace monetarism in policy and impose liberalizing reforms that diminished the state's power to intervene in the economy? The French case is interesting because, compared with other cases examined in this book, it reveals with clarity the impact of international change on the decision to liberalize financial structures and processes. Change in the international monetary system, prompted by the United States' decision to abandon postwar policies of internationalist leadership, forced the French (and other Europeans) to reject inflationary policy and embrace the cause of a strong currency. This shift, in turn, required fundamental reforms in domestic structures to support the new orientation. It also required policy adjustments so that the country could raise the capital resources that inflationary policy would no longer provide. The liberalizing reforms were shepherded through by the state from start to finish; societal support for the reforms was opportunistic and of secondary importance. In this chapter I begin by examining financial interventionism in France as it was practiced prior to the reforms. I then proceed to show how floating rates hampered the use of credit policy as a tool of industrial policy and forced the issue of reform.

## Credit Policy and Industrial Development, 1945–1973

Before World War II, France was one of the world's principal financial powers. It suffered greatly from the destruction and monetary shocks of the two world wars. Following World War I, however, France was able to restore much of its financial might. After World War II, on the other hand, the French made no substantial effort to restore vitality to their financial market or even stability to their currency. Whereas the Belgians, Italians, and Germans pursued rigorous stabilization policies, the French feared the effects of rigor on domestic political stability and thus chose a more lenient path to economic recovery. Pierre Mendès France, minister of finance in the provisional government that took power in August 1944, had advocated a rigorous program of monetary stabilization, but the government of which he was a member rejected his plan in favor of a policy of industrial reconstruction financed through a large and generous sale of long-term government bonds.

In rejecting monetary stabilization, the government acted not out of ideological preference but out of political timorousness. The bond sale not only failed to mop up the inflationary liquidity left over from the wartime economy, it established a policy pattern. According to that pattern, governments, fearful of the political repercussions of a frontal assault on inflation, placed trust in the state bureaucracy's capacity to find increasingly sophisticated ways to keep monetary disequilibrium, which soon became endemic, within manageable bounds. The money supply, which had grown at an annual rate of 14 percent during the years of the leftist Popular Front (1936–38), grew by 30 percent annually under the provisional government and the first governments of the Fourth Republic. Confidence in stocks and bonds never recovered. Bond issues fell from 5.3 percent of GDP in 1938 to only 1.7 percent in 1947. Investment in stocks and bonds remained relatively feeble for the next three decades. Inflation negated the yields offered by interest-bearing assets and thus turned potential investors away, just as it freed businesses from the need to address their demand for capital to the financial market by making it easy to borrow from institutional lenders at interest rates that were typically negative in real terms.

The French could not have sustained this policy orientation for long in a world that was committing itself to eradicating nationalism in trade. Driving prices higher, inflation made French goods less competitive on foreign markets and foreign goods more competitive on the French market, which generated endemic external payments imbalances. Only the financial support of the United States enabled the French to stay their expansionary course without disassociating themselves from efforts to liberalize world trade. The United States came to the aid of the French with direct financial support between 1946 and 1952, easing the pressure created by payments imbalances. The United States also fostered the creation of binding international trade and monetary arrangements, such as the European Coal and Steel Community and the European Payments Union, which sustained the activist thrust of monetary and credit policy throughout the decade.[1] American policy, informed by the ambition of "containing" the influence of communism and the Soviet Union, had the effect not of combating "economic nationalism" or mercantilism, as hegemonic theorists in the field of international relations sometimes claim, but of rendering economic nationalism compatible with an increasingly open trade order.

Even the drift to the right by France's governments after 1948, which brought to power leaders who attached greater importance to stabilizing prices and combating payments imbalances, failed to bring about change in the economy's basic orientations. The fundamental structure of France's credit-based and inflation-prone political economy was repeatedly ratified, and breaches in it were repeatedly plugged, in large part because of the persistent fear of the effects of monetary rigor on

---

[1] Alan Milward, *The Reconstruction of Western Europe, 1945–1951* (Berkeley: University of California Press, 1984), p. 167.

political stability.[2] Elsewhere, I describe France as an "overdraft economy," in which industrial firms were allowed to become highly dependent on credit allocated by financial institutions for their investment capital, and in which growth in the supply of such credit was responsible for about 80 percent of growth in the money supply. Governments sought in activist credit policies the power to reconcile incompatible demands: satisfying broadly based expectations of rising personal income, funding programs that facilitated conversion in traditional sectors, funding industrial modernization, and containing both budget deficits and the danger that deficit spending might cause inflation to spiral out of control.

Two events stand out in this regard: the development of the Treasury circuit in the mid-1950s and the banking reforms of 1965–67. The development of the *circuit du Trésor* during the first decade of the Fourth Republic enabled successive French governments to adhere to an expansionary monetary course while containing the danger of runaway inflation. The keystone of this "Treasury circuit" was the legal requirement that state and para-state financial institutions deposit a part of their resources with the Treasury. Accounts managed by the post office could also be tapped by the Treasury, which in turn kept an account of its own with the post office.[3] The banking system was also partially integrated into this treasury circuit as a consequence of the 1948 requirement that banks retain a certain fraction of their reserves in treasury bonds.[4]

The *circuit* reached out to a large number of public or semipublic financial institutions, such as the Caisse des Dépôts et Consignations, the Caisses d'Épargne, the Crédit Agricole, the Crédit National, and

---

[2] Michael Loriaux, *France after Hegemony: International Change and Financial Reform* (Ithaca: Cornell University Press, 1992), chap. 2.

[3] In France as in many European countries, the post office manages checking accounts and low fixed-interest liquid savings accounts. During the fifties, post office accounts amounted to 18 percent of circulating currency. The Treasury keeps an account with the post office, if only because it facilitates payments of government fees and salaries and the collection of revenues. See François Eck, *Le trésor* (Paris: Presses Universitaires de France, 1982); Dov Zerah, *Le système financier français: Dix ans de mutations* (Paris: La Documentation Française, 1993), pp. 47–52, 200–206.

[4] This minimum was composed of a sum equal to at least 95 percent of the bank's holdings in treasury bonds in 1948, added to which was a sum equal to at least 20 percent of the subsequent variation (growth or decrease) in credits extended to the public. Jean-Pierre Patat and Michel Lutfalla, *Histoire monétaire de la France au XXᵉ siècle* (Paris: Économica, 1986), p. 122. The comparison with Spanish practice is illuminating.

the Crédit Foncier de France. These public or semipublic financial institutions do not depend directly on the ministries but rather function much like public service companies in the United States. Their relationship with the state is defined by a charter that sets out their obligations and privileges. Their management is often largely autonomous, and the capital that sustains their activity is sometimes of state origin and sometimes raised entirely or in part on the bond market. These institutions are all required to keep an account with the Treasury. They are often authorized to make medium-term and sometimes long-term loans within certain spheres of activity: agricultural loans, mortgages, export-development loans. The medium-term loans are accepted by the Banque de France for rediscount.[5] The Caisse des Dépôts et Consignations (CDC) is a peculiar institution in that its capital is legally state owned, composed of consignments and expropriations, but the Treasury does not have immediate access to it. It is as if the CDC were the custodian of a fortune to which its owner, like a legal minor, is barred access. It also manages the accounts of the public savings institution, the *caisses d'épargne*, which, with the post office, comprise France's principal low-interest liquid savings program, as well as the accounts of the various welfare programs and even the French turnpike system. The CDC is the principal source of credit to local governments, public housing authorities, and to a lesser degree, nationalized firms and other financial institutions. It generally does not lend directly to such borrowers, however, but rather buys bonds offered by the Crédit Foncier, which is the direct supplier of most mortgage loans in France. It also buys bonds issued by the Crédit National, which was for a long time the principal source of medium-term loans to industrial firms.

The crisscrossing of liabilities between the Treasury, the post office, the semipublic financial institutions, and numerous other bodies, allowed Treasury officials to draw on multiple accounts to finance public spending without itself issuing bonds or asking the Banque de France to print money. The Treasury used money deposited in post office accounts in much the same way that a bank uses its reserve assets to create more money, by inscribing transfers onto the post office

---

[5] *Arrêté du Conseil Général de la Banque de France*, May 11, 1944. The central bank "rediscounts" a loan when it advances payment on that loan to the lending bank, using the loan as collateral. The bank is still responsible for collecting payments on the loan, and must pay interest on the loan that it in turn received from the central bank.

accounts of households (the salaries of civil servants, for example) and firms (subsidies and grants). But because the money borrowed by the Treasury from one of these institutions to pay off the state's creditors ultimately found its way back to the banks, the post office, or one of the financial institutions that composed the Treasury circuit, a fraction of this money necessarily made its way back to the Treasury. Thus the Treasury had the unusual capacity to feed its accounts *with money of its own creation*. Within this circuit, theoretically, the credit multiplier is negligible.[6]

Properly handled, the Treasury circuit offered policymakers a tool that they could use to redistribute money while both avoiding the political liability of increasing state income through higher taxes and containing the dangers of inflationary financing.[7] The Treasury circuit supplied the state with the capital it needed to finance the state's industrial policy, both through the Fonds de Développement Économique et Social (FDES), which supplied the economy with direct subsidies, or through any number of semipublic financial institutions that were authorized to advance medium-term loans.

When public spending increased the deficit beyond the limits of prudence, as determined by Treasury officials, those officials might instruct the Caisse des Dépôts et Consignations to submit for rediscounting at the Banque de France some of the loans that it had itself previously discounted for the Crédit Foncier, and to deposit the sums it procured from this operation on its account with the Treasury. In this way, the Treasury procured the liquid funds it needed while preventing its account at the Banque de France from going deeper in the red and thus requiring the central bank to print new money to cover its debts. This made it possible for the Treasury to finance a fairly important budget deficit (6.3 percent of the GDP in 1955) without issuing new bonds and yet minimize the inflationary impact of creating the money that was used to cover the deficit. The transfer of Fr 1.12 billion from the Banque de France to the Treasury in 1955, using the intermediary of the Crédit Mobilier, not only helped to diminish the deficit but actually allowed the Treasury to reduce its debt to the Banque de France.

[6]   See Loriaux, *France after Hegemony*, pp. 65–72, 150–53.
[7]   See Edgar Faure, *Mémoires* (Paris: Plon, 1982) 1: 457; Patat and Lutfalla, *Histoire monétaire*, pp. 140–41.

The Treasury circuit was exploited extensively during the 1950s when the financial needs of the Treasury were great. During the four years that the United States provided France with Marshall Plan aid, the Treasury was able to decrease its dependence on the kind of inflationary financing that it had relied on immediately after the war. But when Marshall Plan aid came to an end in 1952, the Treasury was on its own, faced with budget deficits that hovered around 4 percent of the gross domestic product. It had to find the means to finance its economic policies yet eschew the inflationary excesses of the post-war years. In collusion with the semipublic financial institutions, the Treasury was able to supply a sizable fraction of all credit allocated to the French economy. The complex web of crisscrossing liabilities and institutional ties that made the Treasury circuit possible even allowed the Treasury to withdraw gradually from the job of financing industrial investment directly through the FDES, as more conservative governments assumed power and worked harder to contain deficit spending. The Treasury's contribution to the financing of industrial investment fell from 50 percent in 1950 to 35 percent in 1952 to 27 percent in 1956.[8] The state's retreat from direct financing, however, was counterbalanced by the rapid multiplication of medium-term loans rediscounted by the Banque de France, whose part in financing industrial investment increased from 3.3 percent in 1950 to 14.2 percent in 1956.[9]

War in Algeria, however, caused the house of cards to collapse. The budget deficit rose from Fr 630 billion in 1955 (3.7 percent of the GDP) to more than Fr 1000 billion in 1957 (5 percent). The growing disequilibrium in public finances contributed to an imbalance in foreign payments that necessitated an appeal to the International Monetary Fund in 1957.[10]

War in Algeria brought back to power General Charles de Gaulle, resistance leader, leader of the provisional government and prime minister of the first postwar government. The return of this strong, conservative leader, supported by the more presidential constitution of the Fifth Republic, seemed to augur the return of France to greater finan-

---

[8]    Jean-Pierre Rioux, *The Fourth Republic, 1944–1958* (Cambridge: Cambridge University Press, 1987), p. 336.
[9]    Ibid., pp. 332–33. The contribution of the stock exchange to investment financing increased from 4.4 percent in 1950 to 9.2 percent in 1956.
[10]    Patat and Lutfalla, *Histoire monétaire*, pp. 152–53.

cial orthodoxy. De Gaulle was seen as the new Poincaré, the Third Republic leader who stabilized the franc after World War I. But France's credit-based political economy survived de Gaulle's presidency unreformed and even reinforced. The economy's dependence on credit was in fact increased by the very measures that de Gaulle deployed to restore greater orthodoxy to French finance. France under the Fifth Republic became a paragon of fiscal restraint. Budgetary rigor was achieved, however, by transferring financial responsibility for a number of government programs to local governments and private enterprise. Local governments were made to pay more for the upkeep of roads and schools, while firms were made to contribute more to social security and health insurance. Fiscal rigor also caused state support to industry to dry up. The Treasury had allocated nearly seven billion francs worth of credit to the economy in 1963, but gave out less than four and a half billion francs in 1965. Industry was asked to contribute more while receiving less. Industrial firms turned to lending institutions (and to a lesser degree to the bond market) for financial support. The financial consequence of fiscal orthodoxy can be seen in the accounts of the CDC. The importance of government debt in the CDC's portfolio diminished not only in relative but in absolute value from Fr 2.8 billion in 1964 to Fr 2.3 billion in 1972. The volume of long-term credits accorded by the CDC, on the other hand, increased dramatically from 10.1 percent of loans in 1964 to 21.1 percent in 1971.[11]

The French government spent the next two decades undoing with the left hand what it had done with the right. It fought inflation by bringing government expenditures into balance with income, but it incited businesses to raise their prices and to increase their level of indebtedness to deal with the increase in charges. Persistent inflationary pressures incited the government to place administrative caps on bank lending through *encadrement du crédit*, or credit controls. Individual banks were told how much they could increase their lending activity from one year to the next. The state punished banks that exceeded their limit by hiking their reserve requirement. Raising a bank's reserve requirement forced the bank to withdraw a portion of its funds from interest-earning investments, and so diminish its revenues. *Encadrement* was effective in

---

[11]  Antoine Coutière, *Le système monétaire français* (Paris: Économica, 1982), p. 77. See Fernand Braudel and Ernest Labrousse, eds., *Histoire économique et sociale de la France* (Paris: Presses Universitaires de France, 1970–82), 4: 1081.

combating inflation, but it deprived the economy of needed credit in the wake of budget cuts.

The French found it difficult to find a middle ground between inflation and deflation. The bank reforms of 1965–67 were an attempt to find that middle ground. Since World War II, deposit banks had been amassing a voluminous store of private and more or less liquid savings that wartime banking regulations prohibited from being used to support medium- and long-term investment in industry. Apart from the liquid savings amassed in checking accounts, no exploitable source of investment capital seemed to exist. The capital market remained too narrow and the state too committed to fiscal rigor and the fight against inflation. The semipublic financial institutions, already heavy lenders, were ill-suited to meet the more diverse and complex financial needs of the modern industrial economy without thorough deregulation.[12] Hence the government sought to find a way to tap into liquid savings accounts to supply the economy with the financial support it now required more than ever. The reforms were designed to facilitate *la transformation* of liquid savings deposited in banks into pluriannual loans suitable for industrial investment. Banks in the 1960s lagged behind the state and the semipublic financial institutions in their support of industrial investment, in large part because bank regulations limited their right to participate in industrial financing.

Giving industry better access to the liquid assets amassed in the deposit banks required two types of reform. First, bank deregulation was needed to decrease the degree of bank specialization. In 1965, the government validated and reinforced the practice of making certain medium term bank loans eligible for rediscount by the Banque de France by increasing the maturity of such loans from five to seven years.[13] Decrees promulgated in January and December 1966 and

---

[12]   Jean-Pierre Patat, *Monnaie, institutions financières, et politique monétaire* (Paris: Économica, 1982), p. 211; J. M. Levesque, "Economic Planning: The Experience of the French Banking System" (Paris: International Banking Summer School, 1968), pp. 105–16; Peter Coffey, *The Social Economy of France* (New York: St Martin's Press, 1973), p. 93.

[13]   In order to counteract the expansionary impact that this reform would have on the growth of credit, the government tightened the conditions that medium-term loans had to fulfill in order to qualify for rediscount. Tighter conditions actually reduced the volume of medium-term loans being presented to the Banque de France for rediscount—at least for the time being. The new credit facility actually created conditions that facilitated the multiplication of such loans after 1968.

September 1967 put an end to the distinction between deposit banks and business banks, as defined by the legislation of 1944. Deposit banks were given the power to extend long-term loans to businesses, and business banks were authorized to manage deposit accounts.

Second, since the banks were effectively being invited to lend more, and since this involved the "transformation" of short-term assets into medium- and long-term credits, the banks were encouraged to increase their reserves.[14] In 1965 the government abolished the fiscal privileges attached to treasury bonds as well as to savings accounts in certain types of savings institutions. Though a modest reform, it placed the deposit banks on a relatively equal footing in their competition for household savings with savings institutions. Furthermore, in December 1965 the government created an attractive savings instrument called *épargne logement.* This home-savings plan doubled interest paid on savings accounts not drawn upon during a period of four years, then matched the amount accumulated in the account with a low interest mortgage. This new and innovative type of savings plan proved very attractive.

In September 1966 the government set up a financial network that allowed banks and semipublic financial institutions to discount mortgages with a number of institutions endowed with stable resources, such as retirement accounts and the Caisse des Dépôts et Consignations. This modest restructuring augmented the discount facilities available to the banks. In January 1967 banks were given permission to open branches without prior government authorization, and indeed the government encouraged the deposit banks to multiply their branches in order to increase their deposits and augment their reserves. The government also encouraged bank mergers. Simultaneously, however, the government continued to develop financial and fiscal incentives to lure savings away from liquid checking accounts and into more stable, longer-term savings accounts. As part of this effort the government prohibited, in July 1967, the payment of interest on checking accounts and suppressed regulations that limited interest rates offered on less liquid accounts.[15]

Greater bank involvement in the task of providing credit to business meant that the banks would need more ample and supportive refinanc-

---

[14]  Transformation defined in this manner had been going on since 1945, but it had been underwritten by the state and by the semipublic financial institutions. Transformation was now being redefined in a manner that left the banks and the central bank on their own.

[15]  Patat and Lutfalla, *Histoire monétaire*, p. 176.

ing arrangements. To meet this need, the government introduced reforms into the money market. The French actually had no "money market" in the American or British sense of "open market." They had, rather, a small exclusively interbank market for short-term assets and government bonds that helped banks and other financial institutions manage their reserves. Banks could sell assets on this market to augment their cash reserves. The central bank intervened in this market by opening up a "pawn shop" for short term assets, which it would buy at a price and interest rate of its own determination and resell to the bank on demand.[16] The government reformed this system by establishing a more authentic market for treasury bonds. The Caisse des Dépôts et Consignations and the Crédit Agricole were given permission to invest funds on this money market, thereby increasing the volume of very short-term funds available to the banks. Though it is true that only banks and financial institutions were admitted to this auction, the reform, by forcing banks to bid for assets to augment their bank reserves as required, allowed the government to introduce some market discipline into a system founded almost entirely on the allocation of credit through institutional intermediaries. The reform also allowed the government to diminish the financial system's dependence on rediscounting by the Banque de France.[17]

In sum, the Fifth Republic's reforms altered the Fourth Republic's Treasury circuit, which connected specialized financial institutions directly to the Treasury by linking deposit banks to the CDC, to other semipublic financial institutions, and to a lesser extent to the Banque de France. Fiscal rigor robbed the Treasury circuit of its centrality in the French financial system, while the Treasury itself ceased to be the principal source of capital resources for the French economy, though the Treasury—not the Banque de France—remained the place where monetary and financial policy was made. On the other hand, the bank reforms of 1965–67 increased the dependence of France's industry on its banking system.[18] French industrial firms remained as indebted as

---

[16] Loriaux, *France after Hegemony*, pp. 69–71. See also J. Aulagnier, "L'Open Market en France," *Annales Économiques* 2 (1971); Coutière, *Le système monétaire français*.

[17] The efficacy of the reform was reinforced in January 1967 by imposing reserve requirements that obliged banks and other financial institutions to keep an account with the Banque de France, the amount of which varied in proportion to the bank's checking and savings deposits.

[18] Patat and Lutfalla, *Histoire monétaire*, p. 163.

ever. The debt, moreover, was still owed to institutional lenders, not to anonymous holders of financial assets who express their confidence or lack of confidence in firms by buying and selling on a market.

Ironically, this credit-based political economy evolved in part in response to social, economic, and political problems of which credit dependence was itself the source. The bank reforms of 1965–67 sought to address the French economy's relative lack of investment capital, which in turn was the consequence of policies that had discouraged investment in financial assets since the Liberation. In like manner, the fear of successive governments to subject the French economy to a market-driven redistribution of capital resources was aggravated by the militant resistance of certain social categories such as small businessmen and farmers, whose prosperity, power, and economic expectations all had their source in policies that had eschewed the redistributive implications of monetary rigor. It is indicative of the logic of the French political economy that although the bank reforms of 1965–67 aimed to provide a noninflationary source of investment capital for business, they ultimately had the effect of facilitating inflationary policy. In May 1968, general strikes and civil disorder nearly brought down the Fifth Republic. Georges Pompidou, de Gaulle's successor, bought social peace with generous wage concessions, but he used inflationary monetary policy, facilitated by the 1969 devaluation of the franc, to ease the burden of the wage settlement on industry. The resolution of that crisis set the French political economy on a crash course with the 1973 oil crisis, and did so at full inflationary speed.

## Financial Interventionism in the 1970s

For France, the seventies brought two unwelcome changes in the international economic order. The first was the increase in the price of oil and other commodities. The second was the collapse of the Bretton Woods regime of fixed but adjustable exchange rates. The increased cost of oil exacerbated inflation, aggravated the trade imbalance, discouraged investment, and increased unemployment. Flexible exchange rates, though they helped Western industrialized nations confront the immediate challenge of the oil shock, quickly revealed themselves to be a source of new and unwelcome burdens on economic policy.

The French experienced difficulty with several aspects of exchange rate flexibility, the most troubling of which was the appearance of vicious circles of currency depreciation and inflation.[19] The demand for certain imported items, especially for oil and raw materials in the case of resource-poor European countries, is relatively inelastic. Demand for these items remains high even when currency depreciation causes the cost of the imported items to rise. Hence, the increased cost of satisfying local demand for the imported items, expressed in local currency, pushes domestic prices up. Domestic inflation, to complete the vicious circle, causes the currency to depreciate further. Consequently, the depreciation that is initiated by a trade deficit can have the effect of making a trade deficit worse rather than better.

Because of the risk of vicious circles, depreciation did not facilitate payments adjustment in the same way that devaluation did under fixed rates. Although devaluation also had inflationary effects because it raised import prices, the currency's new parity was fixed, and thus was not subject to further vicious circle depreciation, nor was it affected by efforts to suppress inflationary tendencies through policies of austerity. Under the system of floating rates, efforts to contain inflation place upward pressure on the currency and reduce the advantages of depreciation as a way to promote balance of payments adjustment through changes in relative prices. Failure to address imported inflationary pressures, inversely, has no immediate impact on the currency's parity under fixed rates, since the money's value is fixed by international agreement and defended through internationally coordinated interventions on the market. Nor can a government "fine tune" policy to defend a new, depreciated parity under floating rates. The currency market responds with great volatility to a number of stimuli that are not related to a country's external payments position: elections and electoral campaigns, strikes, and international political crises. Currency manipulation, therefore, loses much of its effectiveness as a policy tool. The French, moreover, knew this:

> because of the disorder in the international monetary system, it is no longer possible to control the amplitude of a devaluation as it was until the end of the sixties; the variation in a country's inflation rate, its balance of

---

[19]    For a discussion of vicious circles and bibliography, see Loriaux, *France after Hegemony*, pp. 24–31.

payments deficit, the depreciation of its currency all are excessively subject to speculative expectations. . . . Hence the "spiral" of inflation and depreciation is very difficult to avoid and to control.[20]

Vicious circles such as those described above were in evidence in both Great Britain and Italy during the 1970s. The French, having experienced two vicious circle "scares" in 1973 and 1976, intervened heavy-handedly to ward them off. French officials viewed vicious circles as a serious threat to the French economy and consequently reoriented their external monetary policy. They pegged the franc to the Deutsche mark, the strongest and most sought-after European currency.

The ambition to make the franc a strong currency was not entirely new; indeed, it had informed Gaullist policy through much of the 1960s. The recognition that currency manipulation no longer offered an easy way to balance foreign accounts was new, however, and prompted a sea change in the orientation of French exchange rate policy. The French devalued the franc no fewer than three times in the two decades between 1948 and 1969. In 1954, moreover, French officials used tariff policy to mimic the effects of a devaluation. Suspicion that parities were redefined in order to procure commercial advantage has been voiced on more than one occasion by foreign observers.[21] Change in the international monetary system, however, obliged France to confront the challenge of adjusting its foreign payments position without devaluing the currency, since defense of the currency had become a priority.

When Giscard-d'Estaing assumed the presidency in 1974, he gave voice explicitly to the ambition of making the franc a strong currency within the European joint float, on a par with the German mark. France's subsequent efforts to participate in the float in the face of adversity attest to the seriousness with which this new ambition was pursued. Although the oil crisis of October 1973 forced the franc out of the joint float, the

---

[20]   Commissariat Général du Plan, *Rapport du Comité Financement, Preparation du Huitième Plan* (Paris: La Documentation Française, 1981), pp. 25–26.

[21]   See for example, Robert Solomon, *The International Monetary System, 1945–1976* (New York: Harper and Row, 1977), pp. 25, 163; and Leland B. Yeager, *International Monetary Relations: Theory, History, and Policy* (New York: Harper and Row, 1966), p. 400; see also Jacques Rueff, *De l'aube au crépuscule* (Paris: Plon, 1977), p. 60, for his approach to the question of devaluation; and Mileta Obradovitch, *Les effets de la dévaluation française de 1958* (Paris: Éditions d'Organisation—Éditions Eyrolles, 1970) for an appreciation of the effects of the 1958 devaluation on the French economy.

French implemented a rigorous stabilization plan in June 1974, which allowed the franc to reintegrate the joint float in 1975 at the same parity at which it had left. But the French could not sustain the rigorous monetary policies that were needed to maintain the franc at its elected parity. As austerity became a political liability, reflationary policies were implemented and the franc became once again the weak currency in the joint float. Renewed speculation produced a crisis in the spring of 1976, and the franc was forced out of the joint float yet again. Raymond Barre was then named prime minister and was assigned the mission of implementing policies of rigor that would restore stability to the franc.

The tools that the French employed to stabilize the exchange rate of the franc were characteristically interventionist. Foremost among these was credit control (*encadrement du crédit*). Encadrement had been imposed on previous occasions in order to combat inflation, but only in 1972, as Bretton Woods was collapsing, did it become a permanent feature of France's monetary policy arsenal. Encadrement was relatively effective in slowing the growth of the money supply due to credit expansion (which, as stated above, accounted for about 80 percent of money supply growth in France). It offered two supplementary benefits, as well. First, it conferred upon the government the power to single out certain sectors such as housing and export industries for preferential treatment by exonerating them from encadrement. Banks looked eagerly to these exonerated sectors as a source of income and lent to them liberally, thus diverting the flow of capital to sectors that the government deemed important. Second, since the expansion of credit was, theoretically, contained by administrative injunction, the price of credit had no impact on the demand for credit. Low interest rates did not threaten the economy with runaway monetary expansion. Therefore, governments could support certain kinds of investment by making credit available to them at rates that were below market.

The interventionist response to global disorder was perfected in 1976 by Raymond Barre. The French, following the German lead, began to set yearly targets for money supply growth.[22] By using encadrement to meet

---

[22]   The adoption of such targets, however, does not mean that the French embraced monetarism. Raymond Barre himself refused the monetarist label. See Barre, "L'économie française quatre ans après," *Revue des Deux Mondes,* September 1980. Rather than the implementation of monetarist theory, the new policy translated the government's struggle to contain inflation, given the constraints of the currency market, through gradual reduction of the rate of mone-

these targets, the French achieved an unprecedented degree of coordination among the diverse components of both their monetary and industrial policies. In effect, the interdependence of components of money supply growth—credit expansion, deficit spending, and the balance in foreign transactions—allowed the government to coordinate domestic monetary policy, exchange rate policy, and, to a lesser extent, industrial policy.[23] This was done in the following manner. The government, after settling on a desirable target for monetary growth, forecast with as much precision as possible the contribution of deficit spending and foreign transactions to that target. The remainder determined the limit to be imposed on the growth of credit, which was communicated to the banks. In addition, however, the government had the power to encourage or discourage borrowing on the international financial market by either authorizing or prohibiting foreign borrowing by both public and private firms. Furthermore, by using its influence over the financial activities of public enterprises such as Electricité de France and the Société Nationale des Chemins de Fer, the government exercised some control over the supply of French assets to the international financial market, which increased its control over the final balance of foreign transactions.[24] In other words, the state's estimate of the evolution of foreign transactions was, in fact, part estimate and part target. Moreover, since foreign transactions have an impact on the exchange rate, the government, in making its "forecast" concerning foreign transactions, also determined an implicit target for the exchange rate of the franc. Completing the circle, targets for credit growth were not subordinated solely to monetary considerations but were determined, at least in part, by industrial policy goals.

This approach to monetary policy succeeded in several areas. France actually respected its money supply growth targets better than most

---

tary growth. The approach was more pragmatic than that advocated by monetarist theorists. See Loriaux, *France after Hegemony*, pp. 41–42.

[23]    Transactions on the open market did not affect money supply growth in France for the simple reason that there were none in any conventional sense of the term. See above and note 16 on the interbank money market.

[24]    It goes without saying that trade policy and industrial policy also were designed with an eye to the balance of payments, but they did not constitute a short-term conjunctural policy instrument. Foreign borrowing, on the other hand, supplied a policy instrument that could be used to achieve results over the short term. Before 1976, the government relied heavily on foreign borrowing, especially by state-owned companies, both to sustain the exchange rate of the franc and to bring in needed funds to promote investment and combat unemployment. See Loriaux, *France after Hegemony*, chap. 2.

other countries. After 1976, the franc became one of the more stable currencies. Finally, although both the budget deficit and foreign indebtedness grew, they were kept within moderate limits. Inversely, however, success in taming inflation continued to prove elusive.

The French system was admirable in its highly sophisticated use of state levers to control interdependent monetary quantities. Though the results were not entirely satisfactory, the Barre government did succeed in bolstering the foreign exchange value of the franc, which was its principal assignment. Why then, within the decade, did a decidedly more interventionist-minded Socialist government choose to liberalize financial structures and practices in a way that made such sophisticated use of interventionist tools inoperative?

## Reform

Talk of reform turned earnest in the late 1970s. Study commissions were established by the Commissariat du Plan to prepare the Eighth Plan, and proposals for reform were advanced. The Eighth Plan was to have gone into effect during the period 1981–85, but was shelved following the electoral defeat of the conservative coalition in 1981.[25]

Given the diversity of views expressed on these commissions, one is struck by the extent to which the experts agreed that financial structures and practices needed to be reformed. The experts were particularly critical of encadrement, on the one hand, and the labyrinthine structures of the French financial system, on the other. Though the committee believed that encadrement could not be abandoned as a tool of policy in the immediate future, it nevertheless "clearly affirm[ed] that the suppression of *encadrement du crédit* sometime in the future was necessary."[26] It also claimed that the French financial system was too highly compartmentalized. Numerous semipublic financial institutions specialized in supplying specific sectors of the economy with credit at rates that were only indirectly determined by market conditions. The experts wanted to replace the existing interventionist institutional framework

---

[25]  Commissariat Général du Plan, *Rapport du Comité Financement*; see also Commissariat Général du Plan, *Crédit, change, et inflation, Rapport du Groupe Monétaire Appliquée* (Paris: La Documentation Française, 1979).
[26]  Commissariat Général du Plan, *Rapport du Comité Financement*, pp. 5, 48.

with a single, unified financial market by suppressing the privileges of the semipublic financial institutions. They recommended that the privileges of certain borrowers, such as local governments, be progressively abolished as well, and that the government begin immediately to curtail its practice of subsidizing interest rates.[27]

The discussions that preceded the Eighth Plan are best understood when placed in the context of ongoing efforts to incite households and firms to lend and borrow on the financial market rather than at the bank window, where, ironically, the government exercised its power of control over the flow of credit. In 1979, the *Rapport Mayoux*, a report on the financial difficulties encountered by small businesses, had already argued in favor of the suppression of encadrement.[28] Other commissions and other voices formulated broader complaints concerning the complexity of the French financial system and the related weakness of the French financial market, and proposed that financial practices be liberalized over the long run.

The Socialist victory of March 1981 temporarily silenced all this talk of liberalization. The Socialists pursued an aggressive policy of "redistributive Keynesianism" that increased welfare spending and encouraged wage increases in order to stimulate demand, both to kick-start the economy in the wake of the second oil shock (occasioned by the Iranian revolution) and, over the long run, to revivify French industry.[29] Wages rose at a nominal annual rate of 18 percent in 1982. This policy orientation, however, could not be sustained in an open economy surrounded on all sides by recession. By stimulating demand, the government augmented demand for imported as well as domestic goods, while foreign demand for French goods could not rise in a way that would have offset the policy's impact on France's foreign payments position. Public expenditures rose 11.4 percent during 1981 and 1982, the budget deficit

[27] Patat, *Monnaie, institutions financières, et politique monétaire*, p. 59.

[28] P. Champions, "Le Rapport Mayoux, de quoi s'agit-il?" *Journal des Caisses d'Épargne*, June 1979; L'Association Française des Banques, "Notes de réflexion sur le Rapport Mayoux," *Banque*, no. 388 (October 1979); B. Marguerite, "Le Rapport Mayoux et le redéploiement du système financier," *Issues*, 2d and 3d quarters 1980.

[29] Hall, *Governing the Economy: The Politics of State Intervention in Britain and France* (New York: Oxford University Press, 1986), p. 194; see also Pierre-Alain Muet, "Economic Management and the International Environment, 1981–1983" in Howard Machin and Vincent Wright, eds., *Economic Policy and Policy-making under the Mitterrand Presidency, 1981–1984* (New York: St. Martin's Press, 1985), p. 73.

climbed from 0.4 to 3 percent of the GDP in the same year, and inflation, already aggravated by the 1979 oil crisis, remained high at 12.5
percent in 1981, 11 percent in 1982, and 9.3 percent in 1983 (significantly higher than in neighboring countries, where inflation was falling
rapidly). Payroll taxes, which support many of France's welfare programs, increased rapidly and contributed to a 10 percent decline in
investment in 1981. This inhibited French industry from responding to
the policy-induced rise in consumer demand. Consumers therefore
turned to foreign suppliers, aggravating the imbalance in foreign
trade.[30]

The French economy soon found itself so rapidly and profoundly
ensnared in crisis that the government's critics were shouting incompe-
tence. Mitterrand's first-year dash for growth was reminiscent of the
post-1968 period in its excess. One of its consequences was three devaluations of the franc between October 1981 and March 1983.[31]

The hope that devaluation would suffice to correct the trade imbalance was disappointed, encouraging critics in and out of government to
demand a radical change in policy. The second devaluation in June 1982
brought that change of course. In order to contain inflation, the devaluation was accompanied by wage and price freezes and a reduction in
government spending. Encadrement was tightened, while privileged
credit arrangements that benefited sectors such as steel, refining, or the
public power industry were reduced or suppressed.

The monetary crisis of 1982–83 sealed the fate of France's debt-bur-
dened political economy. The government had been hesitating between
two courses of action in monetary affairs. The first was to unlink the
franc from the mark by withdrawing from the European Monetary
System (EMS) and to allow the franc to depreciate to levels that would
balance the foreign account without jeopardizing the government's
overall economic and social policy goals. The second was to reject those
goals, at least temporarily, in order to defend the franc's participation in
the EMS. A number of high-level officials were favorable to the idea of

[30]    Peter Hall, *Governing the Economy*, p. 198; see also Janice McCormick, "Apprenticeship
for Governing: An Assessment of French Socialism in Power," in Machin and Wright,
*Economic Policy and Policy-making*, p. 51; and Jean-Paul Fitoussi "Comment," in ibid., p. 65.
[31]    Devalued, that is, within the framework of the European Monetary System. See Loriaux,
*France after Hegemony*, chap. 9; Henri-François Henner and Jean-Jacques Yvernault, "Les
dévaluations du franc depuis 1981," *Revue d'Économie Politique* 93, no. 5 (October 1983).

leaving the EMS. It is important to note that ideology was not much in evidence in determining where people stood on this issue. Pierre Bérégovoy, Michel Rocard, and Michel Jobert, on the ideological right end of the government, sided with Pierre Chevènement on the left end, and with Laurent Fabius, leaning that way, in extolling the merits of withdrawal. Outside of government they were supported by Jean-Jacques Servan-Schreiber, a political centrist and confirmed advocate of European integration. The move was resisted principally by Jacques Delors, minister of finance, on the right of the Socialist Party, and by Prime Minister Pierre Mauroy, a centrist. Mitterrand vacillated. A strong advocate of European integration, he resisted the idea of withdrawal when it first came up shortly after he took office, but he came very near to acquiescing at the time of the franc's second devaluation in June 1982. Only determined resistance on the part of some members of the government dissuaded him.[32]

The debate resurfaced when the franc was forced to devalue a third time. This time, however, former supporters of the idea of leaving the EMS crossed the aisle to join the advocates of prudence. Chief among these was the budget minister, Laurent Fabius, who had been a vocal advocate of the government's original expansionist and redistributive policy course. Fabius had requested a detailed summary of France's international financial position from the Treasury, which responded by informing him that central bank reserves, despite two large international loans in the fall of 1982, were desperately low. The Banque de France disposed of a mere thirty billion francs with which to ward off a possible free fall of the franc if it withdrew. To prevent such a free fall, the government might have to raise interest rates from the current 14 percent to 20 percent or more. Moreover, France's foreign debt was high. A depreciation of 20 percent would cause the debt to increase from Fr 330 billion to Fr 400 billion. Finally, it was less than clear that a depreciation of the franc would have a positive effect on the economy. It would have an immediate effect on import prices, but any positive effect on exports would be long in coming, if it came at all. Such considerations caused Fabius, Jacques Attali (a close presidential advisor), and a num-

[32]  Thierry Pfister, *La vie quotidienne à Matignon au temps de l'union de la gauche* (Paris: Hachette, 1985); Philippe Bauchard, *La guerre des deux roses: Du rêve à la réalité, 1981–1985* (Paris: Bernard Grasset, 1986); Julius Friend, *Seven Years in France: François Mitterrand and the Unintended Revolution, 1981–1988* (Boulder: Westview Press, 1989), p. 64.

ber of experts within the President's circle to rally the camp of caution.[33] Their "conversion" was followed by that of other key government figures who had previously been critical of the EMS. Though a more radically nationalist foreign monetary policy was still supported by Bérégovoy and Gaston Defferre (who, like Bérégovoy, was closer to the right wing of the party), Fabius's shift sufficed to lay to rest forever the idea of leaving the EMS.

After 1983, fiscal and monetary austerity became permanent features of socialist economic policy. In 1985, inflation fell to less than 6 percent, compared to an average of over ten percent under Raymond Barre (1976–81). Real wages, which grew by an average of 2 to 3 percent per annum under the Barre government, stagnated after 1983. Unemployment, on the other hand, exceeded 10 percent during the last year of the Socialist-dominated legislature, compared with 6 percent under the regime's conservative predecessors. Long and bitter strikes broke out; large demonstrations brought together artisans, small shopkeepers and the owners of small businesses; a dockers' strike paralyzed foreign trade; finally, student unrest awoke fears of a "May '68 in reverse," that is, a student revolt directed not against a conservative but against a Socialist government.[34]

Liberal reforms in finance accompanied the turn toward economic rigor. The Socialists had come to power with the intention of restoring the state to a more firmly interventionist posture. Beginning in 1983, however, the government reversed course in dramatic fashion.

Prior to the 1983 about-face, Socialist policy had reinforced the French political economy's dependence on institutionally supplied credit. The state signed three-to-five-year "planning contracts" with the newly nationalized firms. Firms were assured the funds they needed if they honored the contract. In 1983, during a period of growing austerity, the nationalized industries still received Fr 20 billion, of which Fr 12.6 billion came directly from the budget. The banks were instructed to lend Fr 6 billion to the nationalized industries, purchase Fr 7 billion in state debt, and maintain their industrial lending rates at 14 percent. The central bank's rediscounting facilities were revived and expanded. In return, the nationalized industries were required to

---

[33]   Friend, *Seven Years in France*, p. 66.
[34]   *L'année politique, économique, et sociale en France, 1983* (Paris: Éditions du Moniteur, 1984), p. 409; see also Hall, *Governing the Economy*, p. 201.

invest Fr 31 billion. This represented about half of all industrial investment in France and significantly surpassed what the firms themselves had planned.[35]

The state, the banks, and the semipublic financial institutions were at the limit of their capacity to provide the French economy with capital, while inflationary financing had contributed to the most serious run on the franc since 1968. The government had to appeal to private capital. To make the French economy more attractive to capital, the government proposed an initial raft of liberalizing financial reforms and innovations.[36] New savings instruments were introduced, such as the *titres participatifs* (certificates of participation), a new hybrid debenture stock that allowed private capital to participate in public sector enterprises, and the *certificats d'investissement* (investment certificates), nonpriority non-voting capital shares. A *second marché* (secondary market) for unlisted securities was created to facilitate access to the financial market by small- and medium-sized firms.[37] "Rules were simplified for new flotations, new financial instruments authorised, the 'monthly settlement' market reformed, securities 'dematerialized'—no more bond and share certificates by the end of 1984, only computerized records—and financial market authorities' powers strengthened."[38] Private banking, banished by the nationalizations of 1981, was allowed to make a discrete reappearance.[39]

Financial liberalization took a "quantum leap forward" after July 1984, when Laurent Fabius was asked to form a new, more pragmatic government. The new government included Pierre Bérégovoy as finance minister, lately a strong advocate of withdrawing from the EMS but now about to become the first minister of finance to visit the Paris Stock Exchange since 1962.[40] Negotiable bank certificates of deposit were introduced, which encouraged banks to raise capital

---

[35]  Hall, *Governing the Economy*, p. 205.

[36]  *L'année politique, 1983*, p. 386.

[37]  François de Witt, "Nouvelle Vague à la bourse: Voici les entreprises qui vont pouvoir profiter de l'ouverture du 'second marché,' " *L'Expansion*, no. 209 (February 17, 1983); *L'année politique, 1983*, p. 362. Zerah, *Le système financier français*, p. 253.

[38]  Philip G. Cerny, "From Dirigisme to Deregulation? The Case of Financial Markets" (paper presented to the International Conference on Thirty Years of the Fifth Republic, Paris, June 1988), p. 20.

[39]  Paul Fabra, "Banking Policy under the Socialists," in Machin and Wright, *Economic Policy and Policy-making*, p. 179.

[40]  Cerny, "From Dirigisme to Deregulation?" pp. 11, 24–27.

beyond their deposit base and to lessen their dependence on central bank discounting and quasi-discounting through the interbank market.[41] Along with the new certificates of deposit, new public short-term instruments were introduced, demand for which rose rapidly from Fr 31 billion in December 1985 to Fr 255 billion a year later. New instruments for interest rate and currency hedging were copied on models supplied by the international markets. The Paris financial futures market, the Marché à Terme des Instruments Financiers (Matif), opened in 1986 to the amusement of journalists, who exclaimed, "Under a Socialist government . . . Paris sees the opening of a futures market: the last word in capitalism."[42] Other reforms liberalized and strengthened the securities market by reducing commissions, by rendering commissions on bond issues freely negotiable, and by reinforcing the powers of the main regulatory body, the Commission des Opérations de la Bourse. As the financial market was modernized, foreign companies like Citicorp wrought further change in the financial landscape by introducing the French to venture capital.[43]

In a reform that attacked the very structural foundations of France's credit-dependent political economy, Pierre Bérégovoy announced on November 5, 1985, that large enterprises would be given access to the money market, which thus lost its interbank exclusiveness.[44] With this reform an enterprise could issue up to ten million francs worth of short-term (from ten days to six months) paper on the money market. In theory this encouraged enterprises to lend and to borrow on the market rather than at the bank window. The finance minister also announced that the market for negotiable treasury bonds would be opened progressively to nonbanks, thus allowing households and industrial firms as well as banks to bid for bonds (in ten-million-franc ten-day coupons).[45]

---

[41]  *L'année politique, économique, et sociale en France, 1984* (Paris: Éditions du Moniteur, 1985), p. 407. Zerah, *Le système financier français*, pp. 97–124.
[42]  "When Pierre Bérégovoy gets his inspiration from Chicago," *Journal des Finances*, February 22–28, 1986, quoted in Cerny, "From Dirigisme to Deregulation?" p. 25.
[43]  Chantal Bialobos, "La finance française découvre le capital-risque," *L'Expansion*, no. 236 (April 19, 1984).
[44]  Philippe Jaffre, "L'unification du marché des capitaux," *Banque*, no. 460 (April 1986). Jean-Charles Naouri, "La réforme du financement de l'économie," *Banque*, no. 459 (March, 1986). Zerah, *Le système financier français*, pp. 73–84.
[45]  *L'année politique, économique, et sociale en France, 1985* (Paris: Éditions du Moniteur, 1986), p. 460.

By decompartmentalizing the money market and rendering it accessible to all, the reforms of 1985 were a step forward in the creation of a more unified financial market, a market capable of handling the supply and demand of very short-term to long-term capital. To feed this new market, the government created new savings instruments. New specialized institutions were created to regulate and facilitate operations.

As structures were reformed, new policy instruments were created and old ones abandoned. In 1985, steps were taken to phase out encadrement du crédit (a process that was completed in 1987 under the conservative successors of the Socialists), and the principal locus of monetary control was shifted from the banks to the new reformed open market.[46] This made it possible to control interest rates and monetary growth through central bank intervention. Monetary control was to be based "on a better control of credit by the banks, which [were] incited to issue bonds in order to avoid monetary creation, which in turn should allow monetary regulation through interest rates beginning in 1986."[47] Finally, exchange controls, reintroduced in 1982, were all but abolished.[48]

While the government liberalized financial structures and processes, it also reduced direct credit allocations by the state. Three-quarters of all loans to business in 1979 came from the state, the semipublic financial institutions, or nationalized banks and their subsidiaries. Forty-three percent of all loans were subsidized by the state, either directly or through the medium of privileged refinancing arrangements enjoyed by such institutions as the Crédit Agricole or the Banque Française du Commerce Extérieur. As interest rates fell, however, the government began to "despecialize" its financial operations. It replaced the institutionally specialized loan subsidy programs managed by the Crédit National, the Crédit d'Équipement des Petites et Moyennes Entreprises, the Crédit Coopératif, and the Sociétés de Développement Régional with a single *prêt spécial à l'investissement*

[46]    Jean Cheval, "Les innovations dans la conduite monétaire en France: Perspectives monétaires 1986," *Chroniques d'Actualité de la SEDEIS* 34, no. 4 (April 1986).

[47]    *L'année politique, économique, et sociale en France, 1986* (Paris: Éditions du Moniteur, 1987), p. 392.

[48]    "Assouplissement du contrôle des changes," *Actualités BFCE*, no. 189 (February 1984); "France: De nouveaux assouplissements au contrôle des changes," *Actualités BFCE*, no. 209 (February 1986); "France: Importante libéralisation du contrôle des changes," *Actualités BFCE*, no. 211 (April 1986). Zerah, *Le système financier français*, pp. 154–68.

(PSI, or special investment loan). In 1986 the PSI was itself abandoned. Subsidized loans henceforward were reserved primarily to small and medium-sized businesses and required no "contractual engagement" on the part of the borrower.[49] In 1985 the Economic and Social Development Fund (FDES) became the victim of willful governmental neglect for the second time since World War II. As stated above, the FDES was one of the principal suppliers of industrial credit during the 1950s. Its role was reduced in the 1960s as Gaullist governments strove to balance the budget, but it was resurrected to help French industry confront the post–OPEC and post–Bretton Woods international political economy of the 1970s. Now it fell victim to socialist liberalization. The FDES, having supplied 9 percent of industrial capital investment in 1981, contributed only 0.29 percent in 1992. Whereas over 20 percent of industrial investment was supported by state funds in one form or another in 1984, that figure fell to 6 percent in 1987 and to 5 percent in 1990. The evolution of the French political economy becomes even more striking if the 5 percent of state-supported industrial investment of 1990 is compared with the 33 percent of 1960 and the 25 percent of 1970.[50]

By 1985 the financial structures of the French political economy were looking distinctly different not only from what the Socialists had envisioned in 1980, but from what they had looked like for the past forty years. Although industry was still highly indebted and dependent on institutional support, it was being nudged away from reliance on specialized programs managed by the banks as well as on more or less specialized semipublic financial institutions, each with its own peculiar credit program. Industry now had to deal directly with a revitalized financial market and a more homogeneous, market-driven banking system that supplied very little in the way of interest rate relief. The banking system in turn, rather than serving as a simple conduit between industry and state institutions like the Banque de France or the semipublic financial institutions, was encouraged to assume the role of intermediary between industry and a reinvigorated financial market, to which they were henceforth considered to be answerable.

[49]  *L'année politique, 1985,* p. 370. Zerah, *Le système financier français*, p. 243.
[50]  See Zerah, *Le système financier français*, pp. 237–42; Cerny, "From Dirigisme to Deregulation?" p. 31.

### International Constraint and Financial Liberalization

International constraint explains reform in France. This does not mean that reform did not have its champions in French policy circles. Reform, however, had had its champions for the past thirty years. Yet no thorough reform of France's credit-based political economy was ever undertaken, even when its advocates, like Jacques Rueff, had the government's ear. In the mid-1980s, however, the issue of reform was pressed hard by the French political economy's nonadaptation to an international monetary environment that had become hostile to inflation in the trade-dependent economies of Europe. The state, however extensive its control over the allocation of credit, simply lacked the capacity to regulate and to control monetary growth in a sustained fashion. Although monetary authorities, prior to reform, skillfully applied their power to control credit allocation and promote and direct investment through subsidized loans and other specialized programs, that power only reinforced the structural weaknesses of France's credit-based economy by validating industry's dependence on institutionally supplied credit.[51] Industrial indebtedness, in turn, became such that industrial solvency depended on inflationary financing.[52]

How great was industry's dependence on institutionally supplied credit? The rate of self-financing (the contribution of business savings to productive investment), fell from a typical figure of 70 percent in the 1970s to only 51 percent in 1981 and to 40.3 percent during the first quarter of 1982. Corresponding figures for Great Britain, the United States, and Germany were 108 percent, 88 percent, and 80 percent respectively.[53] Inversely, industry's need for external funding grew by 17 percent in 1981. The French National Institute of Statistics and Economic Studies calculated that industrial borrowing amounted to nearly 6 percent of gross domestic product in 1982, up from 4.5 percent of the GDP a year earlier.[54] The report of the study commission on

---

[51] Antoine Cachin, "La politique française de déconnexion des taux d'intérêt," *Revue d'Économie Politique* 93, no. 5 (October 1983).

[52] Thierry Chauveau, "L'inflation et les entreprises," *Revue Économique* 36, no. 5 (September 1983).

[53] "Banking on Recovery: A Survey of International Banking," *The Economist*, March 26, 1983.

[54] Ministère du plan et de l'aménagement du territoire, *Rapports de missions au Ministère d'État, Ministre du Plan et de l'Aménagement du Territoire: Le financement des entreprises*

industrial finance for the Socialists' Ninth Plan revealed that "if one eliminates public investment, the growth of which contributed positively . . . up until 1976, it is necessary to speak of a veritable collapse of private sector capital expenditures, which has accelerated the process of deindustrialization in the French economy."[55] Industrial investment diminished in volume by 12 percent in 1981 and by 7 percent in 1982, after having responded weakly but favorably to monetary stimulus in 1979 and 1980 (2 percent and 4 percent respectively).[56]

The redistributive Keynesianism of the early 1980s increased industrial dependence on institutionally allocated credit.[57] Growth in credit allocation grew by 18.8 percent between June 1981 and June 1982. Because credit growth was the principal factor in the growth of the money supply, it comes as no surprise that high rates of growth in credit contributed to rapid monetary growth (12.3 percent over the same period).[58]

It was the need to peg the franc to the mark while assuring the supply of industrial firms with capital, if only to deal with cash flow problems, that led the French economy once again to borrow heavily on the international financial market. France became one of the industrial world's principal foreign borrowers. According to the Organization for Economic Cooperation and Development (OECD), France borrowed $14.5 billion on international markets in 1982. Other observers placed the amount borrowed on foreign markets closer to $23 billion (compared with the United States' $26.5 billion).[59] In 1983, according to the OECD, France, at $13.3 billion, was the world's second largest international borrower—behind the United States ($14.9 billion), but ahead of Japan ($11.6 billion) and Canada ($8.5 billion). Although austerity had begun

---

(Paris: La Documentation Française, 1983), p. 17. The degradation of industry's financial health was caused in part by the increase in the share of value-added, that is, the difference between the income from selling finished goods and the cost of the raw materials needed to manufacture those goods, going to wages and taxes (wages from 6.8 to 7.5 percent and taxes from 2.7 percent to 4.3 percent), and the corresponding decrease in the share going to profits (from 17 to 9.6 percent). Hall, *Governing the Economy*, p. 197.

[55] *Rapport de missions*, p. 15.

[56] Ibid.; see also Michel Fried, "L'investissement industriel et son financement," *Bulletin du Crédit National* 10, no. 37 (4th quarter 1982).

[57] Fabra, "Banking Policy," p. 182.

[58] Alain Redslob, "Un système bancaire socialisé," in Michel Massenet, ed., *La France Socialiste* (Paris: Hachette, 1983), p. 151. On the contribution of credit to money supply growth, see Loriaux, *France after Hegemony*, pp. 66–68.

[59] *L'année politique, 1983*, p. 380.

to reduce the demand for capital, France nevertheless borrowed nearly $13 billion on foreign markets in 1984, bringing total foreign indebtedness close to $70 billion (not counting debts incurred by large public enterprises such as the national electric power company and the national railroad company).[60] Total foreign debt amounted to 9 percent of the GDP in 1984 and imposed an annual servicing burden estimated at $10 billion—which grew to $11.5 billion in 1985 and $21 billion in 1988.[61]

France's industry was caught in a vise of decreasing profitability and increasing indebtedness: "the growth of indebtedness and the reduction, even the disappearance of profit margins is putting a large number of French firms in danger."[62] A report commissioned by the French Senate in 1984 maintained that the nationalization of the banking sector, which was supposed to facilitate the control of monetary growth while increasing the state's power over the allocation of resources to industry, had failed after two years to make good on its promise. Encadrement du crédit (a "profoundly conservative" policy tool that encouraged "lazy solutions" on the part of banks, according to a report submitted in preparation of the Socialist Ninth Plan) had to be tightened rather than loosened, exceptional fiscal levies had to be multiplied, interest rate policy had to be made more deflationary, and the banks had to be forced to make obligatory loans to industry even while being insufficiently capitalized by the state, their principal stock-holder.[63]

Bank profitability dropped dramatically in 1982 and by 1983 barely reached 1981 figures. Banks, though state owned, began to seek com-

---

[60] Ibid., p. 494.

[61] *L'année politique, 1984*, p. 512. Note that borrowing on international markets to finance public sector deficits harbors real short- to medium-term monetary policy advantages. It not only preserves the possibility of pursuing buoyant policies at home over the medium term, but it dopes the exchange rate and thus helps stabilize prices and strengthen the currency. The sale of treasury bills, like the sale of real goods, brings in foreign currency that has to be exchanged for national currency. This stimulates demand for the national currency on the market and places upward pressure on the exchange rate. Only after a period of several years is buoyancy counteracted as debt servicing starts to take large volumes of money back out of the national economy. The French were among the first to figure this out. From the mid to late 1970s, they encouraged government-controlled firms to borrow on foreign financial markets not only to acquire capital not readily available at home, but to bolster the value of the franc on the exchange and ward off vicious circles of currency depreciation and inflation. See Loriaux, *France after Hegemony*, pp. 24–38.

[62] Michel Massenet, Préface, in Massenet, *La France Socialiste*, p. 31; see also Bertrand Abtey, "Les entreprises en péril," in ibid., pp. 254 ff.

[63] *Rapport de missions*, p. 92.

pensation abroad. In 1980 (before nationalization), foreign activity accounted for 22 percent of bank profits; in 1982 it accounted for 95 percent of bank profits.[64] By September 1984 the banking system joined industry as one of the government's major preoccupations. The new minister of finance, Pierre Bérégovoy, met with bank directors to develop policies that would restore profitability and dynamism to the banks. These included reductions in employment, the introduction of new technologies, and the coordination of activities designed to achieve economies of scale. Though modest, the minister's recommendations prefigured the more thoroughgoing liberalization of the financial system that was to follow.[65]

Floating rates compelled the French to slow the growth of the money supply. Industrial indebtedness, however, compelled them to find ways to assure the flow of capital to French firms. But because of the narrowness of the financial market in France—a consequence of its activist credit policy—capital could only be supplied by "printing" new money or by borrowing abroad. It was a case of damned if you do, damned if you don't. The French grasped the bull by both horns and reformed the financial system from top to bottom.

Reform began with deregulation of the financial system. Financial deregulation was intended to accomplish several tasks. First, by abolishing privileged credit lines, it was meant to discourage the allocation of resources to unproductive uses. As mentioned above, many French firms in the late 1970s and early 1980s were borrowing to address cash-flow problems rather than to finance investment, and so were investing less even as they were increasing their level of indebtedness. Second, deregulation was intended in the long run to free a number of well-endowed financial institutions, like the Crédit Agricole, from their narrowly defined sectoral obligations, and make their resources available to a broader fraction of the French economy. Finally, by abolishing privileged lending programs (which depended ultimately on inflationary rediscounting by the Banque de France), it was hoped that deregulation would cause interest rates charged to nonprivileged borrowers to fall. Among these non-privileged borrowers were many small but nevertheless dynamic firms.[66]

---

[64]    *L'année politique, 1984*, p. 447; Alain Chetaille, "L'activité internationale des banques françaises," *Issues* (4th quarter 1984).

[65]    *L'année politique, 1984*, pp. 471–72.

[66]    Fabra, "Banking Policy."

Deregulation ran deeper than this, however, reaching to the heart of France's credit-based political economy. Deregulation encouraged the banks to consolidate their financial base by increasing their capitalization through more active appeal to the financial market (hence the certificates of deposit). It also encouraged banks to regulate their lending activity by relying more heavily on their reserves rather than on central bank refinancing of privileged credits. Though large industrial firms would initially suffer from what would inevitably become more restricted access to bank credit, the cost was compensated by greater direct access to the financial market through the creation of the capital bill (*billet de trésorerie*)[67] and by the greater competition that deregulation would eventually bring to the banking industry. This move was intended to encourage greater bank efficiency, greater market sensitivity, and—it was theorized—lower borrowing costs.[68] Since there was little hope that French industry would become an asset-based rather than a credit-dependent sector, it was proposed that the French political economy evolve toward the German model. According to this model, an asset-based banking sector, composed of "universal" rather than specialized banks, provides for the financial needs of a dependent industrial sector.[69] The banks intervene actively in industrial affairs but regulate their own activity by adjusting to movement in the financial market.[70]

## France after Liberalization

Since 1983, the French have not deviated from their commitment to peg the franc to the mark, despite a rate of unemployment that has at times surpassed 12 percent, two major crises of the European Monetary System, and fears of worldwide deflation. Every French government since 1983, conservative or Socialist, has reaffirmed its commitment to

---

[67] Loriaux, *France after Hegemony*, p. 225.

[68] Étienne Bertier, "Pauvres banquiers," *L'Expansion*, no. 288 (July 3, 1986); Olivier Pastre, "La modernisation des banques françaises: Incertitudes et enjeux," *Banque* no. 461 (May 1986).

[69] Bernard Prudhon, "Intermédiation financière française et intermédiation financière ouest-allemande: Perspectives pour une réforme," *Revue d'Économie Industrielle* 30, no. 4 (1984).

[70] See Commissariat Général du Plan and Ministre du Plan et de l'Aménagement du Territoire, *Rapport de la Commission* (Paris: La Documentation Française, 1984), p. 9.

a strong franc. The results have been nothing short of dramatic. Inflation after 1985 fell below the EC average, and after 1991 even fell below that of Germany. The balance of payments, though it experienced deficits during the rapid growth years 1987–90, was in the black in 1985–86 and again in 1992, despite devaluations of the pound, the lira, and the peseta. Foreign sales of industrial goods, a sector in which France has traditionally been vulnerable, were particularly strong.

Nevertheless, the franc is still not immune to crisis. Uncertainty regarding the outcome of the referendum on Maastricht, market distrust in a British currency that had reintegrated the European Monetary System at an overvalued parity, combined with the pressure that high interest rates in Germany (subsequent to unification) were placing on EMS parities, provoked a major currency crisis in September 1992, forcing both the lira and the pound to drop out. As for the franc, despite the health of the economy's external accounts, it came under heavy pressure and had to be defended by massive purchases by the Banque de France and the Bundesbank. The Bundesbank spent more than $40 billion supporting French currency. The crisis, coming at the time of the referendum, fed a lively debate regarding monetary policy orientation. The strong franc came under heavy criticism by political figures on both the right (notably Philippe Séguin) and the left (Pierre Chevènement).

International constraints, however, afford the French little in the way of credible alternatives to the strong franc policy. Jacques Chirac, after having criticized the hard currency policy both in the mid-1970s and the early 1990s, promptly ratified it upon becoming president in 1995. Despite the currency market's new-found confidence in the franc, it is still the Deutsche-mark that is sought out by speculators in times of currency turmoil and is bid up relative to other currencies, including the franc. But for reasons explored in previous sections, the franc cannot afford to withdraw from the EMS simply because speculators prefer the German currency. Floating is not a viable option. Nor do the strong franc's critics endorse floating, but rather advocate devaluing the franc relative to the mark.

Devaluation is not without its own problems, however. First, it requires German approval, which might well come at the cost of Bundesbank solidarity during times of crisis. Second, it would compromise ten years of efforts to alter the franc's reputation as a weak currency as well as French monetary habits and expectations. It is no small achievement that, as crisis again rocked the European Monetary System in September 1993, speculators were greeted with a joint communiqué from the Banque de France and the Bundesbank expressing their determination to defend EMS parities. The crisis almost brought down the EMS. The band of fluctuation within which EMS currencies were allowed to float was expanded to a meaningless 15 percent. But within this band, the franc has fallen very little. Only the Dutch guilder can boast as good a record in keeping up with the Deutsche mark as the French franc.

Just as France has persisted in its strong franc orientation, it has also persisted in its efforts to give that orientation strong institutional foundation through liberalizing reforms, designed not only to cure French economic agents of their dependence on state-controlled credit allocation but to attract domestic and foreign capital into investing in French assets. Since 1987 regional stock exchanges have been consolidated with the Paris stock exchange. French brokers now operate on a nationally unified financial market. Moreover, the stock exchange was purged of the last remnants of its traditional corporatism and now looks very much like its Anglo-Saxon counterparts. In 1988, the traditional *agents de change*—transaction agents who had been appointed by the minister of finance and were given the monopoly over negotiations between buyers and sellers of stock—were dismissed and their function awarded to private brokerage firms. Transactions are now policed by the Commission des Opérations de Bourse (COB). Though it was created in 1967, the COB's powers were greatly enlarged in the period 1987–89, when the Bourse underwent liberalization, and it now closely resembles its counterpart, the American Stock Exchange Commission.[71]

The last remnants of currency controls were abolished in 1989. French residents were authorized henceforth to hold accounts in foreign currencies in French banks as well as accounts in francs in foreign banks. French firms could now manage multicurrency cash flows and reserves within a single account. This reform intervened merely six years after the most rigorous imposition of currency controls since World War II, when French tourists were prohibited from using their credit card abroad and from spending more than two thousand francs a year on foreign vacations. The lifting of currency controls was accom-

---

[71] See Zerah, *Le système financier français*, pp. 97–104.

panied by the relaxation of regulations governing direct investment by foreign firms in France and by French firms abroad. Legislation passed in 1990 and 1992 accorded firms of the European Union the right to make direct investments in French firms without restrictions, and subjected direct investments by non-EU firms to governmental approval only if the investment exceeded Fr 50 million.[72]

The most notable reform since 1987, however, affected the statutes of the Banque de France. As of January 1, 1994, interest rate policy is no longer determined by the ministry of finance but by a nine-person Monetary Policy Council. Presiding over the council is the governor of the Banque de France, who, like the other members of the council and like their American counterparts, is appointed by the government but cannot be removed by it. The Banque de France, though still a state bank, is now for all intents and purposes autonomous in its decision-making power.[73]

As one can infer from the figures of Table 5.1, one can no longer characterize the French political economy as an "overdraft economy." The figures reflect the declining importance of financial intermediaries and the growing importance of the financial market. As the first item indicates, asset holders have moved away dramatically from liquid savings accounts in savings institutions. They now display a distinct preference for holding interest-bearing stocks and bonds. Item 2 accounts for some of this movement by documenting the growing popularity of investment clubs and firms. Item 3 shows that a similar movement has occurred on the demand side. Borrowers are turning away from institutional lenders and toward the bond market. Banks, as item 4 indicates, are themselves turning to the bond market to raise the capital required for them to play a more active role as intermediaries, not between industrial firms and the Banque de France, the treasury, or the treasury circuit, but between industrial firms and the financial market itself. Items 5 to 8 trace the phenomenal growth of the Paris market, both in absolute terms and in comparison with other European markets.

One of the objectives of liberalizing reform was to incite banks to play a more active mediating role, following the German model, between industry and financial markets. The late 1980s witnessed a number of spectacular initiatives by banks to acquire voting stock in industrial

[72] Ibid., pp. 259–66.
[73] To appreciate the import of this reform, see John Goodman, *Monetary Sovereignty: The Politics of Central Banking in Western Europe* (Ithaca: Cornell University Press, 1992).

*Table 5.1.* From overdraft to asset-based economy

|  | 1982 | 1988 | 1991 | 1992 |
|---|---|---|---|---|
| 1. Percent of liquid and nonliquid assets (all agents): |  |  |  |  |
|    a. Liquid assets | 61.8[a] | 25.3 | — | — |
|    b. Interest-bearing assets | 38.2[a] | 74.7 | — | — |
| 2. Investments in investment firms and clubs (billion francs) | — | 1092[b] |  | 2405 |
| 3. Percentage of credits accorded by financial institutions | 70[a] | 62 | 47 | — |
| 4. Sales of bank bonds (billion francs) | 59[a] | 181 | 149 | 138 |
| 5. Sales of new stock on Paris Exchange (billion francs) | 3.5 | 32 | 46 | 47 |
| 6. Value (billion francs) of titles listed on |  |  |  |  |
|    a. Paris Stock Exchange | 211 | 1484 | 1803 | — |
|       as percent of GDP | 5 | 26 | 29 | — |
|    b. Frankfurt Exchange | 442 | 1490 | 1873 | — |
|       as percent of GDP | 10 | 20 | 24 | — |
|    c. London Exchange | 1394 | 3297 | 5059 | — |
|       as percent of GDP | 44 | 89 | 97 | — |
| 7. Evolution of (index: 1981=100) |  |  |  |  |
|    a. Paris Stock Exchange | 97 | — | 489 | 514 |
|    b. Düsseldorf Exchange | 113 | — | 287 | 281 |
|    c. London Exchange | 113 | — | 363 | 419 |
| 8. Volume of shares traded on Paris Futures Market (million francs) | — | 16.7 | 26 | 55 |

*Source:* Dov Zerah, *Le système financier français* (Paris: La Documentation Française, 1992), *passim.*
[a]   1980 figure.
[b]   1987 figure.

firms. The same years saw a corresponding trend toward mergers and alliances between banks, insurance companies, financial holding companies, and semipublic financial institutions, the purpose of which was to augment the capital that banks and financial institutions could draw on to finance their activities. No less spectacular, however, were some of the blunders that this movement engendered. Following liberalization and bank deregulation, the Crédit Lyonnais, one of France's largest deposit banks, immersed itself in a kind of cowboy capitalism (which, symbolically, included the acquisition of Metro-Goldwyn-Mayer) not unlike that of American savings and loan banks during the same period. The bank sought to become the largest bank in Europe by buying up foreign banks. It invested heavily in the Parisian real estate bubble and bought equity in industrial firms in accordance with the German model. Many of the bank's loans and investments failed during the post–Gulf

War recession, generating losses totaling more than $4 billion by the end of 1993. The bank's losses were such that the state had to devise a bailout plan that engaged more than $14 billion in public money.[74] The crisis of the Crédit Lyonnais is the most serious banking crisis that the French have confronted in modern times. But it is not unrepresentative of what went on in the world of French banking in the 1980s. The Banque Nationale de Paris, Paribas, and the insurance company Groupe d'Assurances National, all state-owned, together suffered losses of more than $4 billion in bad loans and investments.

Though the French have pushed ahead with liberalizing reforms, the state has not entirely relinquished its interventionist role. Indeed, through nationalization, the state became the principal stockholder of most of France's major industrial firms (though many of those firms were returned to the private sector under conservative governments during the periods 1986–88 and 1993 to the present). In general, the state was a good stockholder, injecting more than Fr 100 billion into nationalized industries between 1982 and 1989.[75] Nor did the state limit its aid to industry. The principal insurance firms were opened up to state participation through mergers and collaborative associations with the major nationalized banks, and the state injected billions of francs into the tills of the principal nationalized financial firms, all in an effort to shore up the financial foundations of the French economy. However, the post–Bretton Woods state is obliged to rely heavily on tax revenues and bond sales to finance its interventionism. This has made state involvement in the economy more dependent on the international economic conjuncture. The post–Gulf War recession diminished income from taxes, and the 1993 budget responded by limiting government spending to only 0.3 percent growth in real terms, causing state subsidies to the economy to be cut back dramatically.

Moreover, it would be difficult to discern economic nationalism in any traditionally recognizable sense of the term in state aid to industry even during the period of nationalization. Foreign direct investment was encouraged and facilitated by the Socialist government in order to secure the position of French firms in world markets in response to the massive financial restructuring that was taking place in the European and world markets as a result of deregulation. Table 5.2 shows that

---

[74]  *Le Nouvel Observateur*, February 9–15, 1995, and March 23–29, 1995.
[75]  *Année politique, économique, et sociale, 1989* (Paris: Éditions du Moniteur, 1990), p. 484.

*Table 5.2.* French investment abroad and foreign investment in France (billion francs)

|  | 1985 | 1986 | 1987 | 1988 | 1989 | 1990 | 1991 | 1992 |
|---|---|---|---|---|---|---|---|---|
| French investment abroad | 20 | 36 | 52 | 76 | 115 | 145.5 | 115.8 | 99.6 |
| Foreign investment in France | 20 | 19 | 28 | 43 | 61 | 49.4 | 62.7 | 84.3 |

*Source:* Dov Zerah, *Le système financier français* (Paris: La Documentation Française, 1992), p. 268.

direct foreign investment by French firms increased by a factor of six between 1985 and 1989. In 1987, France occupied sixth place among industrialized countries for total assets held in foreign firms and third place for new direct foreign investments, behind the United States and Japan. France retained that position through 1992. During the period 1981–91, moreover, France held third place with regard to foreign direct investments in national firms, behind the United States and Great Britain.[76] Figures indicate that France is now the G-5 country that is most penetrated by foreign capital. This outcome appears all the more extraordinary as one recalls General de Gaulle's diatribes against American direct investment in France in the 1960s. Finally, massive amounts of French capital were invested in marketable foreign financial assets as well (Fr 46 billion or nearly $8 billion in 1991). Dividends procured through foreign investment have begun to make a positive impact on the French balance of payments.

State aid to industrial and financial firms and state encouragement of foreign direct investment are two facets of a single coherent policy. Although liberalization was prompted by the need to adapt the French political economy to the rigors of a strong currency policy, it produced efforts to restructure the economy more thoroughly and render it more competitive on international markets. Ironically, however, industrial restructuring came at the cost of perpetuating the indebtedness of French firms, a characteristic of the political economy that liberalization was in part designed to attack. It is true that French firms took advantage of the recession of the mid-1980s to reduce indebtedness. The rate of self-financing reached an unprecedented 86 percent in 1988.[77] But industrial

---

[76]   Zerah, *Le système financier français*, pp. 266–72; *Année politique, 1989*, p. 476.
[77]   This was true of large firms. Small to medium firms, on the other hand, had never reduced their level of indebtedness to the same extent.

redeployment, mergers, and foreign direct investment in 1989 and 1990 increased indebtedness, and by 1991 firms once again had to focus their strategies not on developing their productive capacities but on reducing their debt.

Debt reduction by industrial firms had a recessionary impact on the French economy in the mid 1990s. That impact was aggravated by the efforts of the state to reduce public debt. Inflationary financing of government expenditures is less feasible now than it was under Bretton Woods. For this reason, the French government began to borrow heavily in the 1980s to secure funds for its programs. By 1993, the public debt service was the third most important budget expense, claiming 13 percent of the budget. It was surpassed only by education and defense. It should be recalled that France's situation is markedly better than that of most other industrialized nations—government debt represents only 30 percent of the GDP in France. Nevertheless, French officials began to fear that state financial needs were crowding out private borrowing. Subsequently they began to restrict spending, which added to recessionary pressures welling up from elsewhere.

In sum, if we ask how successfully the French political economy has adapted to the post–Bretton Woods order, the signs are mixed. Inflation has been suppressed, the position of the country's external accounts has improved, French industries have markedly improved their capacity to export, and the franc has remained remarkably stable. Yet unemployment has often surpassed 12 percent and shows little sign of abating, and the country still experiences difficulty in finding the capital its firms need to expand and modernize. Policymakers continue to worry about the rate of private savings, which fell from 20 percent in 1978 to 10 percent in 1987, recovering to about 12.5 percent in 1991. This was not enough to prevent the Banque de France from complaining that "insufficient savings is slowing the necessary development of productive investment and rendering our economy dependent [on external financing]."[78]

French officials have therefore not relaxed their efforts to lure savings in ever greater volumes into long-term investment in French industry. This has resulted in a marked supply-side policy orientation in fiscal policy. Between 1988 and 1992, the tax burden, particularly on busi-

---

[78] *Année politique, économique, et sociale, 1992* (Paris: Éditions du Moniteur, 1993), p. 506.

ness and investment, was diminished by about Fr 92 billion. Tax levies on the GDP declined to 14.9 percent in 1992 from 18.1 percent in 1981, though tax reductions were offset by increases in payroll taxes. New savings instruments, such as the "stock market savings plan" (*plan d'épargne en actions*) and the "people's savings plan" (*plan d'épargne populaire*), continue to be created. Such plans funneled almost Fr 60 billion in short-, medium-, and long-term credits at attractive rates to small businesses. The French economy opened wide to foreign direct and portfolio investment. And yet, despite the numerous successes the French have experienced in adapting their political economy to the rigors of the post–Bretton Woods era, the predominant sentiment in 1996 remains one of *morosité*. Frenchmen confess to feeling morose and impotent before the looming constraints and rigors of a more open and less regulated international market.

### France in Comparative Perspective

The French case is significant because it clearly reveals the impact of regime change in international monetary relations on domestic structures and processes. Floating rates compelled the French to make the defense of the franc the principal goal of monetary policy. Defense of the franc, in turn, required liberalizing reforms (*a*) to reinforce the capacity of the marketplace to discipline the actions of banks and firms, (*b*) to attract domestic savings to stocks and bonds, and (*c*) to facilitate access by French firms to foreign capital.

This is not to say that international monetary regime change is the sole explanation of liberalization in France. It is not. There were many factors that conspired to force the issue of reform in France. Many of the drawbacks of extensive state (and therefore bureaucratic) control over credit that were apparent in other interventionist systems were apparent in France as well. First, activist credit policy caused the overall cost of providing credit to the economy to rise in France, as it did in Spain and, if one takes the curb market into account, in Korea. Second, it provoked conflicts of interest between the financial sector and the real economy, as was apparent in Spain and Japan. The Mayoux Report, mentioned above, documented how state control over credit disadvantaged a number of small yet dynamic and internationally competitive firms. Third, there are broadly diffuse but observable disadvantages to any strategy that seeks to socialize economic risk. Bank credit becomes a form of economic insurance for business firms. As such, it cushions firms from the market and can make them slow to respond to the market's guidance, giving rise to "soft constraints," or moral hazard.[79] Moreover, credit-as-insurance either supposes a transfer of resources from firms that are competitive and do not need it to firms that are vulnerable and do need it, or supposes inflationary financing to avoid such a transfer. It is the latter that prevailed in France, as it did in Spain, Korea, and Japan in the 1960s, since it is politically the less difficult path to follow.[80]

These background factors did not await floating rates to make themselves apparent to French monetary officials and experts. Liberalizing reforms were discussed and debated as early as the late 1950s.[81] The only thing that stood between the French and the kind of thorough financial reform that occurred in the 1980s was political timorousness. Credit control in France, as in all the countries examined in this book (with the possible exception of Korea), was designed as much to *prevent* a shift of resources between rising and declining sectors of the economy as to encourage it. Consequently, in France as in Spain, financial liberalization prior to the 1980s was typically a process of two steps forward, one step back, as illustrated by the bank reforms of 1965–67.

Floating rates, then, were not the sole cause of reform, but they did constitute the event that finally rendered reform ineluctable. Without international validation, the French "overdraft economy" was not viable. The French made several attempts to save the overdraft economy under floating rates, but none of them worked. In the early 1970s, they responded to the challenge of defending the franc while allaying the deflationary consequences of the oil shock by implementing a policy of state-guided borrowing by French firms on the international market.[82] When the limits of this policy response became clear, they implemented the plan to combine state control over credit allocation with money supply growth targets, as described above. When the Socialists acceded to power, they nationalized much of industry and most of the banking sec-

---

[79]  This analysis is pursued in Loriaux, *France after Hegemony*, chap. 3.
[80]  A comparison of the French and Japanese "overdraft economies" is found in ibid., conclusion.
[81]  Loriaux, *France after Hegemony*, chap. 6.
[82]  Loriaux, *France after Hegemony*, pp. 34–38.

tor in an effort to strengthen the state's control over investment. It is the persistence of currency weakness throughout this period of experimentation, maintained by the solicitude of state-controlled institutional lenders for their financially strapped clients, that provoked the dramatic turnabout of the mid-1980s.

The clarity with which the French case reveals the impact of regime change on the domestic political economy is matched by the clarity with which it reveals the centrality of the state in the process of reform. This comes as no real surprise to France-watchers, given the pervasiveness, the self-consciousness, and the self-assurance of that country's bureaucratic elite.[83] One sees paler counterparts of this bureaucratic elite in the Japanese and Korean cases, and even in the Spanish case, where Opus Dei solidarities approximated the technocratic autonomy and self-sufficiency of French public officials. But the bureaucratic elite in France has a longer reach than in these other countries. Many of the leaders of France's principal industrial firms are civil servants on leave from their state functions. Similarly, a significant number of France's politicians are also civil servants on leave from their state functions. The pervasiveness of this state elite makes it very difficult to determine where "public" stops and "private" begins.

The state's societal counterparts, moreover, are weaker than in the other countries. France's banks, at the time of the reforms, were nationalized. French banks were not in a position to play the more central role that banks played in other countries. Although they enjoyed a measure of autonomy, they were not in a position to threaten the government with an investment strike. Despite France's success as an exporting nation in the 1970s, French firms were more vulnerable and more dependent on state solicitude than their Korean and Japanese counterparts. They therefore did not assume the more active role that industrial firms did in East Asia. Finally, the less prominent actors—consumers, small businesses, farmers—seem to have played hardly any role at all. Japan appears unique to the extent that such actors were actually important in the reform process.

This brings us to the final aspect of French liberalization that causes the French case to stand out from the others. The French altered policy

---

[83]   See Ezra Suleiman, *Elites in French Society: The Politics of Survival* (Princeton: Princeton University Press, 1978).

and reformed their institutions because the state had lost mastery over monetary policy. It had lost the power to be disinflationary when leaders of a conservative stripe thought it appropriate to be disinflationary, and it had lost the power to be expansionist in a controlled fashion when leaders of any stripe thought it necessary to be expansionist. It lost the former in the late forties and early fifties when the government's preference for highly leveraged policies of rapid growth left the country's industrial firms with a fragile financial base, which both rendered them more vulnerable to deflation and made their sponsors in the ministries more resistant to deflationary policy than in other countries.[84] It lost the latter when change in the international monetary system, occasioned by change in U.S. policy, deprived it of international support in the form of the coordinated determination and defense of fixed monetary parities. If, then, the French government embraced the cause of liberal reformism, it is because it found in liberalism the only means to restore the state's power to dictate monetary policy in an altered international environment.

This is unlike the situation in Korea, where liberalism signified a loss of state power to a capitalist class that was of the state's own making. It is unlike the situation in Japan, where liberalism signified a loss of state power to the market, to the large industrial firms, and, as Calder points out with great irony, to politicians. In France, liberalism gave the state a power it had previously lacked, that of making the franc a strong currency. Nor did liberalization prevent the state, still under a Socialist government, from using its control over budget subsidies to implement a thorough and successful restructuring of industry. One must therefore be cautious in one's interpretation of French financial liberalization. It does not translate in any simple way into a withdrawal of the state from a role of active management of the economy.

What then can be concluded from the French case? The French case suggests that the relationship between state and capital was mediated by a historic event, the rise and subsequent unraveling of the post–World War II hegemonic order. When that order was at its zenith, capital was placed under the guardianship of states brought together in a military and economic alliance for the defense of capitalism. As that order

[84] On ministerial sponsorship of industrial firms and sectors, see especially Jack Hayward, *The State and the Market Economy: Industrial Patriotism and Economic Intervention in France* (Brighton: Wheatsheaf, 1986).

unraveled—the consequence of uneven growth as well as of the decline of the threat of communism—the tutelage of the state diminished. The state in France, after acting effectively in the 1980s to shore up the foundations of its industrial firms, its banks, and its capital market, then relinquished significant parcels of its interventionist powers while retaining the will to exercise tutelage over the political economy. The force that drove liberalization in France was primarily external and structural and assumed the form of a policy constraint. The force that drove liberalization in other countries, notably in East Asia, took the form of a policy opportunity, itself generated by external structural change. We shall return to this observation in Chapter 7.

# CHAPTER SIX

# From Cheap Credit to the EC:
# The Politics of Financial Reform in Spain

SOFÍA A. PÉREZ

In July 1977, only days after taking office, the first popularly elected government of Spain in over forty years enacted a major package of measures to reform the financial system. The aim of these measures was to dismantle the extensive framework of selective credit regulation inherited from the Franco regime. Introduced by way of two executive orders only days after the new legislature convened, the move indicated considerable haste on the part of the government's economic team. Yet the timing of the measures aroused little public debate. Given the close association in Spain between indicative planning and the Franco regime, economic interventionism was associated with political authoritarianism and easily cast as "statism." By the same token, political and economic liberalization appeared to go hand in hand. This connection between democratization and financial liberalization was reiterated two months after the initial measures in the Pactos de la Moncloa, which, signed by all the major political parties, included a commitment to further reform of the financial system.

The move to liberalize the Spanish financial system might easily be interpreted as a direct consequence of the change of political regimes in 1977. Such a conclusion, however, is challenged by two paradoxes. First, although they were introduced immediately following the first democratic elections, the liberalization measures of 1977 had been designed well before, and by a group of policymakers who held positions within the Franco regime's bureaucracy. Second, the liberalization program was championed as a way to facilitate the adjustment of the

Spanish economy by improving the allocative efficiency of the financial system. This, it was purported, would serve the interests of producer groups and secure the political transition to democracy. Yet, for more than a decade after 1977, the reform effort remained partial and did little to improve the market conditions under which Spanish producers were able to raise financing.

Both these contradictions offer important clues to the politics of financial liberalization in Spain. They suggest that economic policy choices on the part of governmental authorities, not changes in the institutions of political representation, were the primary determinants of regulatory change. Indeed, the Spanish story supports the argument Michael Loriaux makes with regard to France: the creation of an interventionist framework of credit regulation in the postwar period and its abandonment in the last two decades were linked to changes in international economic conditions, particularly the diminishing latitude for expansionary macroeconomic policies. However, the Spanish case also suggests that this causal link between international conditions and domestic change is not a mechanistic one. It leaves ample room for the intervention of domestic political motivations in determining the course of regulatory reform.

One of the characteristic features of Spanish financial regulation starting in the early sixties was its close institutional resemblance to French regulatory practices. Some have attributed these similarities to mimicry on the part of Spanish technocrats. Contrary to such a view, I will suggest that the adoption in Spain of French-styled indicative planning and regulatory practices had a much more intricate basis. As in France, financial interventionism in Spain was contrived largely to promote growth through monetary expansion. On the other hand, the abandonment of interventionism in the seventies and eighties was tied in both countries to a change in policy objectives. The central task facing public officials shifted increasingly from directing credit to preferred users toward containing the overall level of liquidity in the financial system. Thus, as in France, the creation of an interventionist regulatory framework in the early sixties and its abandonment two decades later in Spain were closely tied to broader macroeconomic policy considerations.

However, in the Spanish case, this relationship between international constraints and domestic policy choices, and the translation of policy choices into regulatory adjustment, have been strongly mediated by domestic political factors. I argue in this chapter that regulatory change in Spain has been shaped in particular by two domestic political dynamics. First, both the adoption of an interventionist framework in the sixties and its later abandonment were closely tied to shifts of influence within the state's economic policy-making elite. The specific political agenda of the ascendant group within the state bureaucracy determined the character (interventionist vs. market-oriented) that regulatory change took. Changes in the international economic context altered the relative influence of contending groups within the state elite and thus abetted these internal political shifts. But the motivations of reformers in introducing regulatory changes were relatively independent of changes in the international economy. They had their origins in the battles that such reformers had to fight with other groups within the state bureaucracy.

Second, along with this dynamic of change involving the interplay between international constraints and the influence of various domestic elites, Spanish financial regulation has also displayed a strong element of continuity. Both regulation and deregulation were thoroughly conditioned by the politics of reciprocal consent between state elites and the domestic banking sector.[1] While the goals of state elites provided the main impetus for regulatory change (i.e. the creation of an interventionist framework and its subsequent abandonment), the politics of accommodation represent a constant that strongly constrained the course of such change. Thus the course of reform involved both the domestic political agendas of state elites seeking to establish their position of influence within the state, and the politics of accommodation with the domestic banking sector.

More specifically, I suggest here that the origins of liberalizing financial reform in Spain are to be found in a shift in domestic policy leadership away from the Franco regime's technocratic planning elite toward an increasingly assertive monetary authority. This shift began well before the democratic transition. It involved the crystallization of a new elite of central bank reformers starting in the late sixties, an elite that was propelled into a position of policy leadership during the regime

---

[1]  I borrow the concept of "reciprocal consent" from Richard J. Samuels, *The Business of the Japanese State: Energy Markets in Comparative and Historical Perspective* (Ithaca: Cornell University Press, 1987). See pp. 8–9.

transition. The agenda of this new elite centered on the objective of establishing the central bank's control over the Spanish financial system. To advance this agenda, the reformers sought, just like the Franco regime's technocratic planners before them, to establish a working alliance with the domestic banking sector.

Yet, while establishing a compact was relatively unproblematic for the planners, who were using the banks to allocate a rapidly expanding level of liquidity to the economy, it was less so for the reformers, who sought to restrict the level of liquidity in the economy. The accommodation was achieved by placing credit deregulation (essential to the reformers' objectives) far ahead of other reform measures that would have redressed the narrow and oligopolistic structure of the Spanish financial market in such a way as to lower the burden of high real financial costs on nonfinancial firms. Through the 1970s and 1980s, the course of reform in Spain consistently neglected the needs of domestic producer groups. The upshot was that Spanish firms endured inordinate financial costs for more than a decade and that public officials came to rely heavily on foreign capital inflows during the eighties to compensate for the shortcomings of domestic reform.

## Inflationary Public Finance and Private Bank Power

As has been pointed out by a number of economic historians, the story of Spanish economic development is not simply one of late industrialization. It is the story of the failure of industrialization in the second part of the nineteenth century, and hence of arrested development.[2] That century also saw the development of a Spanish banking sector along two lines: (1) credit companies established by French industrial bank capital and primarily engaged in the promotion of the Spanish railways, and (2) domestic banks of issue, which culminated in the Bank of Spain's monopoly of issue in 1874. The failure of the credit companies as a result of the Spanish railway fiasco in the middle of the century left

---

[2] See for example Jordi Nadal Oller, "The Failure of the Industrial Revolution in Spain, 1830–1913," in C. M. Cipolla, ed., *The Fontana Economic History of Europe*, vol. 4, pt. 2 (London: Collins, 1973); and Gabriel Tortella Casares, "Los orígenes de la industrialización española, 1850–1931," in *Banco de Bilbao, 125 años de historia (1857–1982)* (Madrid: Banco de Bilbao, 1985).

a banking sector heavily dominated by the Bank of Spain, whose assets at the turn of the century outnumbered those of private banks by three to one, and which continued to channel its resources overwhelmingly into public as opposed to industrial finance.[3] A number of scholars have linked the stagnation in Spanish industrialization during the last quarter of the century to this overriding involvement of the banking sector in the finances of a waning colonial state.[4]

This scenario changed significantly in the first three decades of the twentieth century, however. The repatriation of colonial capital following the final colonial defeat of 1898 led to the creation of a number of new commercial banks that became actively involved in the promotion of industrial firms.[5] Driving this involvement (both through direct stock holdings and lending) was the banks' role as intermediaries in inflationary public finance. Starting in 1917, the direct monetization of the public debt by the Bank of Spain was replaced by the mechanism of *pignoración automática* (automatic collateral lending), whereby the private banks could automatically obtain credit from the Bank of Spain for up to 90 percent of the public debt that they purchased. This change meant that the public debt was effectively monetized through the private banks, and it allowed the banks to "increase their ratio of productive to liquid assets . . . at a negligible additional risk" and cost.[6] Since the private banks could obtain automatic credit from the Bank of Spain for up to 90 percent of their public debt purchases, they were able to use these purchases to monetize their purchases of industrial assets.

The persistence of this indirect monetization led to the consolidation of a mixed banking system and to Spain's adoption of a bank-financed

[3]    See Pablo Martín Aceña, "Development and Modernization of the Financial System, 1844–1935," in Nicolás Sánchez-Albornoz, ed., *The Economic Modernization of Spain, 1830–1930* (New York: New York University Press, 1987); and Gabriel Tortella, "Spain 1829–1874," in Rondo Cameron, ed., *Banking and Economic Development: Some Lessons of History* (New York: Oxford University Press, 1972).

[4]    Tortella, "Spain 1829–1874."

[5]    The initial stimulus for this involvement was provided by Spanish neutrality in World War I. Neutrality produced a boom in the demand for Spanish exports, and the war forced import substitution on the economy. The result was exceptional profit opportunities for investment in Spanish industry.

[6]    Gabriel Tortella and Jordi Palafox, "Banking and Industry in Spain, 1918–1936," *Journal of European Economic History*, special issue on Banks and Industry in the Interwar Period (fall 1984), p. 88. See also Juan Velarde Fuertes, *La decadencia económica de España* (Madrid: Tecnos, 1967), pp. 621–23.

industrialization model in the early part of the twentieth century. Yet the banks' promotion of industrial activity, based as it was on indirect monetization, tainted the relationship between banks and industry with an "original sin": because industrial investment became a source of extraordinary profits for the banks, they had no need to develop the internal capacity and culture to promote long-term industrial investment strategies. This was reflected in the fact that the banks' direct investments were predominantly in those sectors that were either natural oligopolies (energy) or that had heavy tariff protection. The link between universal banking and export promotion, which has received so much attention in the German case, never developed.[7]

The link between public and industrial finance established in the early part of the century had other enduring consequences for Spanish economic development. The main beneficiary of the *pignoración* was the banking sector itself, whose assets experienced rapid growth in the second two decades of the century. The growth of the sector was accompanied by heavy concentration. "By 1923 the 'Big Six,' numerically just 6.6 percent of the banking population, had over 40 percent of the combined paid-in capital and over 50 percent of the deposits."[8] This newly found economic clout was reinforced through strong personal connections between the new financial capital and the traditional Spanish aristocracy,[9] giving the bankers a powerful political influence under the old regime of the Bourbon *restauración*. Political power, in turn, became enshrined in the regulatory framework. Thus, the Banking Law of 1921 officially sanctioned the existing banking cartel through the creation of the Consejo Superior Bancario (CSB), a body controlled by the Big Six and charged with regulating the sector. On the other hand, although a number of semipublic credit institutions were created in the twenties, these remained heavily circumscribed by the private bankers who controlled their boards, so that there was no state discretion over

---

[7] See Andrew J. Spindler, *The Politics of International Credit: Private Finance and Foreign Policy in Germany and Japan* (Washington, D.C.: Brookings Institution, 1984), chap. 2; Michael Kreile, "West Germany: The Dynamics of Expansion," in Peter J. Katzenstein, ed., *Between Power and Plenty: Foreign Economic Policies of Advanced Industrial States* (Madison: University of Wisconsin Press, 1978), pp. 210–12; and Andrew Shonfield, *Modern Capitalism: The Changing Balance of Public and Private Power* (London: Oxford University Press, 1969), pp. 246–62.

[8] Tortella and Palafox, "Banking and Industry in Spain," p. 83.

[9] Carlos Moya, *El poder económico en España* (Madrid: Tucar, 1975), pp. 55–91.

credit allocation. The basic features of this regulatory framework, i.e., laissez-faire and state-sanctioned corporatism, remained unaltered during the Second Republic, whose leaders are said to have felt a high degree of deference toward the financial aristocracy.[10]

The model of industrialization followed in Spain up to the Civil War thus left the allocation of credit entirely in the hands of the private banking cartel, which by the 1930s was made up of the "Big Seven."[11] The traumatic disruption of the Civil War, however, ended complacency about relative economic backwardness in Spain, just as World War II did elsewhere in Europe. It produced a domestic political shift in favor of a more active state role in promoting economic modernization. Pressure for such a change was magnified by the context of international isolation that the new regime faced in the forties.[12] This constellation made "industrialization" a political priority for the first time in Spanish history, and it led the regime to adopt a defiant policy of economic autarky (*autarquía*) during its first two decades. The perceived inadequacy of private initiative to the task of autarkic industrialization was captured in the preamble of the 1941 law that created the Instituto Nacional de Industria (INI).

> The investment that the production of certain products requires is so great that it often exceeds the framework in which private initiatives are carried out. In other cases it offers such meager profit margins that it provides no incentives for the financial institutions. . . . Institutions apt to finance such great industrial programs do not exist in our nation, as the present credit institutions, given their [commercial] character and specialization in short term credit, are not the adequate ones to back these ends. This creates the need for an agency that is endowed with the economic capacity and legal

---

[10]   Juan Velarde, "Prólogo," in Juan Muñoz, *El poder de la banca* (Algorta, Vizcaya: Zero, 1970), p. 5.

[11]   Banco Español de Crédito (Banesto), Banco Hispano Americano, Banco Central, Banco de Bilbao, Banco de Vizcaya, Banco de Santander, and Banco Popular.

[12]   A UN resolution imposing an economic and diplomatic boycott of Spain was in effect until 1950. At the same time, Spain was excluded by the United States from receiving Marshall Plan aid. In 1953, however, the United States signed a series of agreements with the Franco government whereby the latter authorized the United States to establish military bases in Spain in return for a substantial aid package ($85 million in economic aid and $141 million for military assistance). Although these agreements marked the end of the Franco regime's international isolation, Spain continued to be barred from membership in the EEC until the end of the regime.

character needed to realize and give form to the great programs of industrial resurgence of our nation.[13]

The creation of the INI suggested a deliberate effort to embark on a statist model of development in which the initiative of private financial capital would be supplanted by the state. Yet despite the significant political momentum behind its creation, the model of development that the INI embodied never took hold under the *autarquía*. As the preamble suggested, the INI's architects had intended it to play the role of a large financial holding company modeled on the Italian Istituto per la Recostruzione Industriale (IRI), which would give the state an important market presence in the financial sector. Contrary to this design, however, the Institute's role as a financial intermediary was never allowed to develop. Instead, the INI's activities centered on the creation of a limited number of public companies and on the direct production of basic industrial inputs (principally steel and energy).[14]

The circumscribed role that the INI came to play was the result of internal political conflict among the various factions that supported the regime in its military victory. The Institute's creation was part of the effort by the regime's leadership to assuage its national-syndicalist left-wing, the Falange. Before his death in the civil war, the Falange's founder, José Antonio Primo de Rivera, had called for a program of radical socialization of the economy, centering on immediate nationalization of the entire banking sector. Thus, according to one economic historian, the entire policy of economic autarky adopted by the regime in its first two decades (when the INI was created) is to be understood as the least common denominator to which the various discordant factions of the emerging regime could agree. The scope that the INI could attain within national capital was, however, limited by the strong influence that the private banks held with the new regime, thanks to the support that they had offered to Franco's side during the Civil War. Thus, in

---

[13] Law of September 25, 1941, in *Boletín Oficial del Estado* 280 (October 7, 1941).

[14] The Institute also took direct stock holdings in private companies in these sectors and promoted some joint ventures with foreign capital and the domestic private banks. The most prominent of the latter was the launching of SEAT in 1949, in which the INI joined hands with FIAT of Italy and Spanish bank capital. For discussion of the INI's creation and development see Pedro Schwartz and Manuel Jesús González, *Una historia del INI (1941–1976)* (Madrid: Tecnos, 1978); and Pablo Martín Aceña and Francisco Comín, *INI: 50 años de industrialización en España* (Madrid: Espasa-Calpe, 1991).

sharp contradiction with the Falange's project of nationalizing the banking sector so as to end the retarding influence of "monopoly capital,"[15] the Franco regime sanctioned the banking status quo in 1939 and again in 1941—the year that the INI was created—by legally freezing entry into the sector. And in the Banking Law of 1946 it recreated the corporatist regulatory framework of 1921.

More important yet in limiting the INI's potential role was the perpetuation under the *autarquía* of the use of the *pignoración* and the prewar pattern whereby the monetization of the public debt was directly linked to the expansion of the private banks' assets. The potential for expansion through the *pignoración* was magnified, moreover, by the shift from a metallic standard (an idiosyncratic Spanish mixture of gold and silver) to an unbacked fiduciary standard for the peseta. This allowed the banks to expand their industrial holdings and lending to an unprecedented extent, and it placed them in an excellent position to benefit from the large profit opportunities that the autarkic modernization drive created. The consequence was a new process of concentration in the financial sector. From 1941 to 1960, the Big Seven absorbed as many as seventy-eight smaller banks, leading their share of total bank deposits to rise to 72 percent in 1957.[16] At the same time, inflationary credit expansion dramatically reduced the share of the Spanish capital market in the external financing of the private sector, raising that of bank credit from an average of 30 percent in the prewar period to an average of more than 60 percent in the period of 1941 to 1959.[17]

Far from the statist model heralded in the creation of the INI, the model of industrial finance that drove autarkic industrialization during the first two decades of the Franco regime was based on a vast expansion of private bank credit, fueled by the issuance of public debt. Yet, monetary expansion was not accompanied in this period by state discretion. While the regime imposed a high measure of direct control over product markets during the two decades of the *autarquía*, it abstained from intervening in the allocation of private credit during

---

[15]    Juan Velarde, "La empresa pública," p. 71.

[16]    Arturo López Muñoz, *Capitalismo español: Una etapa decisiva* (Algorta, Vizcaya: Zero, 1970), p. 246; and Antonio Torrero, "La evolución del sistema financiero," *Boletín de Estudios Económicos* 30, no. 96 (1976). See also Ramón Tamames, *La lucha contra los monopolios* (Madrid: Tecnos, 1966), pp. 325–52.

[17]    Mariano Navarro Rubio, *Mis memorias: Testimonio de una vida política truncada por el "Caso Matesa"* (Barcelona: Plaza y Janes, 1991), p. 519.

this period. The absence of selectivity as a means to restrain and canalize the flow of bank credit not only precluded state direction of bank credit allocation, it also lent monetary expansion an untamed character. This was justified by reference to the success of Nazi Germany in using monetary expansion to promote industrial expansion.[18] But the choice to forego state discretion over credit flows seems to have responded foremost to domestic political factors, and in particular to the banking sector's ability to check the advance of the public sector. At a time when the demands for state-led industrialization of the national-syndicalist wing were being addressed pro forma through the creation of the INI, the unregulated character of monetary expansion was a politically opaque but highly effective way of allowing the private banks to maintain their dominant economic position within national capital.

Yet, this regulatory accommodation between the new regime and its clients in the banking sector was only as viable as the economic policies that it served. As a prominent national-syndicalist economist had predicted, the experience of German inflationary finance was inapplicable to Spain, where various structural bottlenecks meant that a rampant expansionary monetary stance could only lead to a "pure inflation."[19] The most important of these bottlenecks inevitably turned out to be the economy's need for foreign exchange. The critical point came in 1957, when two drastic wage increases decreed by the national-syndicalist Minister of Labor, José A. Girón, led to a sharp increase in credit demand from businesses and a rapid fall in foreign reserves. Despite a restrictive fiscal stance and a sharp reduction in the amount of public debt issued during 1957 and 1958, the monetary expansion could not be halted. Banks proceeded to trade in their swollen portfolios of public debt as collateral for credit at the Bank of Spain, so as to take advantage of the surge in demand.[20] The monetary expansion gave way to economic crisis when the level of net reserves turned negative in June 1959. This payments crisis had a profound effect on domestic perceptions. As one

[18] Jacinto Ros Hombravella et al., *Capitalismo español: De la autarquía a la estabilización* (Madrid: Edicusa, 1978), p. 180. References to this example were also part of the justification for the move toward an unbacked currency standard.
[19] Higinio Paris Eguilaz, *Diez años de política económica en España, 1939–1949* (Madrid: CSIC, 1946), p. 129.
[20] Manuel Jesús González, *La economía política del franquismo* (Madrid: Tecnos,1979), pp. 49–82.

author puts it, it seemed to leave no alternative to external economic liberalization other than "an intolerable decline in the standard of living,
perhaps accompanied by a drastic harshening of the political regime."[21]

The dilemma was as much a matter of sheer economic constraint as a
function of the political balance within the Franco regime in the late
fifties. After the signing of the treaties with the United States in 1953
(providing Spain with U.S. financial aid in return for the establishment
of U.S. military bases), the regime had switched from a policy of strict
autarky to a more standard import substitution strategy. This earlier shift
involved an important increase in the economy's import requirements.
Without the assistance of foreign capital and IMF funds in 1959, the
payments crisis would have forced an indeterminate reduction in
growth. Such a prospect was a real political threat to the regime, which
in the years immediately preceding the crisis (1956 and 1957) had experienced a sharp increase in political unrest (most prominently a miners'
strike in 1956, followed by widespread student protests). This wave of
political unrest had been the cause of the massive 1957 wage increase,
which set off the inflationary cycle that eventually led to the payments
crisis. The precondition for IMF membership in 1959 was a significant
step in the direction of external trade liberalization. But at the same
time, the need for IMF assistance strengthened the position of the
regime's technocratic reformers, who favored external liberalization as
a matter of ideological preference.

The result of the economic crisis of 1957–59 was therefore a decisive
shift within the regime's elite in which a group of neoliberal technocrats, often associated with the Catholic lay organization Opus Dei,
were placed firmly in charge of economic policy, permanently displac-
ing the regime's national-syndicalist supporters.[22] The political
change—strongly encouraged by the French devaluation of 1958 and the
onset of Atlantic convertibility at the end of that year[23]—set the stage for

[21]    Ibid., p. 114.
[22]    Though membership in Opus Dei generally remained secret, several of the most prominent members of the new technocratic elite were known to be members of this Catholic lay
organization. See Charles W. Anderson, *The Political Economy of Modern Spain: Policy-
Making under an Authoritarian System* (Madison: University of Wisconsin Press, 1970), pp.
140–41. For a more sociological analysis, see Carlos Moya, *Señas de Leviatán: Estado
nacional y sociedad industrial: España 1936–1980* (Madrid: Alianza Editorial, 1984), pp.
134–41.
[23]    The French move in particular created in Spain "a sense of danger and distancing."
Manuel Jesús González, *La economía política del franquismo*, p. 166.

the IMF-backed stabilization plan of 1959. The stabilization plan marked the abandonment of the autarkic policy regime, and augured the adoption of a new, outwardly oriented development strategy. This new policy orientation, centering on market-oriented trade and price liberalization and on French-styled indicative planning, had important consequences for Spanish financial regulation. Most important, it implied that monetary expansion would have to be kept in line with the new requirements of peseta convertibility. Thus, along with a ceiling on bank credit and cuts in government spending, the stabilization plan included a commitment by the government to permanently abandon the *pignoración* and therewith the mechanism that had been the motor behind Spanish bank-led industrialization in the first half of the century.

**The Introduction of Interventionism**

The abandonment of the *pignoración* was the principal regulatory prerequisite for the move to an outwardly oriented growth strategy. The regulatory implications of outward liberalization went beyond this first step, however. The new technocrats in charge of Spanish economic policy after 1959 had two regulatory options to choose from. First, the German example of export-led growth left allocation of credit almost entirely up to the private banks, which presumably were best able to gauge the long-term efficiency of resource allocation. A similar growth strategy was adopted in postwar Italy, although its banking sector had been mostly nationalized during the twenties in the IRI. In both the Italian and German cases the state refrained from trying to structure the overall character of credit allocation, which was left to market forces. The second option was the French model of selective credit allocation, described by John Zysman.[24] The basic regulatory principle here was an attempt by state authorities to regulate the price of credit selectively, in such a way as to encourage the pattern of allocation that would maximize productivity growth. The course of Spanish financial regulation following the stabilization plan clearly reflected the second option rather than the first.

---

[24]  John Zysman, *Governments, Markets, and Growth: Financial Systems and the Politics of Industrial Change* (Ithaca: Cornell University Press, 1983).

The new regulatory framework was spelled out in the Banking Law of 1962 and in associated legislation that was instituted with the introduction of French-styled indicative planning. The new legislation defined the banking sector as an instrument of the plan and introduced two major changes in the legal framework of banking regulation. The first of these was an attempt to rationalize the institutional relationship between the state and the financial sector and to move away from the corporatist legal framework that had been established by the Banking Law of 1946. Most important in this regard was the nationalization of the Bank of Spain and of the official credit institutions and the formal imposition of a regime of "specialization" (i.e., separation between commercial and industrial banking activities). The second change was the creation of two "privileged financing circuits" that would allow public authorities to selectively regulate the allocation of bank credit.

The first of these two changes had a clear political content, in that it sought to address the growing perception—created during the *autarquía* by the rapid expansion of the banks' industrial holdings—that the banks' "economic power" rendered the regime captive to private interests. One of the objectives of the 1962 law was to formally establish the legal authority of the state over banking regulation, thereby rectifying the perception of political weakness. The formalization of state authority, however, also served the purpose of creating distinct categories of financial institutions which could be assigned different economic functions.[25] This segmentation of the credit market provided the institutional basis for the second main component of the regulatory framework created in the aftermath of the stabilization plan, namely, the creation of the *circuitos privilegiados* (privileged financing circuits), whereby state authorities could exercise discretion over the allocation of bank credit.

The *circuitos privilegiados* were, as their name indicates, implemented in a roundabout way. The new system of credit regulation involved two separate circuits. First, with the creation of the Planning Commission in 1962, the Bank of Spain's rediscounting mechanism was transformed into an instrument of selective credit allocation through the creation of special rediscount lines for credits extended to favored sec-

---

[25]    For a firsthand account of the motivations behind the new law, see the memoirs of the finance minister at the time, Mariano Navarro Rubio, *Mis memorias*, pp. 188–94.

tors. These special lines offered the banks a source of cheap liquidity over and above that of the Bank of Spain's regular rediscount window, thus giving them a strong incentive to lend to sectors eligible for such rediscounting.[26] Along with this first type of privileged financing a second circuit was created by way of a compulsory "public funds" coefficient, which obliged financial institutions to earmark a fixed proportion of their resources for the purchase of securities issued by the public sector. The resources raised by the state in this way were used to finance the official credit institutions, which had been assigned the function of extending long-term investment credit to favored sectors under the new Banking Law.[27] This allowed for a significant expansion of the role of these institutions, and in particular the Banco de Crédito Industrial, in the financing of private investment during the sixties.[28]

The construct of privileged financing created in Spain in 1961–62 bore a remarkable resemblance to that which had been contrived in France in the immediate postwar period, leading some to argue that it constituted a case of wholesale and unabridged institutional importation. Yet, there is more to this extreme parallelism than unadorned mimicry.[29] The key to the double-circuit mode of financial interventionism imported by the Spanish technocrats from France lay in the fact that, while formally separate, the two tracks of privileged financing were functionally interdependent. The special rediscount lines created a new, though more controlled "guarantee of liquidity" for the banking sector. From the banks' standpoint, this strongly mitigated the character of the second circuit, i.e., the compulsory coefficients imposed on financial institutions to finance credit extended by the official credit institutions.

More specifically, the manner in which selective credit regulation was implemented—in essence by subsuming monetary policy—served two critical political purposes in the technocrats' new industrialization drive. It served to reconcile two conflicting aspects of their economic policy

[26]    An additional, non-sector-specific rediscount line was created in 1965 for medium- and long-term credits.

[27]    The list of these favored sectors varied over time according to the objectives set out by the Planning Commission. See Raimundo Poveda, *La creación de dinero en España, 1956–1970: Análisis y crítica* (Madrid: IEF, 1972).

[28]    Gabriel Tortella and Juan Carlos Jiménez, *Historia del Banco de Crédito Industrial* (Madrid: Alianza Editorial, 1986), pp. 238–39.

[29]    See Anderson, *Political Economy of Modern Spain*, pp. 164–67.

strategy, and it compensated the banking sector for accepting state discretion over part of its resources, thus assuring the latter's support for the technocrats' growth strategy.

Discussions of the interventionist framework instituted in the sixties by contemporary Spanish economists tend to suggest that the prime motivation behind the creation of the privileged financing circuits lay in the Franco regime's clientelistic character, or, as one economist put it, in the desire of "politicians" to exercise the "enlightened despotism of discretional credit concession."[30] However, although there is evidence of the clientelistic use of the *circuitos privilegiados* and in particular of the credit extended by the official credit institutions,[31] such arguments provide a weak explanation for the initial creation of these circuits. As the Italian postwar experience suggests, the use of financial institutions for political patronage can be equally, and perhaps more effectively, achieved in less circuitous ways, and it is not invariably linked to monetary expansion (see Tables 6.1 and 6.2).[32] Thus, while patronage may have been the consequence of the privileged financing circuits, it was not its raison d'être.

Rather, the initial creation of an interventionist regulatory framework was principally intended to reconcile two conflicting elements in the economic policy strategy pursued by Franco's technocratic planning elite. As suggested above, the main shift in Spanish economic policy, as set out in the IMF-sponsored stabilization plan of 1959, was the abandonment of an inwardly oriented growth strategy in favor of trade liberalization and the opening of the Spanish economy to foreign investment. This shift to an outwardly oriented growth strategy was meant to address the foreign exchange gap, which was seen to be a fundamental

---

[30]   Enrique Fuentes Quintana, "Prólogo," in Rafael Termes, *Desde la banca*, vol. 1 (Madrid: Ediciones Rialp, 1991), p. liv.
[31]   See for example the discussion of the MATESA scandal by Tortella and Jiménez, in *Historia del Banco de Crédito Industrial*, pp. 155–95.
[32]   Italy's financial interventionism, based on special public credit institutions, was linked neither to the commercial banks, nor to central bank rediscounting in any systematic way. Although Italian inflation rates rose substantially following labor unrest in 1963, financial interventionism was designed in the context of an anti-inflationary policy orientation during the forties and fifties. See Guido M. Rey, "Italy," in Andrea Boltho, ed., *The European Economy: Growth and Crisis* (New York: Oxford University Press, 1982), pp. 505–8. For a discussion of the uses of the special credit institutions for political purposes see Giandomenico Nardozzi, *Tre sistemi creditizi: Banche e economia in Francia, Germania e Italia* (Bologna: Il Mulino, 1983), p. 60.

*Table 6.1.* Inflation averages for 1950s and 1960s

| Years | Italy | FRG | France | Spain |
|---|---|---|---|---|
| 1950–1959 | 2.8 | 1.2 | 6.2 | 5.8 |
| 1960–1969 | 3.4 | 2.4 | 3.9 | 5.8 |

*Source:* Computed from IMF financial statistics.

*Table 6.2.* Claims on banks and savings banks as percentage of total central bank assets

| Year | Italy | FRG | France | Spain |
|---|---|---|---|---|
| 1955 | 3 | 10 | 24 | 21 |
| 1960 | 1 | 2 | 27 | 12 |
| 1965 | 3 | 5 | 19 | 14 |

*Source:* Computed from IMF financial statistics.

constraint on Spanish development. It implied that domestic monetary expansion would have to be kept in line with the imperative of maintaining the peseta's convertibility. This had been the imperative that had led in 1959 to the abandonment of the autarkic mode of untamed monetary expansion through the *pignoración*.

However, despite the basic change in economic policy orientation that the stabilization plan of 1959 augured, the economic policy strategy pursued in Spain during the sixties differed sharply from the export-driven growth strategies adopted in Italy or Germany. Whereas those strategies were premised on domestic price stability and the maintenance of an undervalued currency, Spanish industrialization in the sixties was driven by a continuous expansion in bank credit through the extension of the special rediscount lines, which resulted in comparatively high rates of domestic inflation. This element of relative continuity with the autarkic era reflected a choice on the part of the technocratic planners of the Opus Dei to pursue a "cheap credit" strategy of modernization, such as had been pursued in France starting in the late forties. In the words of one critic, the technocrats' growth strategy was based on "the complete subordination of monetary and financial policy to a policy of 'production.'"[33] The fundamental ingredient of such a strategy was the supply of ample credit at low administratively set cost to industry and other producers. To ensure that such a policy would produce the necessary expansion of productivity, it was necessary to

---

[33] Luis Angel Rojo, "La política monetaria," in Manuel Aguilar Navarro et al., *España perspectiva 1968* (Madrid: Guadiana, 1968), p. 64.

impose some form of discretion over credit allocation. This was the logic that underpinned the interventionist regulatory framework created in 1962.[34] The importation of the French regulatory framework in 1962 thus reflected a prior choice to pursue the French postwar strategy of cheap credit cum convertibility, rather than the German/Italian strategy of export-led growth based on domestic price stability.

As Michael Loriaux has argued for France, the pursuit of an expansionary monetary course to intensify the rate of industrial modernization was facilitated in the postwar period by an exceptionally tolerant international economic context. In the Spanish case, the policy leeway provided by Bretton Woods was augmented by the large and unexpected foreign exchange contribution from the Spanish tourism boom of the sixties, and to a lesser extent from worker remittances.[35] The pursuit of a strategy of cheap credit was also imbued with a certain economic logic in the Keynesian orthodoxy of the day, namely that of facilitating an optimal rate of investment through the maintenance of low long-term interest rates.[36] Nonetheless, Keynesian economic theory can hardly be said to have prescribed as inflationary a policy course as was pursued in Spain during the sixties (see Table 6.1). The costs of such a strategy in terms of long-term trade performance, even within a tolerant international context, point to domestic political factors in explaining this policy course.

In the Spanish case, the pursuit of a strategy of cheap credit even after the stabilization plan of 1959 can be linked to what Charles W. Anderson has described as the overriding imperative of the Opus Dei technocrats, i.e., ensuring the stability of the existing political order.[37] That order had been significantly challenged by the miners' strikes and student protests of the late fifties. On the other hand, trade liberalization, a critical element in resolving the external constraint on economic growth, promised to create its own stresses. Thus the first round of tariff reductions from 1959 to 1962 placed severe strain on the technolog-

---

[34]    The main departure from the autarkic period was that credit expansion could be harnessed through selective allocation and rationing.

[35]    See Manuel Román, *The Limits of Economic Growth in Spain* (New York: Praeger, 1971), pp. 44–48. Such non-trade-related sources of foreign exchange explain why Spain was able to avoid devaluation for almost a decade (until 1967), although the rate of credit expansion and domestic inflation were significantly higher than in France.

[36]    For a discussion of this economic logic, see Antonio Torrero, "La utilización interna de los recursos financieros: Reflexiones desde una óptica Keynesiana," *Economistas*, no. 21 (1986).

[37]    See Anderson, *Political Economy of Modern Spain*, pp. 140–41.

ically outmoded steel and coal-mining sectors, both of which entered a stage of irreversible crisis in the early sixties.[38] At the same time, the regime's ability to control wages through political repression was diminished by its decision to seek associate status in the EEC, in order to make trade liberalization pay off. A partial legalization of collective bargaining thus quickly led the regime to lose control over the sphere of industrial relations, as bargaining between employers and underground unions became widespread.[39]

All of these circumstances, ultimately reflecting the underlying political precariousness of the regime, advised against using orthodox recessionary methods to control wage pressure. Instead they favored using inflation to diffuse the costs of economic change. The economic logic of the strategy of cheap credit which financial interventionism was meant to implement, masked the political logic of a "strategy of inflation." The objective of such a strategy, however, cannot be reduced to mere clientelism. It constituted a formula for counteracting the ability of labor and traditional sectors, in particular agriculture, to limit the accumulation and growth process that the planners viewed as essential to the regime's survival. More specifically, credit expansion and the resulting diffusion of costs through inflation served to pursue two goals. First, they facilitated the shift of resources from some sectors into others.[40] Second, cheap credit to industry, whose cost was diffused by inflation, also served to offset nominal wage increases and, indirectly, the pressure of rising agricultural prices resulting from labor emigration.[41]

The framework of selective credit regulation contrived in the early sixties by the Franco regime's technocratic planners was, therefore, created to make the choice of a cheap credit strategy compatible with external trade liberalization and the maintenance of a convertible currency. At the same time, however, the guarantee of liquidity on which selective allocation turned had a very important second function, namely that of

---

[38]   Arturo López Muñoz and José Luis García Delgado, *Crecimiento y crisis del capitalismo español* (Madrid: Cuadernos para el Diálogo, 1968), pp. 189–212.
[39]   José María Maravall, *Dictadura y disentimiento político: Obreros y estudiantes bajo el franquismo* (Madrid: Alfaguara, 1978), p. 57.
[40]   For an elaboration of this point, see the discussion of the theory of demand-shift inflation in Zysman, *Governments, Markets, and Growth*, pp. 141–44.
[41]   Luis Angel Rojo, interviewed in Salvador Paniker, *Conversaciones en Madrid* (Barcelona: Kairos, 1969), p. 162. For a discussion of the effect of agricultural prices, see also Román, *Limits of Economic Growth in Spain*, pp. 28–39.

rendering the imposition of state discretion over credit flows highly acceptable to the domestic banks. While the technocrats' macroeconomic modernization strategy motivated the change in the regulatory framework after 1959, that framework was underpinned and overdetermined by the politics of accommodation between state authorities and the banking sector. This accommodation rested on two pillars: the provision of ample central bank rediscounting and the maintenance of the status quo in the banking sector. Its most important consequence was that of allowing the Big Seven to secure and expand their position as intermediaries in domestic financial flows during the sixties.

The manner in which selective credit regulation was instituted in Spain had several important consequences for the Spanish banking cartel. First, the ample supply of liquidity to the sector through the continuous expansion of special rediscount lines over the course of the sixties meant that the state continued to underwrite the risk of the banks' loans to industry as well as their direct industrial investments.[42] It thus provided a strong measure of continuity with the past, the only difference (from the banks' point of view) being that monetary expansion was harnessed through selective allocation and subjected to state control. The guarantee of liquidity had a second and very important consequence, however. It effectively negated the opportunity cost that the banks were made to bear as the result of their being required to maintain a fixed ratio of public debt to total deposits. Most important, however, by recreating the old pattern of allowing the banks to reap the benefits of monetization, albeit with greater state control, the expansion of the special rediscount lines made cheap credit to industry perfectly compatible with high profits for the banks.

If monetary expansion through the special rediscount lines served to reconcile the economic policy objectives of the technocrats with profits for the banks, the second track in the privileged financing circuit—namely, the use of the compulsory ratio to finance the long-term credit provided by the official credit institutions—also served the banks' interests. It implied that with the end of automatic collateral lending, the banking sector would not be expected to bear the risk of long-term lending to industry. Rather, by assigning long-term lending to the official

---

[42]    Interruptions to this flow of liquidity during the sixties were limited to short, punctuated stabilizations after which the flow of liquidity to the banks would be quickly resumed.

credit institutions, the state would take over this risk directly. More important, however, the financing of the official credit institutions through the compulsory ratio carried another implicit bargain, namely that these institutions would not be equipped to compete with the banking sector in the capture of funds. Thus, despite the growing importance of the official credit institutions in providing financing to the private sector in the sixties, their institutional character was restricted to that of "mere administrative bodies."[43]

This implicit bargain in the imposition of the compulsory ratio illustrates the second pillar supporting financial interventionism, that is, the effective preservation of the cartel in the banking sector. While the law of 1962 expressed the political will to end the status quo by allowing for the creation of industrial banks, and to limit the Big Seven's power over industry by imposing limitations on their ability to participate in the ownership of nonfinancial firms, neither objective was ever effectively implemented. Specialization never actually occurred for two reasons: the commercial banks were allowed to own controlling stakes in industrial banks, and the creation of new industrial banks was made subject to discretionary authorization by the Ministry of Finance. Thus, of fifteen new industrial banks authorized between 1962 and 1972, nine were owned by the existing commercial banks, and the other six never controlled more than 2.5 percent of total bank deposits.[44] On the other hand, the commercial banks' ability to own stakes in nonfinancial firms was limited only in terms of a ratio to their capital. The banks were thus able to hold onto their industrial portfolios, and even to expand them, by simply issuing new equity.[45]

In addition to the effective limitation to the creation of new banks, competition in the Spanish banking sector was limited in other ways.

---

[43]  Tortella and Jiménez, *Historia del Banco de Crédito Industrial*, p. 198.

[44]  Torrero, "La evolución del sistema financiero," p. 863.

[45]  Such equity issues by the Big Seven were authorized with increasing frequency in the late sixties and became an important new source of extraordinary profits for the banks. The upshot was the *bancarización* of the already defunct Spanish stock market during the sixties, reflected in the share of the banks' own equity (as opposed to their holdings in other firms) in the stock market, which rose from 11.8 percent in 1961 to 39.1 percent in 1974. Given their ability to expand their portfolios of holdings in nonfinancial firms through equity issues, the Big Seven chartered their own industrial banks only to corner that market and to take advantage of the privilege of issuing long-term certificates of deposit (restricted to this category of institutions). See José Miguel Andreu and Carmen Arasa Medina, *Banca universal vs. banca especializada: Un análisis prospectivo* (Madrid: IEP [Ministerio de Hacienda], 1990), pp. 268–71.

First, a discriminatory regulatory treatment was imposed on the domestic savings banks, which in the sixties experienced significant growth in deposits thanks to their rural base. In a clear sign of the subordinate role attributed to these institutions, up to 80 percent of their resources were made subject to a compulsory investment ratio (as compared to the commercial banks' 10 percent). As a consequence, the savings banks' 4 percent increase in the banking sector's total deposits translated into only a 0.4 percent increase in their share of financing to the private sector.[46] Second, the implementation of a 1962 decree authorizing the entry of foreign banks into the Spanish financial market was shelved.[47] Third, access by Spanish firms to international financial markets was sharply curtailed. Instead, when the authorities decided that foreign borrowing was desirable from a current account point of view, the domestic banks themselves were encouraged to raise financing on the Euromarkets for Spanish firms, thus maintaining their position as intermediaries in domestic financing. Perhaps the most blatant expression of the way in which the interventionist regulatory framework supported the Big Seven's cartel, however, was the manner in which interest rates were regulated. While deposit rates were made subject to a maximum, lending rates were regulated in terms of a minimum. This aberrant pattern of interest rate regulation had only one economic rationale, that of supporting the cohesiveness of the banks' cartel in the context of ample liquidity.[48]

The maintenance of the effective status quo in the banking sector and the implicit bargains entailed in the imposition of state discretion over the banking sector's resources both suggest that financial interventionism in Spain was underpinned by a compact of reciprocal consent, in which, to use Richard J. Samuels' words, the banking sector gave up "jurisdiction" in return for "control."[49] The manner in which financial interventionism was instituted (by subsuming monetary policy) meant that state discretion did not interfere with the profit principle of commercial banking. In this sense, it was clearly an alternative to nationalization, which continued to be an objective of the regime's

---

[46]  Torrero, "La evolución del sistema financiero," p. 856.
[47]  The decree was implemented only after the Spanish regime transition.
[48]  It was revised only in 1969, when the orientation of monetary policy turned more restrictive.
[49]  Samuels, *Business of the Japanese State*, pp. 8–9.

national-syndicalist wing. Equally important, the extension of state discretion over credit flows was also an alternative to other, more intrusive forms of statism, and in particular to an expansion of the public sector's role in industrial investment—an expansion that would have limited the Big Seven's role in domestic capital and, with it, their political influence. It is significant that the privileged financing circuits were created at the very same time as the INI's engagement was legally confined to those activities into which private initiative had not ventured, leaving Spain with one of the least significant public sectors in Europe.[50]

## External Constraint, Elites, and the Origins of Reform

Monetary expansion greased the wheels of the Spanish economic miracle, but in the late sixties this strategy came up against a rapidly changing international economic context. Higher international interest rates coincided with growing international capital mobility and an unraveling of the international monetary order. The first signs that the planners' credit-driven growth strategy would not be sustainable in this new environment came with a sharp deterioration in domestic economic activity in late 1967. In that year consumption accounted for the whole increment in final domestic demand, while growth in industrial production came to an abrupt halt after seven continuous years of rapid increases.[51] At the same time, outflows of short-term capital attained such a level as to turn what would have been a basic surplus of $75 million in the balance of payments into a net overall deficit of $140 million.

In line with the existing policy strategy, the Franco government responded by devaluing the peseta by 14 percent. Yet, unlike the case in 1959 when devaluation allowed effective stabilization of domestic prices, the devaluation of 1967 failed to bring domestic demand in line with production. Instead, continued expansion of special rediscount lines caused credit to grow by 20 percent in 1968 and 25 percent in

[50]  Another function that had originally been ascribed to the INI, that of exerting a competitive pressure in oligopolistic product markets, was henceforth discarded. For a discussion of this rollback in the INI's role, see Schwartz and González, *Una historia del INI*, pp. 93–101.
[51]  OECD Economic Surveys, *Spain, 1969* (Paris: Organization for Economic Cooperation and Development, 1970).

1969, as the private banks reduced their liquidity to record lows in order to meet the booming demand for credit. As a result, the devaluation gave way to a strong economic boom during 1968. Meanwhile capital outflows continued to worsen, leading again to a sharp deterioration of the external payments position in 1969.[52]

The events of 1967–69 offered a clear challenge to the cheap-credit growth model whereby the planners had sought to sustain the political regime's viability. Continued capital outflows suggested that the policy of fitting interest rates to growth objectives was untenable in a context of higher international interest rates. The planners proved to be unable to replicate the earlier growth experience. This economic challenge to the planning bureaucracy coincided with a major political scandal in 1969. It came to public attention that MATESA—a Spanish export firm that had been the recipient of more than half of all the privileged export credit granted by the Banco de Crédito Industrial (the most important of the official credit institutions)—was facing default. MATESA became "the sole great politico-economic scandal in forty years of Francoist dictatorship." As one set of observers put it, the affair not only "placed doubt on the central key elements of the economic policy followed after the stabilization plan, and in particular the organization of official credit as it was set forth in the 1962 Law. It also undermined the individuals who had directed and inspired the economic policy of the sixties, and whose common link was assumed to be membership in Opus Dei, an organization to which the management of MATESA was also said to have belonged."[53]

Although the place of the Opus Dei technocracy in the regime was formally affirmed in the cabinet reshuffle of 1969, the scandal, combined with the continued pressure on the Spanish balance of payments in the late sixties, produced a significant shift in policy leadership in favor of central bank authorities. An important factor in this shift had been the appointment of a new Bank of Spain governor in 1965, Mariano Navarro Rubio, a former minister of finance. Though a member of Opus Dei, Navarro Rubio had close ties to the more orthodox

[52]   OECD Economic Surveys, *Spain*, 1971, pp. 5–9; and OECD, *The Capital Market, International Capital Movements, Restrictions on Capital Operations in Spain. Special Report on Capital Markets* (Paris: Organization for Economic Cooperation and Development, 1971), p. 26.

[53]   Tortella and Jiménez, *Historia del Banco de Crédito Industrial*, p. 156.

academic economists who had designed the IMF-backed stabilization plan of 1959, only to be displaced almost immediately by the more politically oriented planners that came to control the Planning Commission. One of Navarro Rubio's first moves as governor was to expand the role of the Bank of Spain's Research Service by recruiting a number of younger academic economists.[54] The presence of this burgeoning elite of reformers in the central bank was reflected in consistent calls for financial reform in the Bank's annual reports starting in 1967.[55]

The continuing pressure of capital outflows became the catalyst that allowed these reformers, backed by the IMF and the OECD, to push through a first reform of interest rates in July 1969. With the stated objective of furthering Spain's "integration with international financial markets," this first reform package linked bank rates to the central bank rediscount rate by way of fixed differentials. However, it failed to establish a connection between the central bank's manipulation of interest rates and the overall rate of monetary expansion. The restrictive effect of the rise in interest rates was therefore effectively negated by a rapid expansion in special rediscount lines, as set out by the Planning Commission's guidelines, forcing authorities to impose a credit ceiling in order to stem capital outflows. This policy incoherence, coming soon after the first reform effort, reflected a standoff between the planning bureaucracy and the emerging elite of policymakers at the central bank. It was not long, however, before the impasse was resolved in the latter's favor. In 1971 a second package of reforms was passed which abolished the special rediscount lines and replaced them by a compulsory investment ratio on bank deposits, thus effectively closing the door on the planners' ability to circumvent the central bank's credit restrictions.

The central bank's new clout, as reflected in the 1971 reform, followed not only from the planners' loss of legitimacy, but also from changes that were taking place within the central bank itself. Most important in this regard were the appointments of Enrique Fuentes Quintana, a highly acclaimed academic economist, to the bank's two boards, and that of Fuentes' protégé, Luis Angel Rojo, to head the

[54]  See Navarro Rubio, *Mis memorias*, p. 304.
[55]  OECD Economic Surveys, *Spain*, 1966, pp. 28–31; Banco de España, *Informe Anual*, 1967, p. 19; 1968, p. 107, 138; 1969, pp. 111–15; and OECD Economic Surveys, *Spain*, 1969, pp. 42–45.

bank's Research Service. Fuentes' and Rojo's appointments signified the arrival of a new, more assertive, and more influential leadership to the central bank. It marked the beginning of a process of thorough internal organizational transformation of the Bank of Spain, the main feature of which was the rapid ascendancy of the Research Service within the central bank's technostructure.[56] The new leadership also brought something else: a clear ideological vision and agenda that clashed directly with the developmental orientation of the regime's technocratic planners. The task of reforming the bank's internal technostructure therefore went hand in hand with that of mapping out an agenda for institutional reform.

As the *Annual Reports* of the Bank of Spain during the seventies suggest, the original objective of this agenda was to secure central bank control over the banking sector's liquid assets, an objective which implied limiting the discretion of other actors within the state over the financial system. Such liquidity control implied a fundamental change in the political use of monetary policy. The necessity of this change followed from what the reformers viewed as the main problem of economic adjustment in Spain, namely the institutionalized use of inflation as a barbiturate for social conflict. Rojo summarized this view in an interview two years prior to his appointment.

> The policy of the government is basically that of covering up holes, a policy of keeping everybody happy. One day the salaries of the workers are increased and the next day the employer gets a special line of credit, so that he won't go bankrupt as a result of the wage increase; with this, the wage increase is destroyed by the price increase. One day protection is granted to one party requesting it, and the next day it is granted to the party requesting counter-protection. In this way tensions are defused. What is the instrument of this policy? Inflation . . . [but] the only thing that inflation achieves is to postpone the problem, which becomes aggravated as time goes by.[57]

[56]  According to Fuentes, Rojo's principal task during the first years following his appointment was that of reforming the technostructure of the Bank of Spain from within, so as to convert it into a powerful monetary authority. This was seen as a key prerequisite for the fundamental change in economic policy orientation that both Fuentes Quintana and Rojo sought. Fuentes Quintana interview, Madrid, summer 1992. For an early statement of Rojo's views, see Rojo, "Política monetaria."

[57]  Quoted in Paniker, Conversaciones en Madrid, p. 162.

Ultimately, liquidity control was thus meant to be a "lever" on the overall character of macroeconomic policy and, in the last analysis, a vehicle for repressing the wage-price spiral to which the technocrats' economic policies had given rise.[58] Achievement of this objective implied the dismantlement of the institutional framework that had given other actors in the state discretion over the financial sector's resources. And this battle could be most effectively approached by tying the central bank's monetary policy objectives into a full-fledged project of financial "liberalization." Such a project, as it began to emerge in the central bank's *Annual Reports*, was easier to promote politically than the reformers' monetary policy agenda because it could be justified in terms of "allocative efficiency" arguments, which were less divisive in their political implications than calls for monetary discipline.

The reform of 1971 was the first salvo in the central bankers' agenda. Along with the end of the special rediscount lines, it also contained a number of institutional reforms, including not only the abolition of the Institute of Medium and Long Term Credit, which had supervised the Official Credit Institutions (an outpost of the Planning Commission), but also the extension of the Bank of Spain's regulatory authority to cover both savings and industrial banks. The combined effect of this early reform was thus to place the central bank in a position to oversee all private credit institutions. And in the clearest statement of the reformers' new position, the Bank of Spain became one of the first European central banks to officially adopt a policy of targeting monetary aggregates rather than interest rates in 1973.

Having significantly limited the planning bureaucracy's ability to interfere with the overall level of monetary expansion, however, the central bank now faced a much more resilient source of resistance from the traditional banking sector. The accounts of some of the principal reformers clearly suggest that their task after 1971 became one of maneuvering around the virtual veto power that the Big Seven held under the Franco regime.[59] The clearest indication of this veto power was the central bankers' inability to promote the creation of a money market in order to gain control over short-term liquidity in the banking sector. When the Bank of Spain created short-term credits in 1974 in

[58]    See Fuentes, "Prólogo," p. liv.
[59]    Interviews with government and central bank officials, Madrid, 1991 and 1992.

order to redress its inability to inject liquidity into the economy in a regular fashion, the banks were able to impose on the reformers a system of proportional distribution of these credits rather than an auction system. This preserved the oligopolistic modus vivendi, and in particular the cornerstone of that modus vivendi, that is, the absence of price competition over the capture of funds. Yet the proportional system also prevented the creation by the banks of a short-term money market, which the central bank would have needed to gauge short-term demand for money. As a result, monetary policy continued to be marred by a pronounced "stop-go" character in the midseventies.[60]

The Big Seven were thus able to obstruct the reformers' policy agenda much more effectively than the planners. Yet whereas the planners could be neutralized by challenging their raison d'être, the banks could not. As the single most important representatives of private domestic capital, the banks could hardly be forgone as policy partners in a neoliberal economic policy strategy such as the reformers' agenda implied. More important, although their ideological project had led the reformers to opt for the Bank of Spain as their institutional base, this choice automatically made them responsible to and dependent on the bankers, who were the central bank's principal institutional clients. It meant that short of nationalization, their political success would depend on establishing a compact of reciprocal consent with the bankers. Yet, the agenda that motivated the reformers clashed head-on with one of the basic elements of prior compacts between the state and the Big Seven, that is, an expansionary monetary policy orientation. In fact, the reformers' objective of reining in credit growth inevitably aggravated the tension between the central bank's two institutional objectives: that of controlling monetary expansion on one hand, and that of ensuring the banking sector's "stability" on the other.[61]

The logic of these policy dilemmas explains what may otherwise appear to be a highly incoherent course of financial reform during the midseventies. This is illustrated best by the liberalization in 1972 of commissions on bank lending. In the context of a banking cartel, this measure made little economic sense, even from the perspective of neoclassical the-

---

[60]    See OECD Surveys, *Spain,* 1974–1977.
[61]    In Spain, where the banking sector had weathered the thirties without any significant crisis and where monetary policy had remained expansionary throughout the postwar period, this was a truly new scenario.

ory. Yet it was a critical sequel to the 1971 reform, because the ending of the special rediscount lines had cut off one of the banks' sources of profits during the sixties, and therefore had undone a key element in the compact underlying interventionism. The liberalization of commissions served in a very concrete way to compensate the banks for the imposition of the coefficient. It meant that while deposit rates continued to be regulated, credit rates on the portion of deposits not covered by the compulsary ratio were deregulated, thus allowing banks to increase their margins.

More than any other measure, the liberalization of commissions foreshadowed the domestic political implications of financial liberalization in Spain. It illustrates a strategy of co-optation by the reformers, with perhaps the underlying calculation that the banks, by accepting some parts of "liberalization," would lend the broader project a measure of de facto validity. This would undermine the banks' ability in the long run to sustain an overtly antireformist stance. Here again, the broadening of the reformers' original policy agenda into a project of "financial liberalization" proved useful. But even more clearly, it suggests the extent to which a reconciliation between the reformers' monetary policy objectives and the political need for reciprocal consent with the banks would have to come at the expense of other groups.

Indeed, what the liberalization of bank commissions did was to support a switch in the banks' business strategy. Instead of receiving a fixed margin on a rapidly expanding pool of liquidity, they would now maintain and indeed expand their oligopolistic profit margins by increasing the cost of financing to their borrowers through the fixing of commissions. This change in business strategy during the seventies was accompanied by the banks' significant divestment from industry.[62] It illustrates the precariousness of the Spanish banking sector's role in industrial finance and the extent to which the guarantee of liquidity had been central to the planners' cheap-credit policy of modernization. That same policy had led Spanish firms to have the lowest self-financing ratios and highest debt ratios in the OECD. In the absence of any other measures to alter the oligopolistic structure of the Spanish financial market, the deregulation of the cost of credit brought to the fore a latent conflict of interests between the financial and real sectors of the economy.

[62]   See Alvaro Cuervo, "Banca, industria y crisis bancaria," and Jordi Blanch et al., "Las relaciones banca-industria y su incidencia sobre la eficacia bancaria," *Economía Industrial,* no. 272 (1990).

*Table 6.3.* Income statements of large Spanish banks (cost and earning margins as percentage of average assets)

| Year | Interest margin | Gross earning margins | Operating costs | Net earnings |
|---|---|---|---|---|
| 1974 | 3.96 | 3.97 | 2.43 | 1.54 |
| • | • | • | • | • |
| • | • | • | • | • |
| 1978 | 4.66 | 5.43 | 3.53 | 1.90 |
| 1979 | 4.33 | 5.53 | 3.49 | 2.04 |
| 1980 | 5.14 | 6.15 | 3.97 | 2.17 |
| 1981 | 5.15 | 6.10 | 4.02 | 2.08 |
| 1982 | 4.82 | 5.82 | 3.80 | 2.03 |
| 1983 | 4.48 | 5.47 | 3.40 | 2.08 |
| 1984 | 4.34 | 5.25 | 3.27 | 1.98 |
| 1985 | 4.18 | 5.22 | 3.28 | 1.94 |
| 1986 | 4.50 | 5.44 | 3.71 | 1.72 |
| 1987 | 4.72 | 6.02 | 3.74 | 2.28 |
| 1988 | 4.73 | 6.07 | 3.46 | 2.61 |
| 1989 | 4.61 | 5.70 | 3.29 | 2.41 |
| 1990 | 4.61 | 5.62 | 3.29 | 2.33 |

*Sources:* 1974–1979: Antonio Torrero, *Tendencias del sistema financiero español* (Madrid: Ediciones H. Blume, 1982); 1980: *Bank Profitability 1980–1984* (Paris: OECD, 1987); 1981–1990: *Bank Profitability 1981–1990* (Paris: OECD, 1992).

This conflict was sharply aggravated by another "liberalization" measure, namely that of bank branching in 1974. In the absence of price competition, this measure, which seems to have been favored by the banks as a way to increase their profits, led to an explosion of bank branches. Fed by each bank's efforts to maintain its share of total deposits within the cartel, the expansion of branches was such that it made Spain the most heavily overbranched country in the OECD.[63] The result was a sharp increase in the banking sector's costs, which was largely passed on to borrowers. Table 6.3 reveals the widening gap between operating costs and gross income margins as well as the rise and subsequent stability of the net income margin. Thus, as the Spanish economy was absorbing the effects of the first oil shock, the course of "liberalizing reform" allowed the banks to shift their burgeoning costs onto their clients, sharply aggravating the burden of adjustment for Spanish firms.[64]

[63]    At the end of 1985, Spain had one commercial bank branch for every 2,300 inhabitants, compared to 3,790 in Britain and 5,500 in France. "Old World Banks in a New Age," *The Economist*, August 22, 1987, p. 73.
[64]    Antonio Torrero, *Tendencias del sistema financiero español* (Madrid: Ediciones H. Blume, 1982), pp. 23–30.

### Financial Reform and the Political Transition

The events of the early seventies greatly strengthened the influence of the Bank of Spain within Spanish economic policy-making. That influence was further bolstered by the regime transition, owing to the transition government's need for economic expertise in dealing with a much altered economic landscape, one in which the threat of runaway inflation figured as a major obstacle to the political task at hand. The clearest indication of the central bank's new status came with the appointment by Adolfo Suárez of Enrique Fuentes Quintana, the principal mentor of the young reformers in the Bank of Spain, as vice-president for economic affairs. Fuentes was assigned the critical task of fashioning a government economic program that would serve as the basis for social consensus during the transition between political regimes. This program, centering on an incomes policy agreement to limit nominal wage increases to 20 percent and the growth of the money supply to 17 percent, was enshrined in the Pactos de la Moncloa, which were signed by all the major opposition parties in October 1977.

With the appointment of Fuentes, the central bank's policy preferences, and in particular its agenda of financial liberalization, were assured the highest priority in the transition process. Financial reform was thus included as one of the central pieces in the declaratory statement of the Pactos. However, the principal package of financial reform measures designed in the Bank of Spain during the previous years had already been passed, in the form of two executive orders, less than five weeks after the first democratic elections of 1977 and two months before the signing of the Pactos.

While there were other circumstances that contributed to place financial reform on the government's agenda,[65] both the timing and course of the actual reforms reflect the importance of the reformers' original agenda, and in particular, their objective of securing the central bank's control over the credit system. First, the timing of the reform package, soon after the first elections, was meant to ensure the market-oriented thrust of the reform process at a time when the main opposition party, the Spanish Socialist Workers' Party (PSOE), still endorsed nationaliza-

---

[65] These include the deteriorating financial situation of Spanish firms in the year leading up to the first elections and the new voice attained by foreign bankers, who provided critical financing to the Suárez government in 1977.

tion of the banking system. The reforms also would preclude a wider parliamentary involvement in the formulation of reform, at a time when the main challenge for the reformers was controlling the inflationary impact of the transition process. In this context the objective of limiting political discretion over the credit system gained a new urgency. The political logic of the timing was spelled out by Fuentes in a recent account of the reform process: "The intention was to catapult the financial reform process far enough so that the advance would be irreversible. From then on, the timing of subsequent steps toward greater freedom and competition could be debated, but it would be impossible to take a step backward without incurring a very high cost and highly criticizable contradictions.[66]

Although the reformers' pursuit of liberalization at the high point of the transition was meant to secure the central bank's agenda for reform and preempt alternative visions, it also had another effect. It rendered the reform initiative hostage to the imperative of assuring the banking sector's cooperation with the transition government's economic program. This constraint did not figure prominently in the reformers' decision because they believed that the success of their reform agenda hinged critically on their ability to establish a working alliance with the bankers. Again, Fuentes' account is instructive: "I was convinced that these liberalization measures were a critical part of the adjustment policies that the country would have to apply to get out of the crisis, and I was even more convinced that, without the support of the Spanish bankers and the heads of the Savings banks . . . those reforms, no matter how adequate they were, would not become a legal reality or inspire the daily practice of the Spanish financial system."[67]

In fact, the actual reform package adopted by the government was formulated during a series of closed meetings between Fuentes and the heads of the Big Seven in the six months preceding the first elections. These meetings centered on the government's imperative of securing the banks' support for the Pactos de la Moncloa and of ensuring that the banks would not undermine the achievements of the wage and price agreements with the opposition. The meetings were marked by the banks' initially strong opposition to the reformers' liberaliza-

---

[66]    Fuentes, "Prólogo," pp. lx–lxii.
[67]    Ibid., p. lxii.

tion agenda.[68] The timing of the negotiations thus inevitably created a linkage between the banks' support for the government's economic program and the content of the financial reform package.

The outcome of the negotiations illustrates the reformers' efforts to advance the central bank's agenda and at the same time establish a new compact of reciprocal consent with the bankers. The principal characteristics of the 1977 reform package was that it salvaged, in the face of significant resistance from the bankers, those aspects of reform that were most critical to the Bank of Spain's original agenda: achieving greater technical control over the banking system's liquid assets, and dismantling the institutional structure of privileged financing that had given other state actors discretion in the financial system. The package included the deregulation of interest rates,[69] the creation of an auction system for the allocation of short-term Bank of Spain adjustment credits to the banking sector, and the imposition of a reduction schedule for the dismantlement of the compulsory investment ratio. It also drastically reduced the number of sectors that qualified to receive financing through the compulsory coefficient, and abolished the Ministry of Finance body that had decided which users could be included under the compulsory coefficient.[70]

In contrast, the reform package of 1977 conspicuously failed to reform the structure of the Spanish credit market in a manner that would have infused it with a greater measure of competition. This failure is particularly apparent in three reform areas. First, although a decree was passed in 1978 allowing some foreign banks to enter the domestic market, heavy restrictions were placed on these institutions, forcing them to raise a large share of their resources on the interbank market, over which the Big Seven exercised a high measure of control.[71] The importance of

---

[68] *El Pais*, March 9 and 11, 1977.

[69] Nevertheless, because of the banks' resistance this measure was initially limited to bank deposits and lending at terms of more than one year. It extended to operations at terms of more than six months in 1981, and only in the late eighties to all operations.

[70] The function of supervising the banks' compliance with the compulsory coefficients was also transferred to the Bank of Spain.

[71] This included restriction on the number of offices that foreign banks were allowed to open and on the amount of resources that they could raise in Spain. At the same time, authorization for entry of individual foreign banks remained subject to the discretion of the Ministry of Finance and the Bank of Spain. See Daniel Alvarez Pastor and Fernando Eguidazu, "La banca extranjera en España: Régimen legal," *Información Comercial Española*, no. 545 (1979). For a more detailed discussion of the consequences of these measures, see Sofia Pérez, *Banking on Privilege: The Politics of Spanish Financial Reform* (Ithaca: Cornell University Press, 1997), chap. 5.

these limitations was illustrated over the following years when several attempts by foreign banks to exert a competitive downward pressure on investment credit rates were foiled after the Big Seven raised the cost of the foreigners' resources in the interbank market.[72] Foreign banks were thus precluded from exerting the kind of competitive pressure that would have produced real change in the financing conditions faced by all but the largest Spanish firms. This resulted eventually in the conversion of the foreign banks to the Spanish rules of the game. They started exploiting oligopolistic market conditions as the only way to make their Spanish operations profitable.

The failure to alter the oligopolistic structure of the Spanish financial market was also evident in a second area of reform, that of the official credit institutions. Despite repeated reports of plans by Ministry of Finance officials to reorganize these institutions in such a way as to allow them to compete with the Big Seven, such a reorganization would not take place until a decade and a half later, when the prospect of European financial integration forced the government to act.[73] The third area in which the reform effort of the transition period failed was capital market reform. Despite the creation of a commission to study capital market reform, no significant attempt to enhance the role of the capital market was made until well over a decade later. This failure is particularly telling because the Anglo-Saxon model of industrial finance, which theoretically informed the Bank of Spain's financial reform program, attributes the critical function of providing long-term investment finance to the capital market. The complete inaction in this area is explained by the reformers' decision to curb the impact of disintermediation on the banking sector.[74]

These failures followed from the reformers' political aim of establishing a new compact of reciprocal consent with the banking sector. Such a

---

[72] The Spanish banks could foil the foreigners because, acting as a cartel, they were able to impose significant increases in the interbank money rates in response to the foreign banks' announcement of rate cuts. See for example *El Pais*, August 19 and September 13, 1984, and August 8, 1985.

[73] Jaime Requeijo, "Los circuitos privilegiados de financiación y la reforma del Crédito Oficial," *Información Comercial Española,* no. 596 (1983), p. 79; and *Mercado Financiero*, September 1982, p. 30.

[74] José María García Hermoso and Sebastián Ubirría Zubizarreta, "Reforma y transformación del mercado de valores," *Papeles de Economía Española*, no. 44 (1990), pp. 137–38. Disintermediation refers to a decrease in the proportion of savings in any given financial system that is intermediated (i.e., channeled into investment) by financial institutions.

compact was believed to be necessary in order to establish a working alliance that would facilitate the central bankers' institutional agenda in monetary policy. The consequence, however, of the compact's unbalanced approach to reform was a sharp deterioration in the financial conditions faced by Spanish firms in the late seventies. Despite the Suárez government's prodding in 1978–81, the banks repeatedly refused to lower the cost of credit to industry.[75] The increase in financial costs was such that starting in 1978 Spanish firms became subject to a negative leverage effect (i.e., the average cost of external financing exceeded the average return on investment), a situation that lasted for more than a decade.[76]

## Socialist Victory and Reform in the 1980s

The aggravation in the financial conditions that Spanish industry faced following the liberalization package of 1977 led, during the final two years of the Unión de Centro Democrático (UCD) government, to a halt in the reformers' agenda. The phasing out of the compulsory investment ratio had to be halted and the amount of credit extended by the official credit institutions had to be increased to compensate for the virtual disappearance of medium-term investment finance coming from the private banks. The setback, which was closely related to the UCD's growing internal factionalism and increasingly precarious parliamentary hold, proved to be temporary, however. The elections of 1982 brought an end to this situation by giving the Spanish Socialist Workers' Party (PSOE) an absolute majority in the Cortes.

Contrary to the expectation of some, the new Socialist government bolstered the central bank's position of policy leadership. This was apparent in several early appointments made by Felipe González, most

[75] In 1979 the government promised unsuccessfully to get the banks to lower their credit rates to industry by 2 percent. In 1982 again, negotiations to get the banks to provide more favorable credit terms failed. See *El Pais*, May 24, 1979, and *Mercado Financiero*, February 1982, pp. 14–15.

[76] Alvaro Cuervo, "Análisis económico-financiero de la empresa Española," *Papeles de Economía Española*, no. 3 (1980). The negative leverage effect was interrupted for only a couple of years in the late eighties before reappearing in 1989. See Juan Antonio Maroto Acín, "La situación empresarial en España (1982–1989)," *Cuadernos de Información (FIES)*, no. 44/45 (1990).

notably the reappointment of José Ramón Alvarez Rendueles as governor of the Bank of Spain and the appointment of Miguel Boyer, a prominent young recruit to the Bank of Spain's Research Service, as minister
of finance. Indeed, Boyer's appointment, and his eventual replacement
by Carlos Solchaga, another member of Angel Rojo's entourage, reflect
the consolidation of the central bank's policy leadership after the 1982
change in government. A number of factors served as precedents for this
consolidation: the moderation of the Socialist party over the previous
years, the virtual hegemony of the central bank's views among Spanish
academic economists, the demonstration effect of the French U-turn of
1983, and the growing dimensions of a crisis in the Spanish banking
sector itself.[77] The consequence was that financial reform under the
Socialists continued to be driven by the central bank's policy priorities
and shaped by the reformers' relationship with the Big Seven.

In the early eighties, the reformers' agenda and the politics of the
compact came to center increasingly on the imperative of finding an
orthodox method of financing a budget deficit that had gone from less
than 1 percent of the GDP in 1977 to 5.8 percent in 1982. The search
for orthodox deficit financing was closely linked to another central
bank objective, namely that of creating a money market in short-term
government securities through which it could control short-term liquidity more effectively. Before 1982, the banks had successfully prevented
the authorities from issuing securities that would compete with their
capture of short-term deposits. This had forced the Bank of Spain to
first monetize the public deficit and then offset this monetization
through the issuance of its own certificates of monetary regulation to
the banks. This arrangement perpetuated the central bank's legal obli-
gation to monetize the Treasury's shortfall; it also made the government
subject to an oligopsony, since the auctions for Bank of Spain certificates were restricted by law to the commercial and savings banks.[78]

The change in government, and the new synchrony between the
Ministry of Finance and the central bank, led to a more assertive attempt

---

[77]    See Pérez, *Banking on Privilege*, chap. 6.
[78]    In the early eighties this became a potent impediment for monetary policy, as the growing
budget deficit forced the Bank of Spain to raise the return on its certificates to over 20 percent. An earlier effort in 1982 to have the Treasury issue bills in its own public auctions was
marred by the banks' decision to boycott these auctions. See "La reforma de un fracaso,"
*Mercado Financiero,* October 1982.

by the reformers to find a way out of this conundrum. The solution was enshrined in a new reform of the compulsory coefficients late in 1983. The original investment coefficient, which the banks were obliged to cover with low-rate credits to privileged users, was further reduced, and a new compulsory coefficient was created obliging the banks to invest 12 percent of their deposits in treasury bills (*pagarés del tesoro* or PTs).[79] What had once been an instrument of privileged financing for industry was thus transformed into an instrument of orthodox deficit financing. This ended the central bank's inability to avoid monetizing the deficit.

The new coefficient was interpreted by some as a return to interventionism and therefore as a setback to the reformers' agenda. Yet, it reflected a new accommodation between the central bank and the Big Seven which was consistent with the pattern of accommodations that had characterized the reform process from the start. The coefficient was drafted by Bank of Spain officials in consultation with the private banks. And, in the domestic economic context of the early eighties, which was characterized by a sharp drop in credit demand, it constituted a nonbinding constraint on the banks. This is illustrated most conspicuously by the fact that for most of the time that it was in effect (1984–87) the banks held PTs well in excess of the required proportion.[80] Indeed, by shifting their resources into PTs during the mideighties, the banks were able in effect to intermediate the disintermediation process that the expansion of a public debt market normally holds in store. This allowed them to sustain oligopolistic interest margins at a point in the economic cycle when the collapse in credit demand would have otherwise forced them to reduce their credit rates (see Table 6.3). Lastly, the new coefficient also represented an alternative to a more assertive attempt by the authorities to raise deficit financing more directly from savers.

The "interlude" in the liberalization process in the mideighties thus reflects an attempt by the reformers to protect the banks' position as intermediaries in the Spanish financial system at a time when this was

---

[79]   At the same time, the already existing reserve requirement ratio, which obliged the banks to deposit a share of their funds with the central bank, was increased. The share of this ratio that was remunerated by the central bank was also increased.

[80]   For the period 1984 through 1986, the banks held an average of 51 percent of the total PTs issued by the Treasury, while the coefficient obliged them to hold an average share of 41 percent. See Carlos Contreras, "Deuda pública, desintermediación, e inovación financiera en España," *Papeles de Economía Española*, no. 33 (1987).

being challenged by the growing financial needs of the public sector. Such an attempt is also reflected in the conspicuous postponement of capital market reform, in the central bank's imposition of a moratorium on new foreign bank authorizations during these years, and in the manner in which the banking crisis of the early eighties was resolved. With few exceptions, the large number of smaller industrial banks that had to be taken into receivership by the Deposit Guarantee Fund were reprivatized not through an open auction system, but in the context of a closed negotiation table consisting of the minister of finance and the Big Seven.[81] Through this process, the Big Seven were able to maintain their share of the banking sector's deposits at a time when this share was being threatened by the expansion of the domestic savings banks.[82]

## EC Membership and the Politics of Financial Reform

The accommodation between the central bankers' monetary policy objectives and the interests of the banking cartel under the first Socialist term in office meant that, as in the previous decade, financial deregulation and the dismantlement of the privileged financing circuits occurred in the context of a largely unaltered financial market structure. The consequence of this accommodation was that Spanish firms continued to endure inordinate financial costs, as reflected in the continuance throughout the mideighties of the negative leverage effect.[83] This situation contributed to the deepening of the Spanish industrial recession and to the stagnation in private investment in the mideighties, at a time when the world economy was on its way to recovery.[84] The watershed in this economic scenario would come with Spain's accession to the European Community in early 1986.

[81] In some cases, such as that of the RUMASA banks, five smaller banks were included, but their share of participation in the privatization was limited to 25 percent. Thus, despite their strong expression of interest, foreign banks were allowed to bid only on those few banks that had been rejected by the domestic cartel.

[82] According to one estimate, the total cost of the crisis was Pta. 1,581 billion, of which the private banks contributed Pta. 365 billion, and the state Pta. 1,216 billion. Alvaro Cuervo, "La crisis bancaria española de los años setenta," in Pedro Tedde de Lorca et al., *El sistema financiero de la economía española* (Madrid: Economistas, 1989), p. 54.

[83] Maroto, "La situación empresarial en España."

[84] Gross fixed investment remained negative throughout 1984, and unemployment continued to rise through the first half of 1985, peaking at 22 percent.

EC membership altered the dynamics of domestic financial reform in a number of ways. First, the prospect of a single European financial market after 1992 created a new exogenous stimulus for financial reform, clearly distinct from the original central bank agenda that had driven the Spanish reform effort up to this point. The prospect of 1992 led the government to act on the long neglected task of capital market reform. Such reform had become necessary if Spain was not to fall too far behind the dramatic over-hauls that were occurring elsewhere in Europe. Thus, after a decade of delay, the 1978 proposals of the Commission for the Study of Capital Market Reform were finally addressed in the Capital Markets Law of July 1988.[85] After years of limiting the competitive effects of credit and interest rate liberalization, the 1992 deadline also impelled the authorities to prepare the national banking sector for greater international competition.

A second effect of EC membership on the course of domestic financial reform was more indirect but equally important, if not more so. It derived from the tremendous impact that membership had on the level of domestic economic activity. EC membership ended the overextended recession afflicting the nonfinancial sectors of the Spanish economy. Recession gave way to a demand boom over the course of 1986, driven by foreign investment. This reduced the nonconstraining character of the Treasury coefficient, and it increased the banks' interest in freeing their resources, which led to the dismantlement of the remaining compulsory coefficients in 1987 and 1989.[86] At the same time, foreign investment became a palliative for resolving the long neglected prob-

---

[85] This law abolished the legal monopoly of state-licensed *agentes de bolsa*, who charged fixed commissions on trading, and replaced these with incorporated brokers and dealers. It also created a new Capital Markets Commission to regulate the market according to a new set of principles of conduct, including the prohibition of insider trading practices. At the same time, the different stock markets in different Spanish cities were electronically integrated, and the Bank of Spain created a book-entry system for the secondary market, thus ending the physical transfer of securities. See the *Economist*, August 1987, and García Hermoso and Ubirría Zubizarreta, "Reforma y transformación."

[86] In 1987 the compulsory investment coefficient, which had already been sharply reduced in 1985, was reduced to 1 percent of the bank's resources, while the PT coefficient was reduced to 10 percent. Finally, in 1989, both of these coefficients were abolished. This left only the reserve coefficient, which during the eighties had also been used as a means of deficit financing. In 1990, this last coefficient was reduced from 18 percent to 5 percent, rendering it a more orthodox reserve requirement. See Raimundo Poveda, "El coeficiente de inversion, 1985–1986," and Poveda, "La reforma del coeficiente de inversion de marzo de 1987," *Papeles de Economía Española,* no. 32 (1987), as well as Rafael Repullo, "La reforma de los coeficientes bancarios en España," *Papeles de Economía Española,* no. 43 (1990).

lems of the Spanish industrial sector. Thus, according to one estimate, the proportion of Spanish manufacturing industry in foreign hands rose from 17.9 percent in 1985 to 31.5 percent in 1990.[87]

The corollary of this implicit strategy of falling back on foreign investment was that the "thinking" behind financial reform became dissociated, even more so than before, from concerns about the needs of nonfinancial firms. Instead, the reformers' attention after 1986 focused sharply on the banking sector's ability to compete in an integrated European financial market after 1992. Thus, while a large share of Spanish industry was being sold off to foreigners, the government (led by the Bank of Spain) set out on an active attempt to promote a set of mergers among the Big Seven. The strong relationship that the reformers had fostered with the banks in the preceding decade, undertaken to promote liberalization, thus ironically set the stage for a new form of financial nationalism in the late 1980s which contrasts sharply with the government's attitude toward the sale of industry to foreign interests.

Paradoxically, however, it was this attempt by the central bank to strengthen the domestic financial sector that produced the greatest degree of strain among the members of the Spanish financial community. In its eagerness to prepare the sector for 1993, the central bank in 1987 endorsed a hostile takeover of Banesto, one of the so-called mammoth banks, by the more efficient and dynamic Banco de Bilbao. The attempt, which broke all the rules of the cartel's modus vivendi, was foiled by Banesto, but it eventually resulted in a defensive merger by two other mammoths (Banco Central and Banco Hispano Americano) following the merger of Banco de Bilbao and Banco de Vizcaya, two more dynamic banks that the central bank had hoped to use as its instruments. Though the central bank was eventually to intervene in the sector through its takeover of Banesto, which faced default in early 1994, most observers of the Spanish banking scene concur that the bank mergers that did take place were guided less by efficiency criteria than by fears of hostile takeovers.

In the face of the authorities' failure in 1987 to impose their designs on the future composition of the banking sector, the default strategy pursued at the turn of the decade was one of continuing to limit the level

---

[87]    José Antonio Martínez Serrano and Rafael Myro, "La penetración del capital extranjero en la industria española," *Moneda y Crédito,* no. 194 (1992), p. 157.

of competition in the banking sector while prodding the banks to modernize their management and to seek international business partners. By doing so, the authorities allowed the banks to exploit their existing privileged position to the fullest, so they could enter the single European market with the highest level of capitalization possible. This approach was encouraged by the realization, in the late eighties, that the banks' main actual source of staying power was, paradoxically, that which also made them least cost-efficient, i.e., their prodigal branch networks, which created an inordinate barrier to entry into the retail banking market for foreign banks.[88] As a consequence, the Spanish banks focused their efforts less on cutting costs than on shifting their lending activities towards those sectors that were least sensitive to high interest rates, i.e., households and construction.[89] Government policy in the late eighties lent support to this banking strategy not only by continuing to restrict the operations of foreign banks but also in more subtle ways, such as through unfavorable tax treatment of collective investment funds, which slowed the process of disintermediation. This allowed the banks to protect their position as the most important institutional investors in the Spanish capital market, which remained considerably narrower than elsewhere in Europe.[90] The result of such policies was that the Spanish commercial banks continued to have the highest profit margins in the EC by the end of the decade, despite their very high operating costs (see Table 6.4).

In the late eighties and early nineties, Spanish economic policy was thus characterized by a stark contrast between the authorities' efforts to protect sovereignty in the financial sector and the wholesale reliance on foreign investment to mitigate the problems of the nonfinancial sectors. In time, this policy logic was extended to the macroeconomic level, leading to heavy reliance on shorter term cap-

---

[88]   The profitability of most foreign banks remained well below expectations, leading some of them to withdraw at the end of the decade. See Philip Sington, "Spain: Defending El Dorado," *Euromoney*, July 1989.

[89]   Antonio Torrero, "La formación de los tipos de interés y los problemas actuales de la economía española," *Economistas,* no. 39 (1989).

[90]   Despite large inflows of foreign capital in the late eighties, the capitalization (total value of domestic securities as a percentage of gross domestic product) of the Madrid Stock Exchange represented only 33 percent of GDP in 1989, as compared to 67 percent for the Frankfurt stock market, 68 percent for Paris, 67 percent for Milan, 143 percent for the U.K., 153 percent for Tokyo, and 82 percent for New York. Based on OECD monthly financial statistics, April 1992.

*Table 6.4.* Costs and margins of large commercial banks as percentage of average balance sheet total (1990)

|  | Spain | France | Germany | Belgium | Italy | Netherlands | U.K. |
|---|---|---|---|---|---|---|---|
| Gross earnings | 5.62 | 2.39 | 3.56 | 1.75 | 4.16 | 2.69 | 5.03 |
| Interest margin | 4.36 | 1.79 | 2.31 | 1.35 | 2.91 | 1.92 | 3.01 |
| Other income | 1.26 | 0.60 | 1.24 | 0.40 | 1.25 | 0.77 | 2.02 |
| Operating costs | 3.29 | 1.56 | 2.25 | 1.21 | 2.72 | 1.86 | 3.37 |
| Net earnings | 2.33 | 0.83 | 1.31 | 0.54 | 1.44 | 0.83 | 1.66 |
| Profits before taxes | 1.72 | 0.31 | 0.83 | 0.33 | 0.90 | 0.51 | 0.65 |
| Profits after taxes | 1.22 | 0.36 | 0.49 | 0.27 | 0.70 | 0.38 | 0.34 |

*Source: Bank Profitability 1981–1990* (Paris: OECD, 1992).

ital inflows to finance the growing current account and domestic budget deficits, in particular after the international boom of the late eighties gave way to renewed recession in 1989. Such capital inflows in turn came increasingly to depend on high Spanish interest rate differentials with other EC countries, and on the imported credibility that EMS membership conferred to the peseta. They also subjected the Spanish economy to a prolonged period of heavy currency overvaluation, which left its mark in the form of slow productivity increases and a dramatic fall in the international competitiveness of Spanish firms. These excesses were revealed in the aftermath of the EMS crisis of 1992–93, when the Spanish economy was once more, as in the mideighties disproportionally hard hit by international recession.

## Spanish Financial Reform in Comparative Perspective

The chapters in this book illustrate the almost universal trend, over the last two decades, toward the abandonment of state-directed credit allocation in formerly interventionist states, lending support to the argument that domestic financial liberalization is the result of systemic changes in the world economy. Yet, they also suggest that there has been great variation not only in the patterns that reform has followed but, even more important, in the domestic economic and political motivations for reform. Indeed, perhaps the most remarkable aspect of the trend toward financial liberalization is the extent to which a common set of economic ideas has served as the vehicle for reforms responding to significantly different sets of domestic economic problems. Nevertheless, comparison of the case studies offered here suggests a number of insights about the postwar sequence of regulation followed by deregulation (or reregulation) of credit allocation.

First, despite the differing domestic political and economic contexts of the countries considered, there are important similarities in their postwar move to state-directed credit allocation. One observes, for example, striking similarities in indigenous policy instruments, such as between the Korean policy loans, the Mexican *cajones*, and the Spanish *coeficientes*, or between the French and Spanish Treasury circuits and the use of the postal savings system for public finance in Japan. More important, other chapters corroborate the point made above about Spain: the construction of a domestic regulatory framework of selective credit allocation went hand in hand with a specific policy orientation, i.e., what has been termed a policy of cheap credit. This policy orientation generally coincided with a "developmental" or "volontariste" policy philosophy which rejected economic orthodoxy, in that it aimed to promote investment above all else, particularly above price stability. One of its by-products was a relatively high and, in most cases, widely fluctuating domestic inflation rate in the fifties and sixties. Yet, if monetary expansion was to produce lasting growth, countries pursuing such a policy of cheap credit needed to address the foreign exchange gap of their economies. Sooner or later governments became aware of the need to tie the fate of their economies to that of the booming world economy, especially since, as Loriaux argues, the postwar international order was exceptionally tolerant of monetary expansion in secondary economies.

Within such an overarching policy orientation, instruments of selective credit allocation served two critical purposes. The first was that of resolving the imbalance between credit demand and supply that followed from low administered interest rates. This was necessary to harness a fundamentally expansionary monetary course in such a way as to make it compatible with balance of payments constraints and, in most cases, currency convertibility. Here selectivity was, as Sylvia Maxfield argues, intended as an instrument of monetary policy. In the Mexican case, where foreign creditors held an important card in economic development, and where foreign assistance was not as gratuitous (tied to U.S. political interests) as elsewhere, selective credit allocation was therefore promoted by the central bank. But the Spanish hiatus of 1959 illustrates the limits of "going it alone" in an uncontrolled course of expansionary monetary policy. Selective credit regulation came hand in hand with the abandonment of an autarkic policy orientation in Spain, because the Franco regime's technocratic planners wanted to emulate the French formula of liberalizing trade relations while maintaining an expansive monetary policy stance.

Selectivity was thus an alternative to more orthodox methods of reconciling national policy objectives with external constraints. But state discretion over credit allocation also served a second objective. It facilitated the pattern of capital allocation which government officials deemed necessary for economic transformation, and which the markets could not reliably produce. It is this second rationale which was most often used to justify the introduction of interventionist credit regulation, and which gives rise to the association between financial interventionism and state capacity or strength in the political science literature. This statist or neomercantilist rationale, however, tended also to be related to the choice in favor of using monetary expansion to promote growth. State-directed credit allocation was meant to gear resources in such a way as to have two effects: expand productive capacity sufficiently to neutralize the inflationary impact of monetary expansion, and produce the change in trade performance that was required to satisfy the foreign exchange requirements of rapid modernization driven by monetary expansion.

The two functions of selective credit allocation (its monetary policy function and its industrial policy function) were thus not, in principle, at cross-purposes but rather were meant to support each other. Their distinction, however, is an important one, because it points to two different political motivations that governments had for pursuing a cheap credit growth strategy. These may be described as, on the one hand, the neomercantilist motivation so often associated with financial interventionism and with (as Meredith Woo-Cumings argues) power politics, and on the other hand the domestic political motivation of using credit expansion in order to meet all demands and ensure domestic political stability. The latter is what has been described above as the political strategy of inflation. The balance between the two types of motives, or the extent to which cheap credit was used to defuse social conflict in different countries, is important in understanding subsequent developments in these countries and in explaining differences in the politics of financial liberalization.

One clear contrast that emerges is between Japan on one hand and the two European countries on the other. The Japanese ability to translate cheap credit into growing trade surpluses, mirrored in the declining demand for funds by Japanese firms and in the excess savings of the Japanese economy, is fundamental to Kent Calder's argument that institutional reform in Japan has been motivated by changes in the interests of different domestic sectors. Such an interest-based explanation is not applicable to state-led financial liberalization in France and Spain, which was driven primarily by monetary policy concerns. On the other hand, in the two European countries a strong argument can be made that the pursuit of a cheap credit strategy followed from an early decision to eschew economic stabilization for the sake of political stabilization. This political purpose informed the logic of both industrial policy and of financial regulation in these countries.

A second insight offered by comparison of the case studies is the extent to which any systemic explanation of financial liberalization must make allowance for the role of domestic conditions. While the Spanish case corroborates the links drawn by Loriaux between change in the international economic environment, domestic monetary policy objectives, and regulatory reform, it also highlights the extent to which this link can depend on domestic political factors. In Spain, the changing international environment played itself out as a shift within the policymaking elite that favored the authority of the central bank over economic policy and weakened that of other state actors. But this shift was well under way by the late sixties, before changes in the international environment had taken on a compelling character. It required the pre-existence of a cohesive group of reformers with a well-defined agenda for institutional reform. And it was strongly aided by factors pertaining to the political regime transition in Spain, such as the loss of legitimacy of the Franco regime's technocratic planners and the association between state interventionism and political authoritarianism in recent Spanish history.

The shift within the domestic economic policy elite explains the early commitment to the principles of financial liberalization in Spain. When combined with the Bank of Spain's efforts to establish a compact of reciprocal consent with the banks, it also explains the Spanish pattern of proceeding with credit deregulation without significant reform of the financial market. This contrasts markedly with the French attempt in the seventies and early eighties to maintain the basic principle of state discretion over credit allocation—in an effort to control inflation without giving up control over interest rates—and with the subsequent comprehensive and simultaneous approach to credit deregulation and capital market reform in that country after 1983. On the other hand, the difference in economic fallout—in particular, the prolonged negative leverage effect in Spain—illustrates the extent to which cheap central bank rediscounting in Spain had served to paper over a latent conflict between an oligopolistic private financial sector and a highly dependent industrial sector in earlier decades.

Lastly, the early commitment in Spain to the philosophy of financial liberalization, and its relationship to a shift within the state elite in favor of the central bank, reflect the extent to which the abandonment of financial interventionism has involved an ideological change concerning the proper role of monetary policy. This ideological shift emerged in Spain as a reaction to the Franco regime's strategy of inflation. In France it was only fully espoused after the protracted failure to limit inflation by other means. It involved, at heart, the use of monetary policy rather than collective bargaining mechanisms to discipline wages. And it was best promoted politically by way of neoclassical "allocative efficiency" arguments that emphasized the collective good to be gained through deregulation, as opposed to the distributional implications of imposing austerity. What is important is that—in a climate of strong inflationary expectations in which the goal of policy became that of repressing rather than channeling monetary expansion—state authorities gained an interest in extricating themselves from credit allocation and in binding themselves to the market. They did so because the old interventionist frameworks of financial regulation politicized the task of disinflation.

It is this political calculation that seems to explain the Spanish Socialists' embrace of the central bankers' policies and the French Socialists' about-face in the mideighties. The irony is, of course, that the economic success stories that have so altered the international context as to turn Europe's leeway for monetary expansion in the sixties into international constraint during the eighties do not demonstrate, as the new economic orthodoxy would tell us, the failure of a cheap-credit strategy but rather, as Woo-Cumings argues, its very success. The difference between the European and the East Asian cases would thus appear to lie not so much in the economics of financial regulation as in its politics.

# Capital, the State, and Uneven Growth in the International Political Economy

## Michael Loriaux

In Chapter 1, I speculated that the abandonment of credit activism is part of the broader global trend toward liberalizing reform in financial affairs. The quasi-simultaneity of credit policy reform in all five cases nourishes the suspicion that some global logic is at work. I surveyed two hypothetical characterizations of that logic. The first stressed the role of market and political pressures engendered by the desire or the need to improve efficiency in the short-term allocation of capital. The second stressed the role of structural pressures engendered by policy shifts in powerful countries, especially the United States.

In this chapter I argue that the evidence forces us to recognize the importance of U.S. policy in fomenting the need for liberalizing reforms. This is not to deny that the desire for (or the requirement of) greater short-term allocative efficiency did not weigh on policy. But politicians are constantly challenged to square the circle and to supply incompatible goods to their societies. The pursuit of short-term allocative efficiency is not always compatible with the development of clientelistic ties with chosen sectors of political society, or with the development of military strength. It is a rare government that can pursue all three goals simultaneously. In the five cases examined here, the apparent and simultaneous preference of all five governments for one goal (short-term allocative efficiency) over others (which, if not abandoned, were at least assigned to second rank) appears largely to have been a response to direct and indirect pressures originating in policy decisions made in the United States.

The case for such pressures would be less compelling if one could invoke Occam's razor and claim that the more parsimonious, market-based explanation must be preferred if it succeeds in providing an "adequate" explanation of the "facts." This line of argument would make it possible, without further examination, to dismiss external political or structural pressures as having done nothing more than facilitate an outcome that was already made imperative by the internal logic of the market. But the parsimonious, economistic explanation deals "adequately" with only the "stylized fact"—to borrow an economist's term—of liberalization in the abstract. The economist's parsimonious explanation is less helpful to the investigator who confronts and tries to make narrative sense of voluminous masses of archival evidence. The fact that some reference to U.S. policy is indispensable to the narrative is, moreover, of central theoretical importance. It empowers the critical observer of political economy to question the ontology of the economist's categories of thought; and it justifies the appeal to Marx, Polanyi, and others who portray the market as the manifestation of power relations. The mechanisms that the economist analyzes are not to be treated uncritically as a "phenomenon of nature" but rather as mechanisms characteristic of a particular sociopolitical order, imposed and sustained by power relations, whose ethical and philosophical foundations can be contested.

The need to incorporate U.S. policy into the explanation of liberalizing reform raises a second issue of theoretical importance. It nourishes the suspicion that another force is at work in the international political economy which is influencing change in U.S. policy. That force is uneven growth. Differentials in long-term growth rates between countries, Robert Gilpin tells us, can have a profound impact on the evolution of the international political economy. For Gilpin, regularity in international economic relations requires stability in the underlying political order. But the underlying political order is weakened if uneven growth favors the rise of countries that contest the rules of international economic relations and if, inversely, it saps the strength of countries that enforce those rules. The current order, Gilpin speculates, is threatened by the end of the U.S. economy's uncontested supremacy in the world economy. That supremacy allowed the United States to play a leadership role in fashioning and enforcing the rules of international relations in the post–World War II era. But the growing strength of the economies of Western Europe and East Asia may undermine respect for the underlying principles of the international political economy. It may also foster efforts to amend those principles so as to give greater recognition to the welfare economics of the Europeans and the nationalist solidarity of the Japanese. Failing such amendments, Gilpin reasons, the economy is threatened by regional fracture.[1]

Uneven growth, in this account, flows like an undercurrent in the international political economy. In time, that undercurrent can disperse and wash away the institutional constructs that ride the waves at the surface. Uneven growth may not be the only destructive undercurrent. Technological change and market rationality may be others. But the concept of uneven growth is particularly suggestive when one examines liberal reform in interventionist states. One might nevertheless resist the notion that the United States, sole military superpower following the collapse of the Soviet Union and well positioned to dominate world markets in growth sectors such as information-processing technologies, declined as a hegemonic power, despite signs of decline as found, for example, in the secular depreciation of the dollar relative to the mark and the yen or the achievement of parity in per-capita gross national product by European and East Asian economies. Such resistance might be justified if it were not the case that U.S. policy has sought more than once to slow or prevent what policymakers themselves have perceived to be a decline of U.S. influence in world politics and the international political economy. The dismantling of credit activism does not necessarily reflect the relative decline of the United States as a hegemonic power. It does, however, bear the imprint of American efforts to prevent that decline from occurring.

Broadly speaking, both credit activism and liberalization in financially interventionist states reflect the making and unmaking of a hegemonic world order, the purpose of which was to preserve the capitalist order from the forces that threatened it. That order was composed of institutions and arrangements that sought to give the state the means to manage and direct capital in a way that preserved political stability within the framework of an open international economic order. Following World War II, political leaders sought to prevent the recurrence of the kind of international economic crisis that threatened the

---

[1]  Robert Gilpin, *The Political Economy of International Relations* (Princeton: Princeton University Press, 1987), chaps. 9, 10.

very survival of capitalism during the interwar period. They hoped, moreover, to arm governments against both the internal political threats and the external military threats that arose from the settlement of the war. This meant creating international institutions and informal arrangements that facilitated state management of the capitalist political economy. States were empowered to direct capital to accomplish political tasks: neutralizing political opposition through subsidies and clientelism, nurturing the development of an indigenous industrial and financial elite, and developing a strong industrial base that facilitated participation in an open trade order and contributed to the military power of participating governments. Uneven growth undermined this protective international order by weakening the willingness and perhaps even the capacity of the hegemonic power to manage and underwrite the institutions and arrangements that supported it. As the United States reacted against its self-perceived decline in the 1970s and 1980s, it unleashed the global shocks in money and finance that produced the pressures for reform documented here.

But uneven growth did not have a coherent or uniform impact on the international political economy. Its impact varied from country to country, and affected the path toward liberalization chosen by national governments in different ways. Nor should it be seen as problematic that a single causal factor should assume multiple guises as it travels from country to country. Global warming is, by definition, a global phenomenon. But it is quite capable of manifesting itself in one region in the form of greater precipitation and a fall in mean temperatures over part of the year, while elsewhere it may manifest itself in the form of desertification and generally higher mean temperatures. So it is with uneven growth. Though a global phenomenon, it has affected Mexico differently than Japan, and Spain and France differently than Korea.

## Safeguarding Capitalism

To understand financial liberalization in interventionist states, one must first have grasped both the political purpose of interventionism and the external validation that it received from U.S. policy. Interventionism had no purpose other than to bolster the foundations of the capitalist order by aggressively addressing threats, both internal and external, to that order's survival. This meant several things. First, it meant promoting growth and keeping people at work. The 1950s were, in every advanced industrialized country and in international economic relations generally, a reaction against the 1930s. Second, it meant silencing capitalism's potential adversaries through compensation and even outright clientelism. Such compensation was sometimes financed through redistribution, but more typically through inflation. Third, in many countries it meant using policy to create or strengthen an indigenous industrial and financial elite. Finally, it meant promoting industrial growth, which was important not because it accelerated GDP growth— this would be difficult if not impossible to demonstrate—but because national elites considered industry the source of military and economic power in international politics. Interventionist financial policy, therefore, not only embodied the Gerschenkronian logic that is generally evoked to explain the link between late industrialization and state activism, but reflected diplomatic ambitions, constraints, and opportunities that had their source in the international political position of each country at midcentury.[2]

The ambition to promote industrialization to bolster national power was most apparent in the Korean and French cases, and in both countries that ambition derived from similar geopolitical concerns. Credit activism was employed in Korea to fortify the Maginot line of capitalism in East Asia. The national territory had been rent by a civil war that bipolarity in world politics congealed into a protracted interstate conflict. The Communist North enjoyed an industrial head start, the legacy of the colonial period. In the 1950s, the pro-American South ignored the blandishments of its American sponsor to integrate its economy into a broader and more interdependent Pacific trade zone, choosing instead to implement policies that were designed to hasten the development of its own heavy industry and to support a military establishment equal to that of its fraternal enemy. That preoccupation became particularly insistent in the 1970s when the Nixon Doctrine, the fall of Vietnam, and the conjunction of an international oil and monetary crisis all pointed to the withdrawal of the United States from its hegemonic role.

---

[2] See Alexander Gerschenkron, *Economic Backwardness in Historical Perspective* (Cambridge: Belknap Press of Harvard University Press, 1962).

Capitalism was not only being defended in South Korea, it was being nurtured. It is there that one finds the most extraordinary effort to create the material foundations that allowed Korea to thrive in a world capitalist political economy and to reform its society in a way that reinforced the chances of that success. The Korean state not only industrialized the country, it created the Korean industrial class. It was the state that transformed the owners of auto repair shops into the chief executive officers of multinational corporations, "a striking substitution of the state for the 'natural' historical process of development."[3] Activist credit policy was the principal tool that the state employed in its experiments with "social engineering" on this vast scale.

France, traumatized by its poor showing against the Wehrmacht in May 1940, similarly resisted the liberalizing thrust of U.S. foreign policy following the war in order to hasten not only the industrial modernization of its economy but the end toward which industrialization was but a means: the "modernisation" (the term that the French planners themselves used) of French political society as a whole. Political modernization, however, was not always compatible with the more immediate need to stabilize newly minted democratic institutions in this ideologically divided country. More than in Korea, which was a military dictatorship for most of the postwar period, activist monetary and financial policy in France was used to blunt ideological struggles. It was used to quiet the enemy within, to combat the ideological restlessness that nourished opposition to the international capitalist order on the left and on the right. Activist credit policy was born of efforts to avoid the political stress of monetary rigor. The tools of credit activism were perfected as the state worked to contain the inflationary pressures that deficit spending generated in the 1950s. Without such tools, weak governments would have had to augment the tax burden or ask the Banque de France to bail them out with inflation, and thus incur the risk of losing whatever moral and political authority they commanded. In the 1960s and 1970s, under a new constitution that gave more muscle to government, interventionism persisted, driven by the need to use liquid savings to finance long-term investment in a political economy in which investment in financial assets was already thoroughly discouraged by activist policy. The

---

3   See above, p. 65.

post-OPEC recession of the 1970s merely exacerbated the need for state-brokered credit.

The "modernizing" ambition formulated by Resistance leaders, however, was not neglected. In France as in Korea, one of the ambitions of state policy was to endow the country with an economic, political, and technical elite that could lead the French economy to a position of competitiveness and even leadership within the more open and liberal international political economy. France was not a struggling industrial upstart like South Korea, but it was concerned with a level of economic and social dynamism, adaptability, and cohesion that suffered in comparison with the political economies of the great powers of Northern Europe. French efforts to modernize the political economy often capsized and transformed themselves into efforts to defuse the political opposition that modernization generated. Nevertheless, throughout the postwar period the state painstakingly nurtured the development of a "modern" technocratic and managerial elite that now fills the corridors of the ministries, the board rooms of major corporations, and the chambers of parliament. It is no accident that credit activism and the elitist École Nationale d'Administration were born simultaneously. Power in the pre–World War II political economy was shared by a conservative business elite, an ideologically quarrelsome political elite, and a sedulous though unimaginative bureaucratic elite. Power in the post–World War II political economy is not shared but practically monopolized by a technocratic elite that has successfully colonized the world of business and politics. The efficacy of liberalizing reform in the 1980s is testimony to the capacity of that elite to pilot France in whatever direction the undercurrents of the international political economy might carry it.[4]

In Spain as in France, credit activism was used both to protect the traditional social order from the shock of transition to a world of open trade and to promote the rise of a technocratic elite that could foster the development of a more dynamic and competitive Spanish economy. Pursuing this goal, a network of technocrats linked to the religiously traditionalist but economically reformist lay brotherhood of the Opus Dei interposed itself between the world market and traditional Spanish soci-

---

[4]   See Michael Loriaux, "Is France a Developmental State?" in Meredith Woo-Cumings, ed., *The Developmental State* (forthcoming).

ety while simultaneously promoting the industrialization of the Spanish economy and its integration into the economic order structured by American hegemonic leadership. It made generous use of inflationary policy to diffuse the costs of economic change and thus help ensure the survival of the political order. Inflation reduced the real cost of satisfying demands for higher wages. It facilitated the supply of life-giving credit to noncompetitive industrial sectors such as steel and coal, which were threatened by the dismantling of autarkic trade barriers. The technocrats, moreover, appealed specifically to the French model to supply the regulatory framework that made "cheap credit cum convertibility" possible.[5] As part of this reform, they adopted selective credit regulations, making them palatable to the banks through the assurance of generous central bank rediscounting and by state recognition of the privileged position of the Big Seven banks.

Capitalism in Japan was not so much nurtured as it was reincarnated in its pre–World War II persona. The nationalist thrust of credit policy in prewar and war-time Japan was revived and validated by the hegemonic power with the onset of the Cold War, on condition that Japan participate in America's anti-Soviet alliance system. In Japan one encounters the same need to finance deficit spending as in Korea, France, and Spain, and the same readiness to dip into state-run savings institutions (particularly the post office savings network) to do so. In addition to industrialization, state control over credit was used to court sectoral, and even clientelistic support for government. This kind of activity is more pronounced in Japan than elsewhere. Specialized lending institutions continue to supply credit on preferential terms to a wide variety of activities in Japan, from agriculture to small businesses to coffee shops and bath houses. Clientelism also explains why the state showed such indulgence toward small banks, often at the expense of the large city banks.

Such efforts as we encounter in these countries to tame and to nurture capitalism domestically depended on some aspect of the post–World War II international order. International financial support for a "cold warrior state," brokered by the hegemonic United States, made possible a strong dose of economic nationalism in Korea. In France, despite early skirmishes with a United States that disapproved of its activist policy

[5]  See above, p. 178.

orientations, credit activism was finally ratified. A key factor was the existence of a monetary order that organized international solidarity around countries experiencing payments imbalances because of inflationary policy. That monetary order itself cannot be understood without reference to the politics of the Cold War or American leadership. In the case of Spain, revived American interest (as evidenced by the construction of U.S. naval and air bases on Spanish soil beginning in 1953 and the subsequent extension of technical and financial assistance) created the conditions for Spain to shed its isolationism and join the Organization for European Economic Cooperation in 1958. That, in turn, inclined the Spaniards to adopt interventionist policies and institutions that, borrowing on the French model, assumed that the Bretton Woods arrangements would endure. In Japan, the Korean War goaded the United States into reconciling itself to the restoration of the pre–World War II developmentalist political economy, which it had tried to dismember in the years immediately following the war.[6] But Japan was in turn cajoled into participating in a unified capitalist order that the United States now defended and refereed more actively.

Not all countries took advantage of external opportunities to embrace activist credit policies as aggressively as the countries studied here. But it is important to note that most countries did take advantage of those opportunities in some way. The response of other countries, like that of the interventionist countries, was mediated by the peculiarities of their various geopolitical situations, domestic institutions, and political priorities.

Great Britain, for example, used Keynesian aggregate demand management to foster stable growth and keep people at work. Keynesian policy requires either a "large country" that sets prices on foreign markets, and so is not threatened by trade deficits when it acts to increase consumer demand; or, as Keynes himself argued, it requires international agreements to police transactions in a way that safeguards the government's power to influence markets effectively.[7] In Britain,

[6] The notion of a "developmentalist" political economy is borrowed from Chalmers Johnson, *MITI and the Japanese Miracle: The Growth of Industrial Policy, 1925–1975* (Stanford: Stanford University Press, 1982).

[7] On the "large country" assumption in economic thought, see William H. Branson, *Macroeconomic Theory and Policy,* 2d ed. (New York: Harper and Row, 1979), pp. 313–14, 332–35.

Keynesian policy gave rise to a generally buoyant monetary policy orientation that clashed with the City's ambition to preserve confidence in sterling. Great Britain experimented with incomes policy, a most interventionist policy tool, in order to address that contradiction. Incomes policy eventually failed, however, because wage settlements, in keeping with the expansionist bias that was embedded in the international political economy, repeatedly overshot their targets.[8]

Italy was a model of monetary restraint immediately after the war, though deficit spending was a problem. The Italian government addressed that problem courageously before 1958, but then monetary policy turned resolutely expansionist until inflation and external payments imbalances made stabilization necessary in 1963. Stabilization did not succeed in slowing public sector spending, however. During the 1960s, the Italian political economy evolved into one in which the Banca d'Italia was called upon more and more to correct the monetary excesses generated by *sottogoverno* (undergovernment) and the appeal to deficit spending to finance political patronage.[9]

In Germany, "economics," in the words of Wolfram Hanrieder, was "the continuation of politics by other means."[10] Economic growth was accorded the highest priority as a way "to solve a number of potentially divisive issues,"[11] but Germany's international situation all but ruled out French-style mercantilism. Institutional decentralization under the federal constitution, moreover, complicated state intervention, even in the form of Keynesian demand management.[12] The government therefore spurred growth by promoting exports, and it promoted exports by pegging the Deutsche mark to an external parity that was undervalued rel-

[8]  Stephen Blank, "Britain: The Politics of Foreign Economic Policy, the Domestic Economy, and the Problem of Pluralistic Stagnation," in Peter Katzenstein, ed., *Between Power and Plenty* (Madison: University of Wisconsin Press, 1978); Michael Surrey, "United Kingdom," in Andrea Boltho, ed., *The European Economy: Growth and Crisis* (Oxford: Oxford University Press, 1982).

[9]  Guido M. Rey, "Italy," in Boltho, *The European Economy;* Alan R. Posner, "Italy: Dependence and Political Fragmentation," in Katzenstein, *Between Power and Plenty*; John B. Goodman, *Monetary Sovereignty: The Politics of Central Banking in Western Europe* (Ithaca: Cornell University Press, 1992), pp. 142–69.

[10]  Wolfram Hanrieder, *Germany, America, Europe: Forty Years of German Foreign Policy* (New Haven: Yale University Press, 1989), p. 225.

[11]  Klaus H. Hennings, "West Germany," in Boltho, *The European Economy*, p. 479.

[12]  Such intervention was difficult despite the relatively large size of the public sector. See Sima Liberman, *The Growth of European Mixed Economies: 1945–1970* (New York: John Wiley, 1977).

ative to the dollar.[13] The expansionist thrust of German policy, though less evident than in other countries, is mirrored in the expansion of Bundesbank currency reserves, which the bank "sterilized"—that is, prevented, by means of a parsimonious discount policy, from leaking out into the wider economy—so it could not threaten the country's trade surplus by fueling demand. The strategy would never have worked had not Bretton Woods conferred on central banks a monopoly on operations on the currency market. Without that monopoly, the Deutsche mark would have been bid up by traders before 1969.

Most industrialized and industrializing countries in Western Europe and East Asia—parts of the world that were of strategic interest to the United States—adapted their economic policies in some way to an environment created and sustained by active American leadership in international economic affairs, an environment that was tolerant and even supportive of expansionist policy. It is therefore the comparison with Mexico that becomes enlightening, since it is Mexico that benefited the least from external, hegemonic support.

Mexico, like other countries, tried to use credit activism to shore up the domestic bases of capitalism, both by using clientelism to indulge potential adversaries and by consolidating the position of domestic financial capital. Shortly after World War II, the Camacho government imposed selective reserve and portfolio requirements on banks, but in return granted them oligopolistic privileges and rents (in the form of higher-than-market interest rates). In the 1970s, as banks began to feel the squeeze created by enhanced state intervention in financial affairs, the Echeverría administration sought to strengthen the position of the banks by encouraging mergers. Credit activism in Mexico was not designed to weaken national finance capital but rather to nurture an indigenous capitalist political economy. Simultaneously, in keeping with its populist reputation, Mexico, like the other countries studied here, developed a number of specialized financial arrangements to win popular allegiance to the state's governing elite. The *fideicomisos* bespeak clientelistic origins, though Sylvia Maxfield shows that they were hampered in their efforts to channel credit to privileged borrowers

---

[13]   Note that the government, not the Bundesbank, was accorded the responsibility for determining the exchange rate of the Deutsche mark under fixed rates. The Bundesbank was only empowered to defend that rate. Hennings, "West Germany," p. 475.

because of the structurally imposed need to control the expansion of credit.

Maxfield's analysis leads us to suspect that the desire to nurture capitalism never found the external validation in Mexico that it enjoyed in the other countries. The structural pressure generated by the close proximity to the world's most dynamic capitalist economy made the ambition of nurturing domestic capital considerably more daunting. Nor could the Mexicans exploit the Americans' geopolitical sensitivities to find a way to ease the tension on those structural constraints. The United States was tolerant and supportive of nationalism at the industrialized frontiers of its sphere of influence, but showed no such solicitude toward Mexico. That ambition could be entertained only when American capital had to retrench, as during the 1930s, or when change in the terms of trade brought a sudden windfall of riches, as occurred briefly during the oil, commodity, and international lending boom of the mid-1970s.

## Uneven Growth and Liberalization

Uneven growth diminished the willingness and perhaps even the ability of the United States to manage an open international system that was tolerant of credit activism. The United States reacted to uneven growth, notably under the administrations of Richard Nixon and Ronald Reagan, with policies designed to defend its predominant position. Those policies triggered four events that contributed directly to the liberalizing turn in world finance: (*a*) the dollar crisis of the late 1960s and early 1970s and the subsequent collapse of the Bretton Woods monetary order, (*b*) the collapse of the hegemonic order in the petroleum market (to the extent that that collapse was fomented by U.S. monetary policy), (*c*) the effort by the United States in the 1980s to defend its military preeminence in the world by borrowing heavily on world financial markets, and (*d*) the effort by the United States in the 1980s to rid the international political economy of the self-discriminatory arrangements that it had itself introduced and tolerated up through the mid-1960s.

The Bretton Woods system collapsed when the United States rejected devaluation as a response to international speculation against the dollar, refused demands by other countries to reinforce international controls on the movement of capital, and demanded that other countries revalue their own currencies. When other countries failed to revalue their currencies, the United States reneged on its commitment to exchange dollars held by foreign central banks for gold at a fixed price. Joanne Gowa underscores the nationalist motivations that drove U.S. policy, which effectively relegated the survival of the postwar international monetary regime to a distant third-place priority, behind the prosperity of the domestic economy and U.S. security objectives.[14]

The collapse of the Bretton Woods system imposed two kinds of stress on other countries. First, it deprived inflationary, trade-dependent countries of international solidarity in defending and readjusting the external value of their currencies by putting an end to the central banks' monopoly on international currency transactions. Currencies (or blocs of currencies) were made to fluctuate on the market, and the power of monetary officials to intervene to control the external value of their currencies was much diminished.[15] Second, floating rates introduced the specter of destabilizing spirals of inflation and currency depreciation. That threat, however, was greater for the more trade-dependent economies of Western Europe (in which about 30 percent of the GDP is traded) than it was for the less trade dependent and better protected economies of East Asia (where about 15 percent or less is traded). For the former, depreciation under floating rates did not supply the monetary "fix" that internationally coordinated and controlled devaluation did under fixed rates. Currency depreciation, like devaluation, raises the price of imported goods. If the demand for those goods is inelastic, currency depreciation can result in a vicious circle whereby depreciation and inflation feed off each other. Inversely, attacking inflation generally causes the currency to appreciate, negating whatever commercial benefits might have been sought in the first place. Overshooting of equilibrium currency values by an inherently nervous currency market rules out finessing this dilemma through "fine tuning."

---

[14]    Joanne Gowa, *Closing the Gold Window: Domestic Politics and the End of Bretton Woods* (Ithaca: Cornell University Press, 1983), p. 23; Gilpin, *Political Economy of International Relations,* pp. 90, 345.

[15]    Michael Loriaux, *France after Hegemony: International Change and Financial Reform* (Ithaca: Cornell Unversity Press, 1991), pp. 24–31; Eric Helleiner, *The Reemergence of Global Finance: States and the Globalization of Financial Markets* (Ithaca: Cornell University Press, 1994), pp. 123–24.

The oil shock was the source of complicated and crosscutting movements that further tested financial and monetary policy throughout the industrialized world. First, it discouraged investment, slowed economic activity, and depressed government revenues while multiplying claims on government insurance and compensation arrangements. Second, the oil shock effected a transfer of real wealth from oil-consuming to oil-producing states, generating policy responses in some countries such as Germany to curb domestic demand for imported goods by clamping down on the creation of new money. Such policies compounded the effect of the monetary shock by exacerbating the growing tension between strong- and weak-currency countries and increased the risk of monetary vicious circles in the latter. Third, the oil shock reinforced inflationary pressures, producing the crisis of "stagflation" characteristic of the mid-1970s. Finally, by spawning large volumes of petrodollars in search of investment opportunities, it fed the growth of offshore banking and generated pressures to deregulate financial activity at home while preparing the ground for the debt crisis of the 1980s abroad.

The impact of Reaganomics on the economies of other countries was also complex. The core feature of Reaganomics was the deployment of a policy of fiscal stimulus at a time when the Federal Reserve was fighting inflation and therefore refused to monetize government debt. The combination of a lax fiscal policy and a rigorous monetary policy caused real interest rates to climb. High interest rates in the United States attracted foreign capital. As foreign capital bid for dollars in order to invest in the U.S. debt, the exchange rate of the dollar climbed to record heights. For countries that had gone deeply into debt in the 1970s, the combination of high interest rates and the artificially high exchange rate of the U.S. dollar triggered the debt crisis of the 1980s. For countries that imported oil and other commodities paid for in U.S. dollars, Reaganomics triggered the equivalent of a third oil shock (the second having come at the time of the Iranian revolution in 1979). In response, all countries raised interest rates and enacted other pro-capital reforms in order to compete for capital with a United States whose economic policies were causing a global capital hemorrhage. The high dollar, moreover, fed U.S. impatience with asymmetric trade arrangements and reinforced the resolve to win freer access to foreign markets for American goods and services, particularly financial services.

Such were the shocks that policy in the United States, driven largely by the effort to forestall the effects of uneven growth on the leading world economy and premier military power, generated in the rest of the world. The countries examined here responded to those shocks in ways that were informed by (*a*) their own position in the world economy, that is, by the degree to which they themselves benefited or suffered from uneven growth, and (*b*) specific institutional features of their domestic political economies.

France, like Europe generally, was not a beneficiary of uneven growth after 1973. European economies were caught between the export-oriented and labor-intensive economies of the developing world and the export-oriented but increasingly capital-intensive economies of the Pacific Rim. France depended to a considerable extent on state-negotiated contracts with developing countries for sales of infrastructure and technology (facilitated by its state-controlled system of credit allocation) to achieve balance in its external accounts. The debt crisis of the 1980s caused that market to wither. The shocks, therefore, hit France particularly hard, and contributed to the brutal turnabout in policy orientation. The principal cause of that turn-about, however, was the shift to floating rates. Credit activism in France had always coexisted with a tolerance of comparatively rapid growth in the money supply and the ever present threat of price inflation. Floating rates made the economy more vulnerable to inflation and ruled out devaluation as a means of dealing with payments problems. The French had to get serious about fighting inflation, and in doing so they recognized that they had to reform financial institutions that had been designed from the outset to facilitate monetary growth. The French state was the author and executor of these reforms.

By adopting a policy of credit activism resembling that of France, Spain imported its strengths as well as its weaknesses. As in France, credit activism presupposed international monetary solidarity and the possibility of relying on external monetary adjustment in the event of payments difficulties. Though elaborated on the foundation of the 1959 devaluation, credit activism did not preserve Spain from the need to devalue yet again in 1967 (just as the French had to devalue in 1958 and again in 1969). But by the late 1960s the Bretton Woods system had already begun to collapse under the weight of the global currency crisis. The Spaniards had adopted a system whose external validation was withdrawn within a decade. Given the growing monetary turmoil of the early 1970s, devaluation of the peseta was powerless to bring monetary order to the Spanish economy.

Despite the similarities, domestic institutional differences inclined the two countries to experiment with different responses to external monetary stress. When Bretton Woods collapsed and the oil market entered into turmoil, the French responded by reinforcing coercive state control over credit allocation; they did not liberalize until 1983. In Spain, in contrast, a different institutional relationship between the state and the banks produced a different outcome. The Spanish response to the shocks of the 1970s was less statist. This was for three reasons. First, the banking sector in Spain was financially sounder and more autonomous. Second, the Spanish state lacked the institutional capacity of the French state, as evidenced by Spain's greater difficulty in disconnecting domestic from international interest rates in the late 1960s. Third, given the greater autonomy of the banks, growing international constraint contributed to a shift of influence within the state to elites who favored pro-banking reform. For all these reasons, Spain embarked on a path of liberal reforms as early as the 1970s. The purpose of reform was not to weaken the state but, as in France, to restore the state's power to conduct monetary policy. Monetary policy in Spain (as in France) was unable to respond efficiently to new external challenges because it was being held hostage by a multiplicity of credit entitlement programs. Nevertheless, the state had to make reform palatable to the banks by confirming privileges that were the source of rents.

Japan, unlike France and Spain, was a beneficiary of uneven growth. Japanese policy responded efficiently to the need to promote exports to cover the higher cost of oil and other commodities. And, unlike France, Japan benefited from a more asymmetric trade arrangement with its principal trade partner, the United States. Japan had open access to the American market, while America's access to Japan's market was tightly regulated through structural barriers. Japan's surplus in foreign trade became a quasi-permanent feature of its political economy. Because Japanese firms swelled with export earnings, they, unlike their French counterparts, were never preoccupied with the hunt for ever new sources of financing. Monetary and energy crises in France produced experiments with new forms of credit activism. When those experiments failed, the French acknowledged the need for radical and costly reforms. Liberalization in Japan was not an act of supreme political will, as it was in France, but rather the effect of fiscal deficits and excess corporate liquidity, which together conspired to make credit activism obsolete as a tool of economic policy.

In this volume as in his other writings, Kent Calder voices skepticism regarding the alleged pervasiveness of the Japanese state. Certainly that skepticism is warranted here. Corporate financing grew, causing corporate interest in state-financed credit programs to wane. The state sought out foreign borrowers to make productive use of funds lying fallow in unsolicited credit programs. The growing obsolescence of its credit policy weakened Japan's resolve to resist pressure by foreign financial firms and governments to liberalize, to revalue the yen, and to invest more abroad to address the trade imbalance. Inversely, because liberalization in Japan was a response to the opportunities created by uneven growth—rather than a response to the constraints imposed by it—smaller and weaker actors within the Japanese political economy were able to defend certain aspects of credit activism with success, particularly after the Liberal Democratic Party lost its monopoly on government in 1993. The result is a financial system that, despite deep liberalization, remains relatively segmented. The contrast with France in this regard could not be more striking.

Korea reacted initially to the political repercussions as much as to the economic consequences of the crises of the early 1970s. Korean perceptions of the decline of the United States as a hegemonic power, visible both in economic affairs and in U.S. reversals in Vietnam, incited the Koreans to reinforce credit activism to promote industrial development, import substitution, and military preparedness through the support of heavy industry. But like Japan, Korea was able to address economic challenges not only by using the tools of the state to promote industrial investment but by taking advantage of asymmetries in trade arrangements with the United States that were similar to those that benefited Japan. Thus Korea, like Japan, was buoyed rather than threatened by uneven growth in the international political economy. By the 1980s, many of the tools that had been developed during the previous decades were no longer of any use in a country that had become one of the most successful exporting economies in the world. Korean capitalism "grew up" and cast off the training wheels that activist credit policy provided. Korean firms became less dependent on state-supplied financing and more impatient with the strings attached to it.

Yet liberalization constituted a more dramatic departure from past practices in Korea than in Japan. Meredith Woo-Cumings insists that liberalization in Korea, like credit activism itself, cannot be understood without taking into account Korea's position in the hegemonic order. Korea and Japan both depended greatly on privileged access to the United States import market. Korea, however, was historically more dependent than Japan on access to U.S. capital, whether in the form of government aid in the 1950s or government-sponsored loans in the 1970s. Korea was, subsequently, more vulnerable to American pressure than Japan. Liberalization in Korea bore more clearly the mark of pressures placed on the Korean government by a United States desirous to increase investment opportunities for U.S. banks and private lenders.

But liberalization also bore the mark of Korea's exasperation with inflation. As in France, liberalization resulted in no small part from an encounter with inflationary pressures that had grown intolerable. But Korea's impatience with inflation was not generated, as it was in France, by external payments difficulties rendered insurmountable by change in the monetary regime. As long as Korea was able to protect its market from foreign competition, it was not change in international monetary relations that rendered inflation unbearable, but rather the unwillingness of domestic actors to give up habits and practices that were no longer adapted to the kind of political economy Korea had become. Inflation as a means of socializing risk was not warranted in a political economy dominated by profitable firms that had acquired the capacity to internalize risk efficiently. Whereas the French, given the indebtedness of their businesses, hesitated to engage in an all-out assault on the forces of inflation and therefore appealed throughout the 1970s to the instruments of credit activism to keep inflation at tolerable levels, the Koreans were ready and for the most part eager to engage in such an assault, and needed only Washington's liberalizing prod to get started. Nevertheless, the absence of the overwhelming monetary constraints that we find in the French case explains that liberalization in Korea, as in Japan, was largely a process of "two steps forward, one step back."

In Mexico, yet a different picture emerges, though one still affected by the repercussions of uneven growth and the crises it unleashed.

Sylvia Maxfield privileges the role of broad structural pressures on the Mexican economy, almost to the exclusion of direct interventions on the part of United States or International Monetary Fund officials. The comparison of Mexican policy in the present with policy in, say, the 1950s lends credence to Maxfield's perspective. Thus the monetary crises of the early 1970s did not have an immediate repercussion on the Mexican economy, since inflation had been a long-standing concern. Mexican officials feared that a depreciation in the real value of their currency would either provoke capital flight, against which they were relatively helpless, or discourage sorely needed investment by foreign capital—especially American—in their economy. The structural dominance of American capital on the Mexican political economy prevented change in the international monetary system from having any significant impact on the way monetary policy was made.

Inversely, the oil and debt crises had a profound impact on the course of financial policy in the 1980s. Mexico was, for a short period, a beneficiary of price movements in the oil market. In addition to oil revenues, the boom made Mexico an attractive place to invest petrodollars, unable to find productive use in the depressed economies of the oil-importing countries. It was the influx of oil revenues that gave the Mexican government the opportunity to extend its involvement in credit allocation policy. Mexican officials and businesses borrowed massively to sustain their more activist policy orientation. But the impact of Reaganomics on world interest rates and on the exchange rate of the dollar threatened Mexico with bankruptcy in the early 1980s. Mexico's crisis provided ammunition to bureaucrats and politicians who were advocating market-oriented reforms, and prompted the dramatic turnabout in credit policy.

It is instructive to compare the Mexican case with that of Indonesia, recently analyzed by Jeffrey Winters.[16] Like Mexico, Indonesia is an industrializing, oil-exporting nation that implemented in the 1970s a state-led, activist credit policy that lasted into the early 1980s. As in Mexico, activist credit policy was made possible by an influx of oil revenues and easy access to borrowed petrodollars. And as in Mexico, the monetary and financial crises of the early 1980s greatly strengthened

---

[16]  Jeffrey Winters, *Power in Motion: Capital Mobility and the Indonesian State* (Ithaca: Cornell University Press, 1996).

state actors that advocated restructuring Indonesia's finances through liberalizing reform. But here the parallels end, for Mexico lies in the United States' backyard, while Indonesia lies in Japan's. We noted above that state-run credit programs in Japan were encountering difficulty finding borrowers, prodding the state to redirect its lending activity toward foreign borrowers. Indonesia was among the beneficiaries of this movement. At a crucial moment in the mid-1980s when the slide in oil prices turned into a plunge, Japan very quickly decided to extend "special assistance" loans to Indonesia to cover its balance of payments shortfalls. The loans were direct cash payments of between two and four billion dollars per year, deposited directly into the Indonesian treasury. The rescue program lasted several years.

Japan's rapid intervention in Indonesia's debt crisis was facilitated by the fact that almost all of Indonesia's foreign loans were sovereign debt. On the Japanese side, it was facilitated by the close ties that exist between the state and the banks. In contrast, in the Mexican-U.S. case, private borrowers and lenders prevailed, complicating treatment of the debt crisis. Whereas Secretary Baker's negotiations with interested parties dragged on for many months, Japanese officials and financiers moved rapidly and efficiently to prevent a dangerous downgrading of Indonesia's credit and investment profile. The Indonesians were given the space and time to introduce reforms that would stimulate non-oil exports. As Mexico spiraled into a prolonged debt crisis, Indonesia found the means to avoid default.

As part of the Japanese rescue, Indonesia was pressured (mainly by the United States and multilateral bodies) to pursue aggressive reforms in trade, investment, taxation, and finance. Seizing the opportunity to outmaneuver President Suharto and his extensive patron-client network, Indonesia's economic ministers rammed through dramatic reforms in banking. State banks lost their near-monopoly on domestic lending across all sectors, and the country's roughly two hundred state companies could now deposit their funds in private banks. For purposes of monetary management, credit ceilings and government control over interest rates were replaced by indirect instruments negotiated on the market. But liberalization in Indonesia was more contested than in Mexico, and the pressures less overwhelming. Therefore, the path toward liberalizing reform, as in Korea and Japan, was marked by detours and U-turns.

## Capital Ungoverned

Despite the more uneven pace of liberalization in the high growth regions of the Pacific rim, capital in the 1990s has been freed from state interference to a degree unequaled in a century. State withdrawal from capital markets, however, was not so much the consequence as it was the cause of capital's growing structural power in the contemporary international political economy. Uneven growth undermined a global hegemonic order that evolved explicitly to safeguard capitalism through regulation. Interventionist credit policies were facilitated by the construction, under U.S. hegemony, of a world economic order that was designed to defend a global capitalist system from its adversaries both within and outside the sphere of U.S. influence. The regulatory constraints that were placed on capital were dismantled or undermined by policies designed to forestall the United States' relative economic and military decline. Chief among these policies were the willful failure to address the growing dollar crisis in the late 1960s, the subsequent scuttling of the Bretton Woods monetary regime, the rejection of international efforts to institute exchange controls to regulate the international flow of capital, and the concurrent appeal to world capital to shore up American military preeminence under the Reagan administration.

Uneven growth and the attendant decay of international regulatory constraints on capital have brought about the collapse of the institutional tools developed by various national governments to constrain and guide the use of capital at the national level. Capital has been freed to create a market that is more vast and homogeneous than anything the world has known. It remains to be seen whether capital has been freed as well from the threats and dangers that the hegemonic order was designed to dispel.

There are reasons to doubt that politics will continue to be as acquiescent in confronting the forces of liberalization as it was in the 1980s. Global financial liberalization compels governments to pay for policy with borrowed funds and tax revenues. Paying for state activism and redistributive policy is more problematic than it was when states had more discretionary control over the creation and allocation of credit. Moreover, liberalization has reinforced the structural power of capital by exacerbating government fears of frightening away investors. The disinflationary implications of the new monetary regime and capital's new-found mobility, while apparently contributing to the advent of a more integrated and internationalist world order, have, ironically, weakened internationalism's most active and committed political advocates of the Center-left and Center-right. Paulette Kurzer, for instance, has shown how capital mobility affected relations between labor and capital and threatened the vitality of corporatism in Europe.[17] The French sociologist Alain Bihr, commenting on the rise of a more nationalist and even racist right in France, attributes it to the state's growing incapacity to determine economic policy and the popular sentiment that people "are no longer defended by their representatives."[18] The French have coined the term "pensée unique" (single doctrine) to refer to neoclassical economics' new status as the uncontested orthodoxy. Though uncontested by a viable rival doctrine, this pensée unique has nevertheless become a burning issue in French political life, dividing both the Right and the Left.

It is common to confuse the idea of liberalization with the idea of "liberation" from arbitrary and inefficient state interference. Thus liberalization, in the minds of many, is equated at least rhetorically with a certain idea of freedom. Neoclassical economists have been known to make the leap from rhetoric to philosophical doctrine quite readily.[19] But as we examine the dismantling of the decades-old capacity of states to influence and direct productive investment, we see not the contestation of power but the exercise of power. And as interventionist institutions are brought down by powerful actors, we are reminded of the Hegelian claim that human freedom flourishes not outside the realm of the state but within it. Without engaging in debate regarding the philosophical merits of claim and counterclaim, we can nevertheless conclude by asking whether humanity, or some subset of it, will not see fit one day to reclaim its "freedom" to act from forces that have, at least temporarily, contrived to take that freedom away. And because the power politics of both liberalization and contestation is affected by uneven growth in the international political economy, we are invited to speculate how the persistence of uneven growth will inform the answer to this question.

[17] Paulette Kurzer, *Business and Banking: Political Change and Economic Integration in Western Europe* (Ithaca: Cornell University Press, 1993).

[18] Quoted in Marie-France Etchegoin, "La vague fasciste," *Le Nouvel Observateur*, January 5, 1994.

[19] Milton Friedman and Rose Friedman, *Free to Choose* (New York: Harcourt Brace Jovanovich, 1980).

# Index